PAUL MASON

Live Working or Die Fighting

How the Working Class Went Global

VINTAGE BOOKS
London

Published by Vintage 2008

2 4 6 8 10 9 7 5 3 1

First published in Great Britain in 2007 by Harvill Secker

Vintage
Random House, 20 Vauxhall Bridge Road,
London SW1V 2SA

www.vintage-books.co.uk

Addresses for companies within The Random House Group Limited
can be found at: www.randomhouse.co.uk/offices.htm

The Random House Group Limited Reg. No. 954009

A CIP catalogue record for this book
is available from the British Library

ISBN 9780099492887

The Random House Group Limited makes every effort to ensure that
the papers used in its books are made from trees that have been
legally sourced from well-managed and credibly certified forests.
Our paper procurement policy can be found at:
www.rbooks.co.uk/environment

Mixed Sources
Product group from well-managed
forests and other controlled sources
www.fsc.org Cert no. TT-COC-2139
© 1996 Forest Stewardship Council
FSC

Printed in the UK by CPI Bookmarque, Croydon, CR0 4TD

For
John Mason (1927–1986)

Contents

Introduction

A man is scrambling in the dark across the pits and trenches of a massive building site. He is a foreman on the Liverpool docks, a man reputed for toughness and clean living. It is a warm night in the summer of 1904. The next day, on this spot the city's business elite will watch the King lay the foundation stone of the new Anglican cathedral; history will record the pomp of the ceremony in deferential detail. But it will not record what happens tonight.

Guided by a worker from the site, the docker digs a hole and buries a tin time capsule just below where the foundation stone will be laid. It contains articles from obscure labour newspapers and a message written in the flowery script and language of the self-taught working man. It says:

> To the Finders, Hail! We the wage slaves employed on the erection
> of this cathedral, to be dedicated to the worship of the unemployed
> Jewish carpenter, hail ye! Within a stone's throw from here, human
> beings are housed in slums not fit for swine. This message, written
> on trust-produced paper with trust-produced ink, is to tell ye how
> we today are at the mercy of trusts . . .[1]

Trusts were then what global corporations are today: powerful companies with a finger in every pie, held responsible for all the poverty in the world by some, all the progress in the world by others. Slums we still have – one billion people live in them – and though they are more than a stone's throw from the rich cities of Europe and America, thanks to blogs, television and mobile phones the contrast between squalor and wealth is just as obvious to us as it was then.

Then, as now, there was an anti-corporate movement, and it was global. Its agitators spread their message on the street corners of slum districts, in the steerage cabins of migrant ships. It boycotted unethical goods, got its head broken on demonstrations and lived an alternative lifestyle that shocked mainstream society. This was the labour movement in the years before fists replaced flowers as its main symbols. Its true history has been buried as deep as that Liverpool docker's time capsule; its narratives, heroes and epics have been lost or, worse, simplified beyond meaning.

That history needs to be rediscovered because two sets of people stand in dire need of knowing more about it: first, the activists who have flooded the streets in Seattle, Genoa and beyond to protest against globalisation; second, the workers in the new factories, mines and waterfronts created by globalisation in the developing world, whose attempts to build a labour movement are at an early stage. They need to know what happened to the original labour movement during its long upward sweep not in order to relive it or piously to 'learn lessons' from it. They need to know, quite simply, that what they are doing has been done before, where it can lead and what patterns of revolt, reaction and reform look like when you view them over decades. Above all they need to know that the movement was once a vital force: a counterculture in which people lived their lives and the main source of education for men and women condemned to live short, bleak lives and dream of impossible futures.

I have written this book to tell that story. There is no attempt to be comprehensive; I have just picked out some of the major events that happened during the great advance of the first hundred years, followed by the crisis and catastrophe of the inter-war period.

Because the first 150 years of industrial capitalism took place in countries that were mainly white and produced trade unions that were largely male, this is a story mainly about white, male workers in Europe, America and the Far East. Because it relies on memoirs, oral histories and the work of academics who themselves rely on these sources, I have concentrated on countries where such sources are accessible and trustworthy. I have not given any more than a rough sketch of the situation in mainstream politics in each chapter; if you want to know more about Louis-Napoleon, Franklin Delano Roosevelt or Giovanni Giolitti, just type them into Google and press 'Enter'.

For a long time a book like this seemed to me unnecessary. When there were strong labour movements in Europe, America and the Pacific based in stable communities with an oral tradition, everybody knew the basic history. The workers I grew up with in an English coal and cotton town seemed to have been – as George Orwell wrote – 'born knowing what I had learned, out of books and slowly'. Nobody needed a book that explained the basics then. And in any case, all the best stories had been told, I thought.

I was wrong. Leigh, the town where I grew up, was not so different in the 1960s from how it was when my grandfather went down the pit in 1913: it was a world of white manual workers, devout Sunday marchers for Catholicism and Methodism, brass bands, rugby and the annual Miners' Gala. It is totally different now: twenty years of globalisation have shorn away most of what was permanent and certain. The miners' union was destroyed, manufacturing has moved to China, and if you look for the union activists now you will find them mainly in education and local government. The labour market in which workers from Leigh compete starts at their doorsteps and ends at a bus station in Bangalore or a slum in Shenzhen.

A culture that took 200 years to build was torn apart in twenty. There is no point mourning that but it means the new working class of what campaigners call the 'global south' is being born unconscious of the stories of the past. And the anti-globalisation movement is not in any shape to supply the narratives – its oldest legend tells of a day in Seattle in November 1999.

Today, in place of a static local workforce working in the factories and drinking in the pubs their grandfathers worked and drank in, a truly global working class is being created. This is happening for a number of reasons. First, because since the collapse of communism the whole world's workforce has shared the experience of working in a market economy: there is no longer an 'iron curtain' dividing workers into two completely different ways of living. Second, practice in the workplace is becoming standardised across the globe: the quality circle in a UK car factory discusses the same things as one in China; the work involved in making a Big Mac is the same in Sheffield and Shanghai, even if the wages and human rights are different. Third, with the emergence of global union federations there is the beginning of cross-border collective bargaining. Finally, by pitting the low-waged workforce of the developing world against the high-waged workers of Europe, America and Japan, globalisation has forced labour organisations to think internationally, even if they are slow to act internationally.

Objectively, the global working class exists. Subjectively – in the minds of the people on the factory floor – things are more complicated. In the global south, millions of peasants and shanty dwellers are being sucked into the exhilarating and brutal world of wages, overtime, company dormitories and consumer capitalism. They are going through what the first generation of factory workers went through, but in an economy where information flows like quicksilver and consumer culture is global.

In trying to document the lives of this new global workforce I've met Chinese workers crippled because of inadequate safety standards; I've met Bolivian miners working in conditions worse than my grandfather's generation would have tolerated; I've met Indian garment workers who recognise the labels on the sportswear they are finishing but have no idea who their employer is, or when they're getting paid.

This book sets their stories alongside those of previous generations. The aim is not to draw crude parallels or preach about 'lessons of the struggle' but to show how scrappy and unresolved history is when you are living it in the first draft, and how you have to stand back to make sense of it. Right now in London there are Somali, Kurdish and Brazilian migrant cleaners trying to form unions inside the headquarters of investment banks, but they are still having trouble with the city's geography, let alone its history. They have no idea that the Irish and Jewish migrants who lived in the same streets 100 years ago had to fight the same kind of battle, or how they won. And why should they? Amid relentless change we can no longer rely on word of mouth, family, tradition and community to keep working class history alive.

As a journalist I've learned that the story you uncover when you listen to people is always more interesting than the one you thought you were after. If you do this with workers' history you get startling results. You find that Lancashire cotton workers at Peterloo, the first ever industrial workforce, discovered nearly every type of organisation and tactic seen during the next 200 years. You learn that the 'doomed' silk weavers of Lyon were not fighting a hopeless battle against mechanisation but defending a highly efficient network economy. You find that the revolutionaries of the Paris Commune were really just boring union officials, opposed to strikes. You realise that the Jewish Bund – an organisation that disappears from official Marxist history after 1903 – went on to create one of the most highly developed working class cultures ever seen.

If there is a recurrent theme amid all this, it is control. Politically, the labour movement has debated strategy in terms of reform versus revolution. Practically, to the frustration of advocates of both approaches, workers have been prepared to go beyond reform but settle for less than revolution. Once you understand the deep desire for control within the workplace and for the creation of parallel communities within society, you understand the dynamics, and the limits, of the rebellions narrated here. The great discovery of the grass-roots worker activists was this: that 'power' was just as big a question as 'class'. It was a woman with a rifle from the slums of Montmartre who warned the world 140 years ago:

> There are millions of us who don't give a damn for any authority because we have seen how little the many-edged tool of power accomplishes. We have watched throats cut to gain it. It is supposed to be as precious as the jade axe that travels from island to island in Oceania. No, power monopolised is evil . . .[2]

I decided to end the historical part of this book at the year 1943, with half the workers of the world living under fascist dictatorships,

the other half in alliance with American capitalism or Stalinist communism. By then, many of the individuals Orwell described as the 'flower
of the working class' had been cut down, if not by fascism then by
Stalin's secret police or as casualties of war. When the international
labour movement revived after 1945 it was a different creature. For
the next four decades trade unions and socialist parties commanded a
place at the decision-making tables of the Western democracies, but
much of the gut anarchism and self-taught romanticism you will meet
among the people featured in this book was gone.

To me the experience of labour's great upward surge, when the
ideologies of republicanism, socialism and anarchism jostled amicably
across the tables of working class bars, seems more relevant to the
present than the experience of 1945–89. But there is no law of history
that says the new workers' organisations in the global south have to
repeat the long process of organisation and self-education we saw in
the 19th century. They may fast-forward, and create the most developed, advanced and modern forms of organisation from scratch. They
may also fail.

If a new global labour movement does emerge then the stories in
this book will turn out to be the prehistory of the working class. The
white male rebels gazing out from 100-year-old photographs will be
seen as precursors of a much bigger, multi-ethnic movement centred
on India, China and Latin America which communicates by text
message in real time and in which women are the majority. But that
is not inevitable. It is possible that, among the world's new workforce,
the will to organise will prove weaker than the combined strength of
market forces, autocratic governments and the dream of getting rich;
writing this book has reinforced my view that there is no such thing
as the 'unvanquishable number' Shelley fantasised about in his famous
poem on Peterloo. If the new labour movement fails to thrive and
the old one continues to decline, the least we can do is preserve the
story of those who built the original.

Like the man who buried that message on a summer night in 1904.
At the time all he'd done was sell socialist newspapers, get himself
arrested for street corner speeches and jump ship in Montevideo in

pursuit of teenage kicks. He thought at the time that trade unionism was a 'played out economic fallacy'. But he would go on to organise the strike that for the first time bridged Belfast's religious divide; he would paralyse Dublin at the height of Ireland's biggest ever labour conflict. He would be sentenced to ten years in New York's Sing Sing prison for 'criminal anarchy'. He would warn his judges that 'the ways of the broad highways have been my ways and I have never been encompassed by walls'. His name was Jim Larkin. The labour movement turned him from a studious, romantic nobody into a figure that could demand a hearing from the leaders of powerful nations.

Today the arms of his statue spread out above the main thoroughfare of Dublin, its fingers forked like black lightning. His story is part of a national legend and needs no retelling. But the stories of thousands like him have been lost. Most of them were driven by the same simple sentiments scribbled into the note he buried. It ends:

> In your own day you will, thanks to the efforts of past and present agitators for economic freedom, own the trusts. Yours will indeed, compared to ours of today, be a happier existence. See to it, therefore, that ye too work for the betterment of all, and so justify your existence by leaving the world a better place for your having lived in it.

That message still lies where it was buried. It was addressed to the kids in combat trousers protesting outside a Nike store in Seattle, to the rake-thin teenagers sewing trainers in Cambodian sweatshops and to migrant cleaners resting their exhausted heads against bus windows as dawn breaks in London. Few of us can imagine what that message cost to write, in terms of hardship and self-sacrifice. Or the joy experienced on those rare days when the downtrodden people of the world were allowed to stand up and breathe free.

1. Rise like lions
The Peterloo Massacre, Manchester, 1819

> Rise like lions after slumber
> In unvanquishable number!
> Shake your chains to earth, like dew
> Which in sleep had fall'n on you:
> Ye are many — they are few
> > Percy Bysshe Shelley
> > 'The Masque of Anarchy', 1819

Shenzhen, China, 2003

When they came into the room the guys were sheepish and so was I; every one of them was missing a limb. I had dragged them across the city to meet me in this tatty rooming house because, for a Western journalist, going to Longgang — an industrial suburb of Shenzhen — is only possible with a government minder. And they did not want to meet one.

'I was loading cotton into the front of a mattress machine when somebody at the back switched the power on,' Cao Xian-yi tells me, indicating the stump of his arm to complete the story. 'There were only twelve skilled workers left — all the rest were new recruits. Some of them knew nothing about the job.'

Yuan Yun-zu was making electronic circuits when the machine he was using fell on him. His left hand is missing. With compensation and physiotherapy he might get another job but, like many of the workers injured in China's small private factories, there was no insurance to cover his accident. He is, like the others, a migrant — one man on the road along with 150 million others. He could go back to his village, but he doesn't want to:

It's hard enough for a healthy person to find a job; how do you think it is for a disabled person? In the countryside I couldn't do farm work any more, and if you open a shop in the countryside, it's very difficult to survive, as the economy is terrible there.

Li Qi-bing had been working for 12 hours without a break, making plastic flowers, when a machine sliced his leg off below the knee:

The factory hadn't bought insurance for us. We took the factory to the law courts, but they refused to hear the case. We had to go to the Labour Bureau for arbitration, but the Labour Bureau refused to hear us. We were kicked around all over the place, like a football. Nobody looked after us.

They were all young, they were all migrants, they were all sacked. They are part of the new Chinese workforce which has been scraped together so quickly and cheaply that, in the space of 20 years, it has changed the world. Yet they have so few rights and so little freedom of expression that the world has hardly heard from them.

Disabled sweatshop workers from Longgang turned to Zhou Li-tai for help. In the absence of trade unions or a factory inspectorate with teeth, this compensation lawyer was on a one-man mission to clean up the city. But in 2002 the authorities revoked Zhou's licence. He had launched a legal action on behalf of women who objected to compulsory body searches at the factory gate. Zhou, a self-taught former worker, is blunt about the causes of Longgang's high industrial injury rate:

First, old equipment. Second, the workers don't get training. Third, they're exhausted because of long overtime. Finally, lack of government regulation. In the labour market, supply is greater than demand. It's much easier to attract workers here than it is to attract employers. The local government is keen to develop the local economy. As long as they keep the employers happy and they continue to invest, they don't care about the benefits of the workers at all.

In any other developed industrial economy workers would have the right to do something about this situation: they would be able to negotiate, collectively or individually, to strengthen their position. But only 10 per cent of Chinese migrant workers have ever seen a contract of employment. And, says Zhou, the official trade unions are part of the state:

> The Chinese workers' union behaves like a part of the government, not a union. The union's money comes partly from government, partly from the employers. On top of that, a union rep is still an employee of the company and if he does something wrong he'll be sacked.

Twelve years in jail is the standard punishment for trying to form a free trade union. For workers, basic rights like accident insurance or being able to refuse overtime become scarcer the further you go from the big, shiny factories and the nearer you get to the backstreet sweatshops. And the political rights that would allow them to voice their thoughts about all this are non-existent. Democracy has been off the agenda since the massacre in Tiananmen Square in 1989, and the Chinese middle class has, for now, lost interest in pursuing it.

The scale of what is happening is hard to comprehend, even standing in the middle of a factory complex like BYD in Longgang. Only from the aerial photograph in reception can you see that BYD consists of five giant units, identical and virtually windowless. Between them are sparse concrete thoroughfares along which components and managers are ferried in customised golf buggies. The site is dotted with neat tropical shrubbery, washed in sunlight, and feels deserted. Then, on the stroke of noon, without any signal, 17,000 workers stop work and go to lunch.

They don't march in step like they do in the sweatshops – this is a showcase factory producing for Western brands whose managers have corporate social responsibility pledges to maintain. But they do march in line: single file from the blocks to the main queue, five deep once they've joined it. The queue builds to 100 metres long, then 200 metres – a wide ribbon of bright blue uniforms. Ninety per cent are women aged 17 to 24 ('Men fight too much,' says the company secretary). As the workers squeeze together towards the canteen barrier they hold up ID cards bearing barcodes and digital photos to be scanned.

They live in dormitories, two to a room, and eat three meals a day in the canteen; they are scanned in and out of every sector of the site.

3

This system is not a hangover from communism but has been introduced during the last 20 years, as China's economy has been marketised. It is known in China as 'modern management'. As Lancashire factory owners found in the 1800s, a live-in workforce brings two advantages: it can be paid less and disciplined more easily. The average wage is the equivalent of £40 a month. 'Live like a family, play like a team, work like an army' is the company motto, and since the vast majority would be lucky to take home £40 in a whole year back in their villages, that is what they do. In this single plant, they produce one in seven mobile phone batteries in the world.

Dong Zhen-zhen, an 18-year-old woman, has worked all morning in the 35-degree heat of the battery-charging plant. It's not production line work – the new recruits do that, with red-shirted supervisors peering over their shoulders. Dong, together with three or four hundred others, runs between racks of batteries being charged, checking them, stacking them, slotting in the next batch. She is from a village:

> I'm from Da Sheng in Anhui province. I knew Shenzhen was developing fast so I decided to come to Shenzhen. I've been to a lot of places before that. I worked in Changzhou and Zhouhai, in electrical factories. They weren't as good as this. This factory is better. I couldn't see any future in the other places: here it looks like a garden.

What Dong Zhen-zhen has lived through, ten million Chinese peasants every year will have to endure for the next thirty years simply for China to maintain its planned rate of economic growth. The push factor is rural poverty. You can feel the pull factor when you look beyond the uniform at Dong herself. Like everyone else she's wearing flip-flops, but like everyone else's they are personalised: hers have a Disney character printed on the blue plastic strap. She's wearing a plastic ring, the kind a Western child might get out of a bubblegum machine. Like others she's got a stick-on tattoo, a harmless gesture of revolt just high enough up her arm for the uniform to cover it. Hers is a butterfly; others prefer cartoon characters. If she goes out it will be on a Sunday afternoon rather than at night. There's a midnight curfew and a six-day working week. She will, if she can afford it, wear Western-style shoes and clothes on her night off. There's a mass consumer market now, with prices targeted so that if she manages to save half a month's salary she can buy a pair of kitten heels meticulously ripped off from a Jimmy Choo design.

Becoming a worker means acquiring new ways of living – new disciplines and new freedoms. However tough it is for Dong Zhenzhen she's the first woman in her family with money enough to worry about high-heeled shoes and, like the maimed men from the sweatshops, she sees this as a one-way journey.

But there is a kind of laid-back discontent in the air; you can feel it when you walk the streets of Gangxia West, a working class district in the heart of Shenzhen City. It has slums, street life and, if you peer down the backstreets, sweatshops. It is a concrete warren of ten-storey tenements where families live forty to a block, sometimes with the welding rods of an unofficial factory arcing and fusing on the floors above. The shocking thing is not the state of the buildings but the fact that they are rarely more than two metres apart. In most alleyways you can stretch your arms to touch both sides and the darkness makes it difficult to tell where the public space of street ends and the private space of families begins. If you are a stranger you probably don't want to find out.

In 1980 Gangxia was a field. Through its cracked sidewalks and collapsing drains it is easy to see what lies below – nothing but red earth. Gangxia's archeology consists of a single layer one foot deep, the Deng Xiao-ping dynasty. Deng decreed that Shenzhen should be a rule-free frontier town for China's new capitalists. In less than three decades it has become the workshop of the world. Surrounded by glittering skyscrapers Gangxia already looks like a relic.

But in the evening it pulsates with life. Every available storefront is a shop – pots and pans, a hairdresser, a bar, fruit and vegetables, children's writing books. Every available step becomes a seat for men and women in T-shirts, chatting, smoking or watching football on TV. There are few old people here; it is a district of teenagers and young adults. On any 50-metre stretch of the narrow main street there will be over a thousand people. You are never more than three or four feet away from somebody else.

In just 20 years Gangxia workers have built a community as tightly knit as in the fearsome slums that terrified English social reformers during the Industrial Revolution. The big difference is the total absence of a political public space. There is a chalk mural in Gangxia extolling the virtues of the People's Liberation Army, but nothing else. The public arena, such as it exists, is the mobile phone network or the Internet cafe, where each PC has a sticker on the monitor warning that 'subversion' is a crime.

But Gangxia people are street smart. In November 2001, when the authorities made a sweep, they confiscated ten television modulators which, they said, were being used to broadcast 'underground TV networks' with foreign content. Three years later the *Shenzhen Legal Daily* revealed that, yet again, unofficial TV networks had been busted in Gangxia, with 'more than 10,000 subscribers'.[1] And everywhere there is graffiti with the telephone numbers of people selling fake IDs: on the walls, on telephone boxes, on scaffolding. Migrants need a fake ID to get and keep a job in the city even though it is Chinese government policy that they should move off the land and get that job.

The new Chinese workforce has so far done everything its predecessors did except organise trade unions and fight for its political rights. Although there has been a wave of workplace protests, these have been mainly in the old factories of the Chinese rust belt, in the north, as market forces closed them down. Workers in the old state industries were once a privileged class with nurseries, hospitals and decent housing; the party and the state-run factory looked after them from cradle to grave. As their lifestyle has died that of the export-sector workforce has been created. Young workers in places like Shenzhen have been too busy making their own future to worry about anybody else's troubles. But this is changing.

The DeCoro plant in Longgang is the biggest sofa factory in the world. In October 2005 the Italian bosses at DeCoro cut wages by 20 per cent. A ten-man delegation from the workforce complained and had their ID cards confiscated. A sit-down protest at the factory gate escalated into violence. Workers claim Italian managers punched and kicked them. Three were hospitalised. Then all 3,000 workers went on strike, shouting, 'Stop violence, restore justice, protect our human rights!'² They were dispersed by riot police. It was not the pay that angered them – skilled workers here can earn the equivalent of £70 a month – it was the attitude of foreign managers.

The Chinese industrial workforce is now the biggest in the world. In the years since Tiananmen Square management styles have been draconian in the knowledge that every act of resistance can be labelled as a 'threat to social order' and severely punished. Shenzhen's workers are to global capitalism what Manchester's workers were 200 years ago. What they do next will shape the century.

Manchester 1819

It was 8 a.m. on Monday 16 August. The factories stood silent and in the weavers' cottages the looms were still. For Samuel Bamford, a weaver in the Manchester suburb of Middleton, the key thing was to avoid any excuse for violence. The employers feared the new industrial workforce and today would be the most decisive day in its history. At the appointed time

> not less than three thousand men formed a hollow square, with probably as many people around them, and, an impressive silence having been obtained, I reminded them that they were going to attend the most important meeting that had ever been held for Parliamentary Reform.³

They set off for Manchester marching in battalions of 100 and with a three-tier command structure. This was the opposite of a mob; it was a highly disciplined demonstration dressed in its Sunday best, with all but the elderly forbidden to carry traditional walking sticks.

> First were selected twelve of the most comely and decent-looking youths, who were placed in two rows of six each, with each a branch of laurel held presented in his hand, as a token of amity and peace; then followed the men of several districts in fives; then the band of music, an excellent one; then the colours: a blue one of silk, with inscriptions in golden letters, 'Unity and Strength', 'Liberty and

Fraternity'; a green one of silk, with golden letters, 'Parliaments Annual', 'Suffrage Universal'; and betwixt them, on a staff, a handsome cap of crimson velvet with a tuft of laurel, and the cap tastefully braided, with the word *'Libertas'* in front.[4]

This was the cap of liberty – the international symbol of republicanism made popular by the French Revolution, which the British army had just spent the best part of 30 years in combat with. It was like unfurling the hammer and sickle in 1950s America.

Columns like this headed towards Manchester from sixteen of the surrounding towns while the city's workers left their factories and lined the streets. When Bamford's contingent ran into another, amid sun-dappled woodland, 'We met – and a shout from ten thousand startled the echoes of the woods and dingles. Then all was quiet save the breath of music; and with intent seriousness we went on.'[5]

They were going to hear a man called Henry Hunt advocate ideas considered impossible at the time: votes for all, annual elections and the scrapping of import controls designed to keep food prices high. The movement's leaders were middle class professionals but its members were overwhelmingly manual workers and their families, 100,000 of whom assembled around the wooden platform in St Peter's Field, Manchester. Here a collection of lawyers and journalists sat in expectation of Hunt's arrival. This was the biggest crowd Manchester had ever seen.

But it was not the first radical demonstration of that summer. In July the people of Birmingham had held a mass meeting that had sent waves of fear through the English aristocracy. They had not only called for the right to vote but actually taken a vote there and then. Most big cities were not recognised on the voting maps but Birmingham had elected a 'legislative attorney' – an unofficial Member of Parliament for a seat that did not yet exist. It was a declaration of intent. Now the authorities feared Hunt was going to repeat this stunt in Manchester. They had banned one meeting, a week before, and stood ready to disperse this one if anybody mentioned voting.

It was hot. Hunt arrived at the platform and began to speak. He was a cult figure among the Manchester working class; at radical

Sunday schools monitors wore lockets with his portrait around their necks instead of the traditional crucifix. But when Hunt started speaking, Samuel Bamford did something that working class activists will often do when called upon to listen to a long speech on a sweltering day. He headed for the pub.

> I proposed to an acquaintance that, as the speeches and resolutions were not likely to contain anything new to us, and as we could see them in the papers, we should retire awhile and get some refreshment, of which I stood much in need, being not in very robust health. He assented, and we had got to nearly the outside of the crowd, when a noise and strange murmur arose towards the church. Some persons said it was the Blackburn people coming, and I stood on tip-toe and looked in the direction whence the noise proceeded, and saw a party of cavalry in blue and white uniform come trotting, sword in hand.[6]

This was the Manchester Yeomanry, a civilian posse recruited for the purposes of putting down working class unrest. In preparation for action their sabres had been sharpened, as had their courage; they had spent the morning in a bar. Thanks to a contemporary radical newspaper we know the name and occupation of every one of the 101 men who took part in the charge. The most common job title is publican; there were thirteen bar owners in the saddle that day. The regiment's eleven mill owners and seven butchers also stand out.[7] It was the city's business mafia on horseback. Hunt told the crowd to give them three ironic cheers. The terrified magistrates, observing from the window of a nearby house, interpreted this as 'most marked defiance'. The horsemen pushed through the crowd. The magistrates marched forward through a tunnel made by two lines of constables. They arrested Hunt and several others on the platform, all of whom went quietly.

Now the Yeomanry, whose horsemanship was suffering under the influence of drink, got into trouble. Surrounded by the crowd, punches, bricks and sticks were thrown. The magistrates decided the Yeomanry were 'completely defeated' and called for the regular troops who had been put on standby in the backstreets. The 15th Hussars, veterans of

Waterloo, formed up and charged. The charge, wrote one officer who took part

> swept this mingled mass of human beings before it; people, yeomen and constables, in their confused attempts to escape, ran one over the other; so that by the time we had arrived at the end of the field the fugitives were literally piled up to a considerable elevation above the level of the ground.[8]

Through the cloud of dust, onlookers saw sabres rising and falling. Samuel Bamford was on the receiving end:

> For a moment the crowd held back as in a pause; then was a rush, heavy and resistless as a headlong sea; and a sound like low thunder, with screams, prayers and imprecations from the crowd-moiled, and sabre-doomed, who could not escape.[9]

Within ten minutes the field was clear. Bamford remembered that the 'sun looked down through a sultry and motionless air'.

> Several mounds of human beings still remained where they had fallen, crushed down, and smothered. Some of these still groaning, others with staring eyes, were gasping for breath, and others would never breathe more. All was silent save those low sounds, and the occasional snorting and pawing of steeds.[10]

The streets of Manchester were filled with wailing people running in the direction of the towns they had come from, 'their faces pale as death and some with blood trickling down their cheeks'.[11]

The newspapers named it the 'Peterloo Massacre' in a satirical reference to the presence of Waterloo troops. By modern standards it was unspectacular: eleven killed, 400 injured including 140 by sabre cuts. The news arrived in London two days later and by 5 September had reached the man who would immortalise the event in English literature.

As a place of self-imposed political exile, the Italian port of Livorno was not a bad choice for Percy Bysshe Shelley. He had set himself up on a terrace from where he could hear peasants singing and a water-wheel creaking, while, at night, fireflies glowed. It was in this romantic setting that he opened a package of London newspapers sent by express post in which Peterloo and its political aftermath were described. With a 'torrent of indignation . . . boiling in my veins' Shelley began writing *The Masque of Anarchy*, which he completed in 12 days and posted immediately to his publisher.

It has been described as 'the greatest poem of political protest ever written in English'.[12] Its final verse, which begins 'Rise like lions after slumber', has entered the culture of the British labour movement. When the firefighters went on strike against the Labour government in 2003, 'Rise Like Lions' was the slogan they printed on their union T-shirts. But the victims of Peterloo did not have the chance to hear Shelley's poem. Amid a welter of prosecutions that saw both Hunt and Bamford jailed, most radical publications closed and mass meetings banned, Shelley's publisher deemed it unwise for the poem to see the light of day; it did not appear until 1832.

For all its greatness, *The Masque of Anarchy* has one major flaw: Shelley knew nothing about the working class movement that had organised the Peterloo demonstration. In Shelley's heart-rending descriptions of its economic misery the working class appears as a naive mass, noble in poverty but too poor to think; demoralised by the scale of the injustice they faced, incapable of going beyond passive resistance without exchanging 'blood for blood and wrong for wrong'. Shelley's view of the working class dictated the course of action he advocated:

> And if then the tyrants dare
> Let them ride among you there,
> Slash, and stab, and maim, and hew,—
> What they like, that let them do.
> With folded arms and steady eyes,
> And little fear, and less surprise,
> Look upon them as they slay
> Till their rage has died away.[13]

This was the same strategy of passive resistance being advocated by Hunt and Bamford in the aftermath of the massacre. But it was being rejected as early as the night of the 16 August itself.

In New Cross, a slum area of central Manchester, the Hussars formed a 'strong night picket' to maintain order:

> As soon as it had taken up position a mob assembled about it, which increased as the darkness came on; stones were thrown at the soldiers, and the Hussars many times cleared the ground by driving the mob up the streets leading from the New Cross. But these attempts to get rid of the annoyance were only successful for the moment, for the people got through the houses or narrow passages, from one street to another, and the troops were again attacked, and many men and horses were struck with stones.[14]

After ninety minutes of this the troops opened fire. An infantry company fired three volleys, leaving four rioters seriously wounded. By the next day Manchester was a city under military occupation: 'The streets were patrolled by military, police and special constables; the shops were closed and silent; the warehouses were shut up and padlocked; the Exchange was deserted; the artillery was ready.'[15]

Despite this there were riots again on 17 August, not just in the city slums but in the nearby towns of Stockport and Macclesfield, where one policeman was killed. On 19 August there were clashes in New Cross and 'on the 20th the mob of this locality fought a pitched battle with the cavalry'.[16]

Bamford, an opponent of physical force, described the atmosphere in industrial suburbs in the days following Peterloo:

> I found when I got home, that there had been general ferment in the town. Many of the young men had been preparing arms and seeking out articles to convert into such. Some had been grinding scythes, others old hatchets, others screw-drivers, rusty swords, pikels and mop nails; anything which could be made to cut or stab was pronounced fit for service. But no plan was defined – nothing was arranged – and the arms were afterwards reserved for any event that might occur.[17]

The meekness and intended pacifism of the working class at Peterloo were central to Bamford's legal defence when he was tried for sedition and became accepted facts among socialists in the mid-century, who saw the Peterloo generation as political beginners, naively attached to their middle class leaders. Shelley's poem did not help, surviving while the press accounts faded and perpetuating the idea that the movement assembled at St Peter's Field was simply a vast crowd of disorganised workers.

Closer examination of the sources reveals a different truth: in the months leading to Peterloo the workers of the Lancashire cotton industry built a network of organisations so sophisticated that they foreshadowed anything achieved by the labour movement in the next 200 years.

'Human nature in its worst state . . .': So what was new about the men and women at Peterloo? The answer is more complex than the fact that they earned wages or operated machinery. There were in fact two kinds of worker present: weavers like Bamford who did piece-work at home on hand-powered machinery, and spinners who worked in factories. The key to understanding the terror they inspired among the upper classes is the alliance they formed. The spinners were the first modern 'proletariat'; the weavers an older working class elite whose privileged lifestyle was in decline. Until they jointly adopted democracy as their slogan, it had seemed like a lost cause to the middle class lawyers and journalists who dreamed of it.

The cotton spinners of 1819 were the first workers to experience the impact of a system in which they did not control the speed and process of production. Once cotton spinning was mechanised it moved from the home to the factory, and men replaced women as the core of the spinning workforce. As the machines got bigger, the skill of tending them became more complex and more highly paid. The final brick in the wall was the replacement of water power by steam, which allowed factories to increase in size and to be built in towns instead of next to village streams. By 1800 a core skilled workforce of adult male spinners existed, supplemented mainly by children recruited from orphanages, who were 'indentured' to factory owners and made to live in dormitories.

Coercion, in many forms, was the defining feature of the new industrial work. Labourers had been pushed off the countryside by laws abolishing common land. Poverty had been criminalised. The new poor were compelled by poverty to put their children into orphanages, from which work in a factory in Lancashire seemed like liberation.

Once inside the factory, workers became part of a disciplinary system modelled on prisons and armies, a system needed because for the first time in history machines dictated the speed of human movements. The transition from childhood to work, from the field to the factory, from home-working to industrial discipline – all this etched itself into the memories of this first generation of child factory workers, including Sarah Carpenter, aged ten:

> They took me into the counting house and showed me a piece of paper with a red sealed horse on which they told me to touch, and then to make a cross, which I did. This meant I had to stay at Cressbrook Mill till I was twenty-one . . . The master carder's name was Thomas Birks; but he never went by any other name than Tom the Devil. He was a very bad man – he was encouraged by the master in ill-treating all the hands, but particularly the children. I have often seen him pull up the clothes of big girls, seventeen or eighteen years of age, and throw them across his knee, and then flog them with his hand in the sight of both men and boys. Everybody was frightened of him. He would not even let us speak. He once fell poorly, and very glad we were. We wished he might die.[18]

Robert Blincoe, whose life story became a best-seller in the years after Peterloo, would never forget his first day at the mill:

> They reached the mill about half past five . . . The moment he entered the doors, the noise appalled him, and the stench seemed intolerable . . . The task first allotted to him was to pick up the loose cotton, that fell upon the floor . . . Unused to the stench, he soon felt sick, and by constantly stooping, his back ached. Blincoe, therefore, took the liberty to sit down; but this attitude, he soon found, was strictly forbidden in cotton mills. His task-master (Smith) gave him to understand he must keep on his legs. He did so, till twelve o'clock, being six hours and a half, without the least intermission.[19]

The power structure of the early factory was not simply 'them and us'; Blincoe's memoir shows that brutality flowed through two conduits. There were the factory overseers and dormitory captains, who had the power to beat, fine, hire, fire and, hints Blincoe, rape. Below them were the skilled male spinners, who hired child helpers and were allowed to terrorise their charges:

> It is a fact, too notorious to be denied, that the most brutal and ferocious of the spinners, stretchers, rovers &c have been in the habit, from mere wantonness, of inflicting severe punishments upon piecers, scavengers, frame-tenters, winders and others of the juvenile class, subjected to their power, compelling them to eat dirty pieces of candle, to lick up tobacco spittle, to open their mouths for the filthy wretches to spit into . . . What has a tendency to display human nature in its worst state is that most of the overlookers who acted thus cruelly had arrived in the mill as parish apprentices and as such had undergone all these offensive inflictions.[20]

Factory workers became visibly bent and shrunken. The most common industrial diseases were crippled knees, failing eyesight and curvature of the spine; many had limbs torn off by the machines. In many factories there was a pervasive subculture of violence, rape and casual sex, 'a licentiousness,' one reformer observed, 'capable of corrupting the whole body of society like an insidious disease, which eludes observation, yet is fatal in its effects'.

That was how they worked. This is how they lived: out of 7,000 houses surveyed in Manchester not long after Peterloo 2,220 had no toilet and 900 were deemed uninhabitable. 'What little furniture is found in them is of the rudest and most common sort, and very often in fragments,' reported the surgeon Philip Gaskell. They slept on beds of straw, many to a room. 'The demoralizing effects of this utter absence of social and domestic privacy must be seen before they can be appreciated. By laying bare all the wants and actions of the sexes, it strips them of regard for decency and modesty.'[21] But these were not the lowest of the low. Twenty thousand people lived in the basements of these tenements, frequently alongside livestock. They were mainly Irish weavers, bricklayers and street sellers: 'all are ragged, all are filthy, all are squalid', wrote Gaskell.

The impact of moving to the militarised factories and fetid slums would leave a particular stamp on the way the spinners organised once they began to fight back. But that came later. Like the migrant workers of Shenzhen today, they were too busy earning and spending the kind of money that, as farmers, they had hitherto only been able to dream about. It was the home-working weavers who first formed 'combinations', organisations for mutual assistance which would lobby Parliament for increased wages. In the thirty years before Peterloo the weavers' wages fell rapidly until all they had left was their pride. Bamford's home was a two-roomed house: one room contained hand looms for his wife and himself, the other the status symbols that separated the life of the weaver from that of the spinner:

> An humble but cleanly bed, screened by the dark, old-fashioned curtain, stands on our left. At the foot of the bed is a window closed from the looks of all passers. Next are some chairs, and a round table of mahogany; then another chair, and next it a long table, scoured very white. Above that is a looking-glass, with a picture on each side, of the *Resurrection and Ascension*, on glass, 'copied from Rubens' . . .[22]

This was a privileged culture in decline: mechanised spinning meant there was more cotton and it was easier to weave. An influx of demobbed soldiers from the Napoleonic Wars was destroying both the culture and wage levels enjoyed in the 'golden age' of hand-loom weaving. By the time cotton weaving itself was mechanised in the early 1830s the weavers had become the lowest of the low; an entire craft and culture had reached its nadir. The process generated incredible discontent.

When petitions failed, strikes broke out. In 1799 the government responded with the Combinations Act, effectively outlawing trade unions for the next 25 years. In response the discontent flowed down more anarchic channels. In 1808 Manchester weavers rioted, struck, clashed with the army and were defeated. It dawned on cotton bosses that this was the first 'mob' in Manchester that had not marched for Church and King. By 1812 Manchester was in the grip of the Luddite movement:

frame-knitters in Nottinghamshire had seized control of their villages, smashing the mechanical looms that were supplanting them and their skills. Lancashire weavers joined in, with attacks on the few factories where automated weaving had begun. The movement was put down at the cost of seven executed and 17 transported to Australia. Meanwhile the spinning workforce stood and watched, and got steadily bigger.

It was economic recession that ignited the spinners into action: once wages stopped rising there was nothing to offset the brutality of factory life. Between 1817 and Peterloo the spinners and weavers of Manchester created trade unions, night schools, militias, local parliaments and incipient political parties. While the workers' movement in the later 19th century would insist on rigorous distinctions between politics and economics, the spinners at Peterloo took only two years to work out they are inextricable.

The first sign of trouble was the ill-fated hunger march of 1817. Three hundred men with blankets assembled at St Peter's Field to march to London with a petition for the Prince Regent. Twelve thousand people turned out to see them off. The whole thing was dispersed by the army. Eight leaders (including Bamford despite the fact that he had opposed the march) were charged with high treason. After months in jail the charges failed to stick and they were released.

Now the momentum switched from politics to economics. Between July and September 1818 the whole Lancashire industrial region was gripped by strikes: first the spinners, because their promised pay rise had failed to materialise, then the weavers. Though unions were banned by law the spinners organised their strike by marching from one factory to another, starting around 4 a.m. Their aim, reported local magistrates, was to 'carry off by force or intimidation, though without any violent breach of the peace, the hands who might be disposed to go to work'.[23] These were the first flying pickets in history. As they assembled, the mill owners saw the shocking consequence of all the discipline and brutality they had meted out at work. A half-literate police spy reported:

> The plan they take is as follows, one man from Eich shop is chose
> by the people and he commands them he forms them in Ranks

and attends them on the march and as the soal Command and the[y] obey him as Strickley as the armey do their Colonel and as Little Talking as in the Regiment.[24]

The report conveyed further alarming details. 'The whole of the spinners is out, except about 500,' the spy told his handlers, adding that the pickets' march took 'twenty-three and a half minutes' to pass a point. Their average height was five feet two inches – the physical impact of poverty and factory work meant 'those that should have appeared as men were like boys of fifteen and sixteen'. The police spy offered a final piece of advice. Noting that the reformer Robert Peel had been pressing for the reduction of the working day to eleven hours, he wrote, 'If his Majesty's Minesters could see the people that day or either of the days since the[y] would have past Sir Robert Peel's bill.'[25]

The radical leaders, released from jail, now got involved with the spinners' strike. When the employers started legal action against the strikers they responded with a leaflet calling for a 'General Union'. This document stands as one of the first ever manifestations of 'class consciousness' – recognition that workers from different workplaces, towns and trades had an overriding common interest. It urges the workers to model their actions on those of their employers: to call meetings and to 'coldly and religiously' fulfil whatever is decided on.

> Every branch of labourers, namely Husbandmen, Weavers of all classes, Dyers, Fustian Cutters, Calico printers, Spinners of all classes, Hatters of all classes, Machine makers, Joiners, Bricklayers, Masons, Shoemakers, Tailors . . . ought immediately to call district meetings and appoint delegates to meet at some convenient central place . . .[26]

On 19 August 1818 the delegate meeting took place. It decided to form a General Union, led by an elected committee of 11 men which was to be insulated against bureaucracy by 'rotation every month so that the whole committee is changed every three months'. No individual trade was to strike without getting permission from the rest; once agreed, the whole resources of the union would support any section that went on strike. At this stage all mention of politics and religion was banned in meetings 'under a forfeit of threepence for the first offence and sixpence for the second', to be paid on the night.

The General Union, and the strike itself, did not survive two weeks. Starvation and legal action forced the spinners back to work, with a cathartic riot and shootings signalling the end of things. The committee, which had been in daily session from 7.30 a.m. to 8 p.m. in a pub called The Rifleman, was arrested, and the union collapsed.

In September the weavers struck. They paraded peacefully and at their mass meetings refused to hear any of the radical agitators speak. Their petition, drawn up at a delegate meeting, quotes extensively from the free-market economist Adam Smith. Their strike too was outlawed. The leaders were arrested and sentenced to two years jail. As late as the autumn of 1818 the weavers had been determined not to get involved with the spinners, the General Union or radical politics in general, but with this second mass arrest of their elected leaders this changed.

'The promotion of human happiness . . .': In May 1819 'patriotic union societies' sprang up all across northern England. One, the Stockport Union for the Promotion of Human Happiness, was described in detail in the radical press. Its rules, as with the General Union, were designed to prevent the formation of a permanent bureaucracy. The town was divided into twelve sections, each of which elected a delegate. Each section was divided into 'classes' of 12 people, who would meet once a week and pay a penny subscription. Central rooms were hired, and on four nights a week they were used to teach adults reading, writing and mathematics. On Saturdays there were poetry recitations. On Sundays they were used as schools for children. The purpose of the whole operation was 'to promote by all just means . . . a radical reform of Parliament by means of suffrage in all male persons . . . Parliaments having a duration not exceeding one year and of elections by ballot'.[27]

For reading material the union societies had radical newspapers like the *Manchester Observer* and the ultra-radical *Black Dwarf*, in whose pages one correspondent explained the purpose of all this book learning: 'We are endeavouring assiduously to inform ourselves and others, by all means in our power, [so] that when we are called upon by circumstances we may be able to act as lovers of our country and mankind.'[28] They were preparing for political power.

A member of the Stockport Union describes the meetings in detail:

> We generally read at a class meeting for about half an hour, if there is anything in the course of the reading that anyone present does not understand it is fully explained to him . . . After reading, a general conversation takes place for about half an hour more, when each member states his opinion and ideas of government . . .[29]

Women were present in large numbers; this was an era in which sexual harassment of women at work was common and even in the upper echelons of society they were second class citizens. At a meeting on Saddleworth Moor Bamford made a proposal considered at the time revolutionary – for women to be allowed to take part in voting:

> This was a new idea; and the women, who attended numerously on that bleak ridge, were mightily pleased with it, and the men being nothing dissentient, when the resolution was put the women held up their hands, amid much laughter; and ever from that time the females voted with the men at the radical meetings.[30]

Elsewhere women–only union societies were formed. Blackburn's women organised with the stated aim 'to instill into the minds of our children a deep and rooted hatred of our corrupt and tyrannical rulers'.[31]

When, two months before Peterloo, a delegate meeting of union societies took place in Oldham, 28 towns were represented from all across the industrial north. This was the movement that marched to Peterloo.

Within the space of two years the Manchester working class had moved from hunger marches to strikes, to a General Union expressly forbidden by law, to political organisations fighting for radical democracy. In the process they repeatedly used delegate structures to prevent a bureaucracy emerging. They gave women the vote almost exactly

100 years before the government would. They spent their evenings – following twelve to fourteen hours at work – educating themselves to be citizens in the democratic state that seemed close at hand. And that was not all . . .

'We rushed to the sweet cool air . . .': It was the union societies that, in the high summer of 1819, organised the 'drilling' of contingents for the Manchester meeting. At his trial Samuel Bamford played down the drilling. A pacifist on trial for sedition, fearing he was about to be hung out to dry by his co-defendants, it is easy to see Bamford's motivation. But to others the drilling was done with revolutionary intent. Thousands of people swarmed across the moors around Manchester in the evenings to take part in a whole new form of mass activity:

> When dusk came and we could no longer see to work, we jumped
> from our looms and rushed to the sweet cool air of the fields, or
> the waste lands, or the green lane-sides. We mustered, we fell into
> rank, we faced, marched, halted, faced-about . . . or, in the grey of
> a fine Sunday morn we would saunter through the mists, fragrant
> with the night odour of flowers . . . [32]

One report by police informers captures details of the drilling sessions at a key moment, the night Hunt's original Manchester meeting was banned:

> After they had done exercising they formed a circle around their
> commander, who told them that the intended meeting was put off,
> on account of their paper being illegal, but that would give them
> more time to drill: he then said they must have a colour and that
> they must subscribe . . .[33]

Thousands were involved, usually led by 'old soldiers of the line'. A consistent detail in police reports was the simulation of firing musket volleys by clapping hands. It is hard to accept Bamford's explanation that this was a 'joke'. A witness statement taken by magistrates on 10 August described 3,000 men drilling near Middleton:

The right wing advanced first, and the words of command, 'Fire, front rank kneeling' and when the word of command Fire was given, they clapped their hands; the leader then advanced the left wing in the same order as the right, and ordered them to fire; this was repeated several times.[34]

Even if the union society leaders saw the drilling as simply a way to maintain order, without doubt a large section of the Lancashire working class took the activity at face value. They intended to march to Manchester in military order; they intended to defend themselves if attacked along the way. They expected that the time was near when they might have to fight with firearms, probably as part of a wider republican uprising.

James Norris, the magistrate who gave the order for the massacre, wrote six weeks before the event, 'The lower classes are repeatedly heard to murmur threats that in a few weeks some explosion is to take place . . . for which I fear there is little doubt numbers are preparing themselves with Arms of various descriptions.[35]

The rulers of Georgian England were convinced they would face a general insurrection in 1819, and this is why they engineered the pre-emptive strike at Peterloo.

'If we had met all over England on that day . . .': The movement did not end at Peterloo. It ebbed during the winter that followed, amid trials, cover-ups and a political split. Bamford was by now in jail awaiting trial. He was among the majority of activists who favoured passive resistance. A radical minority agitated for the launch of a national insurrection on 1 November 1819, but Hunt ordered its cancellation. Trade picked up, Parliament passed a series of emergency laws banning public meetings, weapons, drilling and the radical press. Finally, in a coup de grâce, government spies suckered a handful of radical leaders in London into a conspiracy to blow up the cabinet 'to avenge the blood of Manchester'. Though Manchester workers had nothing to do with the plot, its exposure put the lid on the movement. The weavers reverted to their moderate stance.

A police informer described the Manchester workers' movement at the exact moment when the argument between reform and revolution was being resolved, right after the cancellation of the 1 November uprising. At a delegate meeting of the Manchester Union Society representing a membership of 12,500 there was 'much regret on the part of many' that the rising had been cancelled. Some were heard to say they had armed themselves in preparation. One man shouted at opponents of the rising that 'he should teach his children to curse them for not bringing it forward . . . [For] if we had met all over England on that day the business would have been done before now.'[36]

At this point the owner of the rooms told them they could no longer go on meeting as they were disrupting the school based there. This was overflowing with children expelled from mainstream schools for wearing white hats, symbols of mourning after Peterloo. The meeting ended in acrimony with an argument about money, and that was the end of the Manchester Union Society.

'Masters, not so much of others as themselves . . .': Samuel Bamford served two and a half years in jail for his role at Peterloo. On his release he tried to go back to cottage weaving but these were the dying days of the hand-loom industry. He became a journalist, was accepted into the Manchester middle class, and promptly disowned the radical republicans. He would write:

> Instead of wishing to create sudden changes, and to overthrow institutions, it were better that ignorance alone, the fruitful mother of arrogance and hard-heartedness, were pulled down. The masses should be elevated; instruction becoming the handmaid of God's grace . . . Whatsoever was offensive to right feeling, or opposed to the well-being of mankind, would then disappear and become absorbed in the great uprising of the mind. Many who are now but as atoms in the dust would then become exalted . . . many would become masters, not so much of others as themselves . . .

These words are a classic expression of what would become 'moral force' socialism and later Labourism, but would be a cry in the wilderness until, in the 1860s, the upper stratum of workers was granted the vote.

When we look back at Manchester in 1819 we can see the beginnings of everything that has happened since in workers' history: grassroots trade unionism, a workers' militia (albeit lacking guns), the general strike, the world-within-a-world of the socialist education club and above all delegate structures designed to combat bureaucracy. Most of the downsides are foreshadowed too: the orators who mesmerised workers with calls to action but refused to act themselves, the man who absconded with the money of the spinners' union in the middle of the strike, the brutality of skilled spinners towards unskilled women and children. As for the animosity which arises between an old, privileged workforce and a new one, greedily exchanging its poverty and freedom for wages and brutality, look no further than modern China to see how the pattern persists.

'Unity and strength,' said the banner Samuel Bamford carried to Peterloo. The event left behind a residue of class consciousness, a great poem, a working class legend – but little else. The memory of the organisations that made it happen disappeared. All that was left was a gut feeling that Lancashire workers would pass down the generations: at the very start of it all, something terrible was done to us and we will never forget.

2. Everything connected with beauty
The silk weavers' revolt, Lyon, 1831

> I was exceedingly surprised at finding among the weavers them-
> selves and among their children, and amongst everybody
> connected with the production of patterns, an attention devoted
> to everything which was in any way connected with beauty.
>
> John Bowring, Parliamentary testimony
> on the silk industry of Lyon, 1832

Varanasi, India, 2005

It was Lenin's grandfather who decided to call him Lenin. Now he
has ditched his high-caste family name of Raghuvanshi and quit
medicine, so the weavers of Varanasi call him simply Doctor Lenin.
He runs an NGO that specialises in rescuing child workers. But now
he's facing a bigger challenge: 'Before, our main focus was child
labour, but now that's not a problem because there is no labour at
all.' It is September 2005 and the hand-loom silk weaving industry
of Varanasi is slowly rotting away. Over the past five years, as India
has opened its domestic market to foreign imports, cheap Chinese
silk has flooded in.

A Varanasi sari was once, to the Indian bride, what a Savile Row
suit is to the modern chief executive. They have been weaving silk
here for at least a thousand years but the present-day system is only
200 years old. Traditionally, silk weaving was done by a Muslim caste,
and it is to the Muslim weaving district in the centre of the ancient
city that Lenin leads me.

Anwar Ali calls us in to his workshop. It is a single room filled by
a single loom, lit by a single lightbulb. The humidity, which hangs like

25

invisible damp washing in the alleyways, is ideal for silk weaving. Ali is 36, with a wife and five children. He learned weaving as a child and, to look at him in his vest and tattered trousers, does not seem to have much going for him. But when his hands touch the loom, you see him in a different light.

In a silk workshop light itself is the raw material; it streams through the door, lending a deep glow to the purple warps. These stretch horizontally, along the full length of the loom, running away from Anwar's midriff. He sits on the floor, his legs dangling into a shallow pit. He presses a pedal with his foot and, above his head, a heavy mechanism of wood and iron clunks; a belt of coarse, brown cardboard squares punched with holes moves along a click. The cards look like relics from an early computer but the technology is much older. This is the mechanism invented by Joseph Jacquard in the French city of Lyon in 1801, the Jacquard loom.

The holes in the cardboard work like the roll of a pianola, plucking some warps up an inch, leaving others. And through the space between them Anwar Ali throws the shuttles. There are three: wooden, black, six inches long, canoe shaped. Inside each there is a bobbin of silver silk. He never has to look or think as he throws the shuttle; it seems to land in his left hand at the very moment it leaves his right. Next he pulls a crossbar towards his stomach with a soft clunk. This pushes the three wavy lines of silver weft into place. What was a mess of thread has just become a few millimetres of organdie – shimmering, pale translucent silk – with a two-inch band of floral silver braid at either edge.

Nothing else in the room is beautiful: not the mud walls, not the scabby children peering in from the street, not Anwar Ali himself. But the silk sari he is weaving – it will take him three days to make one – is the highest embodiment of India's oldest craft. 'Look,' he says in Hindi, gesturing to the silver effervescence and the sheer bright purple of the cloth. Then he points modestly to his own chest and lowers his gaze, as if to take a bow.

There are 250,000 looms like this in the Varanasi silk industry. The problem is, only half of them are working:

In the last five years there the position has gone backwards. Employment is falling. We are getting less money. Inflation is increasing. Power-loom stuff is cheaper and the hand-loom sari is expensive. Nobody's buying it. We don't know what to do.

By now, Lenin has rustled up a whole street full of weavers. Like Ali they are quiet men. The youngsters, respectful at the back, let the middle-aged do the talking. 'We are living from day to day. Sometimes we have to go without food. The hungry man cannot sleep; he can only stay awake at night. I'm the only one who's working and I have a whole family to look after.'

It's tempting to think of this as the sad end of an industry in long decline, but wrong. Over the past 20 years there has in fact been massive growth in the hand-loom workforce. As India's big weaving mills closed during the market reforms of the 1990s weaving moved to home workshops or small factories. This, plus falling living standards among poor farmers, boosted the number of weavers locally by about 70 per cent. Now there are about 500,000 people within 80 miles of Varanasi living off hand-loom work. As well as the traditional Muslim weaving caste in the old city, there are now hundreds of thousands of Hindu *dalits*, from the 'untouchable' caste of village poor.

Varanasi silk is stiff, stiff with its hallmark gold and silver thread. Stiff because it has been made by hand, with tiny imperfections reflecting the day it was made and the man who made it. By contrast, Chinese silk is buttery, uniform and cheap. It is woven on machines that can make 500 metres in a day and, Lenin alleges, the Chinese government is dumping the stuff on the Indian market. Because Varanasi sari designs are not protected, unlike Cheddar cheese or French champagne, the Chinese have copied them with impunity.

Lenin takes me to a weavers' convention where about a hundred community leaders, NGO workers and activists debate the cause of the recession. Some blame the arrival of power looms, some the Chinese, some the government. Lenin himself – in a piece of flaming oratory worthy of his namesake – blames the World Trade Organisation. He wants textiles exempted from the trade rules under discussion at the WTO. At the end he whips the crowd up into a loud but orderly chant: 'WTO go to hell! Long live the Weavers' Association!'

We drive to the nearby village of Shankarpur to meet a weaver called Vishambar. A *dalit*, aged 40 and dressed in bright white robes, his name got into the local papers when he decided to hand over his three surviving children to an orphan charity. He takes me to see his former workshop, a bare shack now. Then he crouches down beside his new home – a hut made of branches which contains his last possessions: a wooden bowl, a brush made of twigs and a cup.

> I got a government loan but I could not pay it back. Ten years ago I took the loan, to start up as a hand-loom weaver. But for the last five years there's been hardly any work. Whatever I earned I used first to feed my children and I would take what was left. If there was nothing left I just drank water and physically became weaker and weaker.

His wife was the first to die, then his daughter. Indian officials call these 'starvation deaths' but looking at the village you can see that if this is a famine it is highly selective. There are no kids with bloated bellies; the surrounding fields are lush with grass, rice and corn. Fat oxen are being herded between lush rice paddies and there is a store of grain for them to eat. But in the twelve months to September 2005, 39 weavers in the Varanasi district were officially recorded as dying of starvation or suicide due to poverty. A rope slung over the top bar of the loom is the traditional way.

I ask them how it happens that people starve to death amid all this. 'The problem is our feudal pride,' says Vishambar. 'He means,' says Lenin, 'the caste system. Weavers would rather starve than beg – though he lives by begging now. They get so hungry they can't think straight. They won't tell their neighbours they are starving.'

Lenin, despite his name, does not want to overthrow the capitalist system; he wants to bring it in. He wants to eliminate feudalism but preserve the art of weaving, using the Internet to market handcrafted silk. For this he needs to unravel the free trade agreements made by the Indian government under the WTO.

This is not a Ghandian type of thing, this is a capitalist thing: we want to create a weavers' trust, a joint company to cut out the middlemen and sell our produce to the world direct. I want to eliminate the feudal system but in the feudal system some things are good. Nobody wants to destroy the Taj Mahal for instance! In the same way I think it is possible to preserve our economic status, our social rights and our art.

There are 12.5 million hand-loom weavers in India with the majority weaving cotton rather than silk. After agriculture it is the country's biggest industry. If hand-loom weaving is destroyed it will not be because of technological progress but because of an economic policy: the removal of trade protection, which has unleashed globalisation on an industry crippled by the caste system and semi-feudal finance arrangements. When it is finished economists will say that hand weaving on the Jacquard loom was always doomed and that people like Doctor Lenin, Anwar Ali and Vishambar were fighting a losing battle. What happened in Lyon in 1831 suggests they could be wrong.

Lyon, France, 1830

The city was drawing workers to it like a magnet; they were arriving on foot from Switzerland, Italy and the rest of France. Joseph Benôit, aged 18, had been doing the traditional journeyman's 'tour', wandering from town to town seeking work:

> I arrived in Lyon, stripped of all resources, at the end of the cold and rainy winter of 1829. I would endure the rise of hunger, cold and many other privations which my profession entailed. I stayed for two nights under the beautiful stars, behind a hedge in the plain of Brotteaux.[1]

His profession was silk weaving and Lyon was the silk capital of the world. The city had grown dramatically thanks to Jacquard's invention. By 1810 there were 11,000 Jacquard looms in France; by 1830 there were 30,000, most of them in Lyon, which outsiders were calling the 'Manchester of France'.

But this was no Manchester; there was only one factory of any size, an experimental establishment that was rapidly going out of business. The job of turning silk thread into satin, velvet, tulle, brocade or organdie was done in small workshops by skilled men and women on machines driven by pedal power. Apart from the lack of electric light, they could have been in Varanasi today.

Jacquard's invention had automated not the physical labour of weaving but the process of implementing a design. Far from deskilling weavers Jacquard had preserved the skill of their hands and made them capable of producing 'fast fashion'. That is what preserved a business model in the silk industry that all the economic geniuses of the time believed was doomed.

Four hundred silk manufacturers formed the top layer of the Lyon system, known as the *fabrique*. They would buy the spun silk, commission the designs and sell the finished product into the booming fashion market at home and abroad. They were capitalists without factories and without a direct workforce. It was a standing joke that they didn't manufacture anything. Most of their capital was locked up in silk and in the punchcards that held the designs. Their physical presence in Lyon was marked by the tall warehouses that lined the quaysides of the rivers bordering the city.

The next layer down was the 8,000 master craftsmen who owned their workshops and two to six looms. The typical set-up was for both the master and his wife to weave – there were 7,000 women weavers on the census – while the rest of the looms would be worked by journeyman weavers and apprentices, numbering about 20,000. The journeymen were known as *compagnons* – a word that can mean both mates and comrades; they formed a distinct layer with their own subculture of pubs and punch-ups. What they all had in common was work: sitting for 12 to 14 hours at the loom, powering it with a treadle, taking a light blow to the stomach up to 30,000 times a day. The world that Benôit had arrived in was the social opposite of a squalid factory city:

Habitually, in the era I speak of, the worker lived and ate at the home of the master workman and became, in this way, part of the family ... The Lyonnais workers are the most moral in France because of the family life that surrounds their daily work.[2]

The total workforce with their hands on looms numbered 40,000, and with tens of thousands in allied trades more than half Lyon's 140,000 population were dependent on the silk trade. They were known collectively by the derogatory term *canuts*. Adolphe Sala, one of the city's grandees, wrote with pride, 'No bell calls the *canut* to his loom in Lyon ... the Lyonnais worker displays a moral independence which no other manufacturing town could comprehend.'[3]

This is how the system known as 'collective manufacture' appeared to an aristocrat, benign and naturally conducive to social order. To the *canuts* the attraction was different; it allowed them to control their own work, set the price for it and generally stay out of direct contact with their bosses.

> He is trusted to work; he is free to decide the method of execution. Master of his own time, and of his will, he has only to be subject to his own judgement or needs. In the warehouse of the Lyonnais silk manufacturer you find only the products of the workers he employs: you never see him direct their behaviour or their work.[4]

This is the classic system of workers' control that prevailed in all craft workshops during the pre-industrial era and by preserving it, the Jacquard loom had preserved something else – the *canuts* brought an age-old culture and tradition with them into the industrial era. They were 'dreamers inclined to mysticism and outbreaks of violence'.[5]

Though the *canuts* were not crammed into factories they were concentrated into housing districts. Jacquard looms needed high ceilings and these were to be found in the cliff-like tenements of the Croix-Rousse district outside the city, as well as in four other suburbs across the river. The contrast with what the factory system had created could not be greater. Louis-René Villermé, who had documented the horrors of industrial slums, wrote of the *canuts* that 'far from being morally degraded and of meagre intelligence as has been said, they are on the contrary men most advanced in true civilization'.[6] John

Bowring, an English economist sent to find the secret of Lyon's success reported:

> I was exceedingly surprised at finding among the weavers ... an attention devoted to everything which was in any way connected with beauty, either in arrangement or in colour. I have, again and again, seen the weavers walking about gathering flowers, arranging them in the most attractive shapes. I found them constantly suggesting to their masters improvements in their designs.[7]

Silk weaving did not produce brawny fighters. Windows were closed to protect the silk; children grew up with spinal curvature and scrofula. The general atmosphere was sickly. It was as if the soft and pliant quality of the fabric had worked itself into the very being of the *canuts*. Master weaver Pierre Charnier complained to his colleagues:

> There are too many timid people among us. Timidity, as you know only too well, is the character of the silk worker. No other profession is less outgoing than ours. It's our sedentary lifestyle ... which shapes our morale. It is etiolated, just like our bodies. In order to remedy this double weakness, we have to create within our profession an esprit de corps. And there's only one way to get there: organisation ... When we fully recover our human dignity, the rest of the city ... will stop using the word *canut* as a term of abuse.[8]

Charnier set up the Society of Mutual Duty – which he described as a kind of 'working class freemasonry' – in 1827. It worked to a strict plan of organisation: fourteen 'companies' of twenty, each with a commander known as a syndic and two secretaries. Only workers over 25 years old could join. They had to have been a master weaver for at least a year and have a good reputation. But as a secret society there was little it could do except complain about the falling price of silk and bolster the spirit of 'mutualism' through intense cafe discussions. Then, in July 1830, the silk manufacturers were obliged to stage a revolution of their own.

Between the tricolour and the *tarif*: Jean-Claude Romand was a tailor whose business had collapsed, propelling him from the ranks of the lower middle class into those of the *canuts*, and to the tables of their radical cafes.

> I would pass the evenings in houses I knew where people met to discourse very freely on politics ... I got a taste for discussions animated by a very pronounced liberalism. You could read opposition newspapers, and sometimes pamphlets ... we sang songs by Berenger and got worked up against the established order of things.[9]

Educated and literate, Romand would frequent theatres, libraries and opera houses when he had money. When he did not he would wander along the river bank, dreaming of 'a mass revolt in which I could not wait to take part'. On 29 July 1830 his dream came true:

> I found myself one day on the bank of the Rhône, near the Café de la Perle, in the middle of a large crowd, when the mail coach from Paris arrived, which ran up before our eyes a small tricolour flag, which was greeted by cheers from the multitude. I rushed up ... but an old man nearer the flag got there first: he embraced it many times. I could not get to touch it. I could see he was an old soldier of [Napoleon's] *Grande Armée*.[10]

The tricolour was, at this point, banned. The Bourbon dynasty, its ample backside restored to the throne after the Battle of Waterloo, had spent fifteen years trying to govern France according to the old principle of lofty indifference – 'Let them eat cake' – and under the old flag. But this was a different France, an industrial economy with a rising middle class determined to make the country modern.

When the Bourbons tried to deny the middle class the right to vote, Paris revolted. In three days of street fighting the last Bourbon was overthrown and replaced with a 'Citizen King' called Louis-Phillipe – the Princess Diana of his day. Now, along with the tricolour, the July revolution arrived in Lyon. To the disappointment of young workers like Romand and Benoît it was more about street theatre than street fighting. The manufacturers 'stopped all the looms, ordered the workers to form up, armed, in the main squares to support the movement on pain of being sacked if they did not take part. The workers received their orders with joy and put all their strength behind their bosses'.[11] City Hall was seized and an alternative government set up without bloodshed.

Having stripped the main square of cobbles and built a massive barricade of coal wagons and barges, the workers cheerfully took it all down again. Benoît, bemused and depressed by the passivity of it all, decided to liven things up by shouting 'Liberty!' and 'Republic!' but he was howled down by the majority of the crowd.[12] The city's new mayor stood on a balcony and proclaimed 'a new era of prosperity' for Lyon.

A recession began immediately. Regime change wrought havoc with the fashion sense of the upper middle classes. Suddenly, orders for silk dried up. Now Benoît began to see the negative side of the Lyon business model:

> The worker is at the mercy of the industrialist who has no contractual obligation to him; the relationships are temporary and don't create in any way the kind of solidarity that exists in other industries between the boss and the worker. It is useful to be aware that this arrangement, which in appearance involves the independence of the worker, is in reality a cause of his ruin.[13]

The rate for weaving plummeted, throwing thousands out of work and their families onto the streets. Benoît remembered:

> Through the successive cuts in the price of products, the workers were reduced to the most miserable and precarious position . . . you could see in the streets and public squares workers with blemished and suffering faces, their wives and children in rags.[14]

As the misery dragged on, the *canuts* had to suffer the humiliation of seeing their family life and respectability defiled. Benoît raged: 'Sadly for the young girl, for the young mother who had kindled the lustful fires of the exploiters, she was always facing the fatal alternative of death through starvation or survival through dishonour.'

Benoît was thrown out of work for eight months in the winter of 1830: 'I never left a table other than hungry.' Romand, his business ruined, spent most of his time parading with the National Guard – which after the July revolution had been expanded to include skilled workers: 'It was good for my ego, bad for my wallet.' To Charnier it seemed that the July revolution had been a fake: 'The order of things had changed: but despotism, driven out of the palace, had found refuge in the [silk manufacturer's] cash till.'[15]

Lyon had ways of coping with economic crisis. There was the Chamber of Commerce where the silk manufacturers met; there were the mayor and the prefect – both empowered to meddle in commercial affairs. There was an elected industrial tribunal dating back to the Napoleonic period. There was also a precedent for the solution: in 1786 the weavers had been granted a minimum price list, known as the *tarif* and backed by law. This is what they wanted now, with wages plummeting and the workday stretching to 18 hours.

To strengthen their arm in the negotiations for the *tarif* the Society for Mutual Duty, still at this point secret, did three things: they formed a public organisation called the Workers' Commission, joined the National Guard, and set up the first workers' newspaper in history.

On 25 October the mayor summoned the silk bosses and told them to agree a *tarif*. As they assembled in the city's splendid prefecture, they noticed that a crowd of six thousand weavers had quietly appeared in the square below:

> An immense multitude had descended silently and in good order from the heights of Croix-Rousse, crossed the city and filled the squares . . . These were the starving masses who had come to learn their fate. They stood the whole time without uttering a word. There were no guns, no sabres, not even sticks. Just a single tricolour floated above their heads.[16]

Watching from the window, one of the silk merchants noted: 'Their leaders were getting them to execute marches and counter-marches with the facility and precision of generals.'[17] Faced with this, it took just four hours for the meeting to adopt the *tarif*.

The first issue of the weavers' newspaper, *L'Echo de la Fabrique*, was rushed out that evening, with a full five pages devoted to the new price list. It carried a song composed for the occasion, which was sung late into the night in the workers' districts. And – being the first ever workers' paper – it naturally included a column of offbeat news in brief, entitled 'Blows of the Shuttle', which playfully described the bosses' predicament that day: 'We hear that a deputation had to go incessantly to the Café d'Idalie to ask Monsieurs the academicians to look up the word "tarif" in a dictionary.'[18]

As activists crept out before dawn to nail copies of the new price list to warehouse doors, it seemed that Lyon's resilient social network – stretching from the bosses' cafe right into the home of the poorest labourer – had averted disaster. But Romand knew better.

> Two master silk workers who I knew well . . . assured me that a new silk workers' protest would have to be organised immediately because the tarif would not be implemented; and that this time there would be a serious conflict. I started trying to procure ammunition, reasoning that I could arm myself later if it became necessary.[19]

On 10 November, a letter signed by 140 manufacturers renounced the *tarif.* The city authorities, under pressure, announced that it had only ever been intended as a guideline.

'Live working or die fighting . . .': *L'Echo de la Fabrique* never actually called for an uprising but its gossip column of 6 November proved remarkably prophetic:

> It has been rumoured . . . that the masses are ready to rise up; that the Croix Rousse is about to march with a black flag to attack City Hall, and that it will go next to the homes of certain manufacturers whose names figure on a supposed blacklist.[20]

On Sunday 20 November the National Guard was called to a parade in Lyon's main square. The units were recruited by district. The city centre legion included mainly silk manufacturers and their clerks but units based in the weaving districts were recruited from master weavers. The top brass besported themselves on the platform oblivious to the fact that there were, in reality, two rival militias; meanwhile the ranks got to exchanging insults about the quality of each others' uniforms.

The following morning the black flag appeared – the Workers Commission had called a strike to enforce the *tarif*. Four hundred journeymen swarmed into the alleys and tunnels of Croix-Rousse to stop the looms. At 10 a.m. a National Guard unit appeared and its officer ordered the 'rabble' to disperse. In one of those twists of fate on which epochs turn this happened to be the most fashionable unit in the city, composed completely of silk manufacturers. Romand witnessed the stand-off, which began as the troops were enjoying a mid-morning glass of wine:

> The National Guard, emptying their glasses, were imprudent enough
> to propose humiliating toasts to the silk workers who were just a
> few yards away. 'Your health, *canut*! White-cheese eaters! . . . You
> want the *tarif*? Damn you – it is in here!' And with these last words
> they waved their cartridge pouches.[21]

As the militia fixed bayonets, the workers pelted them with cobblestones, forcing them to retreat, some without their weapons. Now a big crowd began to march down the hill, arms linked and singing. But they ran into another National Guard unit, which opened fire. All over the city, workers now took to the streets shouting, 'They have killed our brothers.' One contingent carried a black flag. At that point it had no anarchist connotations but was simply a symbol of mourning. It was Romand who dreamed up the slogan on the flag, words which were to make the *canuts* famous across continents and centuries: 'Live Working or Die Fighting'.

A company of regular infantry was now deployed but refused to fire; many were Bourbon supporters who hated the middle class and their trendy King more than they did the workers. At midday the prefect, together with the commander of the National Guard, led a column up the hill. Pushing past the barricades in full regalia they stood on a balcony in Croix-Rousse to call for the crowd's dispersal, and were promptly taken prisoner. Later a force of dragoons and artillery managed to establish a front line halfway up the hillside but by this time all the weavers' units of the National Guard had gone over to the insurgents.

At 8 a.m. on 22 November, the city authorities tried to advance with regular troops. Romand arrived with a rifle hidden under his coat and was at first mistaken by the crowd for one of the bosses:

> I took two steps back, seized my carbine in two hands by the end of the barrel and raised the butt in the air: 'The first person who comes near will regret it. Fools, do you think that I have come here stupidly to fight you? No, I am of the people and for the people!' With these words, their confidence returned. I realised the soldiers were preparing to fire. I charged my weapon, advanced a few paces along the street and the report of my rifle was greeted by the cheers of those who the instant before had wanted to disarm me.[22]

Romand was not the only one with military experience; earlier that year a corps of 700 'Rhône Volunteers' had staged an abortive attempt to 'liberate' the Italian provinces of Piedmont and Savoy. They were a unit devoted as much to drinking as to drilling and, having averted an international incident, the French authorities were happy to let them go on doing both. But now three master weavers who had been officers in the Rhône Volunteers led a counter-attack. Skirmishes began across the bridges on the north and south sides of the city, close to the centre of power and the silk warehouses.

At one bridge the insurgents were led by an African silk dyer called Etienne Stanislas, who is shown clearly in one of the popular engravings that circulated later. Jean-Baptiste Montfalcon, a local doctor who became the city's main pro-government journalist, described the scene using all the tools of his new profession:

> This hideous Negro . . . choosing his victims from the Pont Morand and with his eyes aflame, his mouth foaming, his arms covered in blood, giving a barbarous cry and jumping for joy every time his lead, skilfully aimed, toppled a dragoon or artilleryman.[23]

That night the army evacuated the city, leaving the workers in control. More than 100 soldiers had been killed and 263 wounded; on the workers' side, there were 63 dead and double that number wounded. The workers' leaders now formed a provisional general staff to run the city which drew on two sets of people: on the one side were master weavers and Rhône Volunteers, on the other were middle class republicans – politicians, journalists and lawyers. The republicans had been taken by surprise at the insurrection but now dived in with the aim of leading it.

From City Hall the provisional government issued decrees against looting, set free those imprisoned for debt but kept common criminals in jail, called for the election of new magistrates and promised elections to 'primary assemblies'. But there was basic disagreement over the way forward: the weavers wanted the *tarif*, the republicans wanted the republic and were counting on the rest of southern France to march to their support. As the arguments dragged on late into the night, the workers' delegates slipped back to the Croix-Rousse, where they set up a new headquarters. Romand observed the political crisis first hand:

> The silk workers had achieved victory but they did not know what to do with it and they folded their arms, seeing their task as finished; whereas the men who had excited them, and who hoped that they would serve as a vehicle for their rise to power, were indignant to see them calm down so quickly.[24]

Romand complained that the men now running the city were strangers to the workers' districts. He tried to strike up a conversation with the republican leaders but, he says, was met with insults:

> These chancers were already putting on airs and graces, displaying ideas more aristocratic than the old city magistrates who my rifle had helped depose. I was for them just a simple tailor, just a prole-tarian, just one of their tools to be used and discarded afterwards.[25]

After three days the revolt petered out and the city was reoccupied. On his way to prison, Romand noted that the republican leaders were given special treatment:

> . . . the rest were chained two by two, but it's fair to say that each was allowed to choose his comrade . . . I chose the negro Stanislas,

who had, it is said, on the Pont Morand borne the brunt of the enemy attack on his own. It seemed to me that his circumstances were closer to mine than all the others . . .

There were arrests but no systematic reprisals; there were even significant concessions made to the weavers. The Society of Mutual Duty continued its work, sending Charnier to Paris to seek an audience with the Citizen King. The city's newspapers hurried to forget the incident. But in the streets and bars of Croix-Rousse the workers talked up the legend of the black flag. The journalist Montfalcon, with his ear to the ground, summed up the problem:

> The victory in November gave Lyon's workers a pride and an audacity that made it impossible to deal with them. It will be for centuries the favourite story in the workshops, tradition will transmit this great event from generation to generation, and the last weaver will enthusiastically tell the last apprentice: 'Once upon a time we drove out the silk manufacturers and the garrison, and took the city.'[26]

Socialism discovers the workers: During the next two years the workers' organisations grew and became radicalised. *L'Echo de la Fabrique* declared itself the paper not just of the silk workers but of the whole 'proletariat'. The journeymen set up their own association, modelled on the master weavers' society. Membership of the National Guard declined, with many of the workers now barred and the manufacturers distinctly unenthusiastic. The revolt made the *canuts* famous all over Europe and a Parisian journalist who had witnessed it first hand shocked the continent with his account:

> The Lyon uprising has revealed a fundamental secret, that of the internal social conflict between the class that owns things and the one that does not . . . The barbarians who threaten society are not in the Caucasus or the steppes of Tartary; they are in the suburbs of our manufacturing cities.[27]

The existence of a class struggle as the central threat to social order was an astonishing new idea. It certainly caused excitement at a derelict monastery on the edge of Paris, where a small group of socialists were living in a commune and practising free love. These were the followers of Count Henri Saint-Simon, a dreamer-up of socialist utopias, recently deceased. He had left his followers a large amount of money and instructions to set up a new religion that could remake society according to scientific principles. The church was led by two 'fathers', Prosper Enfantin and Michel Chevalier. Members wore a blue tunic buttoned at the back, a white waistcoat with their name printed on it in red, a red collar, white trousers, a red beret, a shiny black leather belt and a flowing scarf. Since everybody else in France except clowns wore mainly black or grey, recruitment had been slow. But now they had a cause.

Enfantin decreed, 'For us theoretical politics are now finished; the life of practical politics begins!' He sent emissaries to begin lecturing among the *canuts* and a local Saint-Simonian doctor began writing for *L'Echo*. Meanwhile, master weaver Charnier, sent to Paris to lobby politicians, hooked up with the sect in the time-honoured manner of shop floor activists who find themselves among socialists advocating free love.

By November 1832 the plan had become ambitious: to move the entire commune to Lyon, together with its costumes, theatrical spectacles and secret rites. In a pamphlet entitled 'To Lyon!' Chevalier ordered, 'Forward to Lyon, the giant worker; he will give us a "baptism of wages", and we will pour forth our balm on his fevered head . . .'[28] He promised, 'We will enter wearing the beret of peace, which is the transformation of the red bonnet of terror.'

They arrived during the first anniversary of the uprising and paraded through the streets in full regalia on horse-drawn carts. But they faced two pressing problems: all Saint-Simon's money had been spent and both Chevalier and Enfantin were now in jail. So they became the first of many generations of middle class socialists to 'go to the people': this mixture of cross-dressing poets, doctors and musicians got themselves jobs as trainee *canuts* in the workshops. But the baptism of wages proved heavy going. Emile Barrault, the interim leader of the sect, complained,

From five in the morning to eight at night, I worked as a machine hand for 40 sous a day. My hands became hard, my limbs grew strong; my body became accustomed to the work; thanks to my moral strength my physical force did not give out the first days of work.[29]

After less than a month at the loom, Barrault decided that Lyon was too small a stage for such a big idea as socialism. He ruled that the church should now move to Asia and be renamed the Guild of Women (it would, along the way, make the first attempt to dig what we now know as the Suez Canal). Joseph Benoît, who watched them leave, summed up the impact of the very first socialist 'intervention' into the working class:

> Saint-Simonianism was nothing more than a brilliant meteor illuminating society for an instant with its uncompromising lucidity. After having shaken up the intelligentsia and agitated the population of Lyon, it was limited to a small group of faithful and soon had only a contested influence on the workers. The religious dogmas that its followers had adopted – going so far as to wear costumes – turned it into a sect outside of society . . . The republican idea had more in its favour: it was a form of government which had been tested and which had followers and a tradition. The workers of Lyon, taught by the experience of 1831, became devoted to republican ideas.[30]

The reckoning: 1833 was a record year for silk production, and as the economy blossomed so did workers' organisations. The active membership of the Society of Mutual Duty doubled. A new, more militant generation of leaders took over. *L'Echo de la Fabrique* reported the formation of mutual societies among printers, goldsmiths, stone-masons and hatters, raising a strike fund for the latter. A new workers' newspaper was launched called *L'Echo des Travailleurs*, which accused its rival of being too moderate.

The *canuts* withdrew from the industrial tribunal. Seeking a more permanent solution to the insecurities of the trade cycle they proposed a 'Central House', a cooperative in which each loom entitled you to a single share and where you worked for a fixed daily wage in addition to a share of the profits. One hundred and seventy years later the silk weavers of Varanasi would think of the same idea.

In February 1834, in response to a new downturn in orders, the manufacturers slashed the going rate for woven silk, prompting a general strike which, at its height, stopped every loom in the city. After six days, faced with a united front of manufacturers and government, the weavers voted to retreat in good order. Now the government rushed through legislation based on the English anti-union laws: all unions to register with the police; membership of secret societies to be punished with a year in jail; bars found to be hosting secret meetings to be closed down. Six of the weavers' leaders were put on trial.

Outrage at the imposition of these laws and the indignity of seeing their own men dragged before the courts now pushed even the most moderate of the master weavers into alliance with the republicans. A joint committee was formed and demonstrations called to coincide with the start of the weavers' trial. On 9 April 1834 the second Lyon uprising began.

This time it was armed from the start and led by the republican underground. A full-scale battle lasted six days. Once the workers had captured artillery – and worked out that the powder should go in before the cannonball – heavy weapons were used on both sides. Some 131 soldiers and 192 workers were killed.

One silk worker, a former soldier and the president of a secret society, left an anonymous diary of the fighting. It sums up the political journey the *canuts* had made from trade unionism to working class republicanism:

> Yes I am a republican; yes, my friends who fought alongside me were all republicans; no, we did not attack, nor did we go looking for combat – though we never feared it. But we responded to force with courage and in the name of the Republic, the only form of government where a people can find a guarantee for their rights. So recognise this, Mr

Journalist: this handful of brave men, who survived under the fire of 5,000 soldiers for six days, could not have held on 24 hours under the influence of any cause other than the Republic.

He spelled out the link the silk workers had forged between republican politics and social justice:

Vying with each other in zeal and courage, they decided to die in defence of their rights: at the end each one did his duty as man and citizen. The gauntlet thrown down to us, we were forced to take it up, not only in the hope of winning, but also to show to our oppressors that we care about the well-being of the country, and that we could break our chains at the very moment they thought they had forged the final link.[31]

The socialism of skilled workers: Shortly after the first uprising, one follower of Saint-Simon told readers of *L'Echo de la Fabrique*,

In my opinion the silk industry must sooner or later go the way of the cotton industry, and that is why I am asking my fellow citizens to pay particular attention to what is happening in Manchester and Lancashire . . .[32]

He was not the last socialist to conclude that the factory system – with thousands of workers, machine power and mass production – was the natural business model for capitalism and the most fertile ground for revolution. Skilled artisans came to be viewed by revolutionaries of the mid-19th century as living dinosaurs, doomed to extinction, their craft mentality an obstacle to 'class consciousness'.

With the benefit of hindsight we can see the *canuts* in a different light. The Lyon system looks a lot like Silicon Valley today: a network of skilled specialists and entrepreneurs, capital locked up in designs not machinery, a culture of autonomy and invention in the workplace. Skill – and the right to upskill – was seen as the property of the workers, not the bosses. Innovation and collaborative competition were as central to the business model of Lyon in the 1830s as they are in Silicon Valley today. And in every decade of the intervening period there has been a workforce, usually in the most dynamic corner of the world economy, where skill, radicalism and self-respect have gone side by side.

The *canuts* had a lot more than their chains to lose, namely a room full of expensive looms, a home and hard won social status. But they knew, possibly better than any group of factory workers in the same period, that there was 'a world to win'. *L'Echo* taught the *canuts* that they were part of a new class, the 'proletariat', that it was global and had global interests.

The *canuts* practised what has been called the 'socialism of skilled workers', where democratic rights and the struggle for decency take precedence over the basic issue of wages. Not long after the first insurrection *L'Echo de la Fabrique* began to carry regular guides to self-education, with extracts from the classics that would form a basic reading list for any college course in Enlightenment philosophy and literature today. Having recovered from the shock of free-love feminism as practised by the Saint-Simonians, the editors of the *Echo* were, by mid-1833, advocating greater legal rights for women.

For the skilled worker, the biggest thing they had to lose was control in the workplace, control that was the result of their monopoly on skill and training and their ability to set wage rates. They would defend this with their lives, up to the point of insurrection. But as long as it was there to be defended they had a stake in the capitalist system that the factory wage slave or the slum poor did not. They were not hostile to socialism, but tended to see it as an answer to 'What if?' rather than 'What next?'

In the revolt of the *canuts* we see for the first time the three 'big asks' that drove the formation of a global labour movement: self-betterment, workplace autonomy and democratic rights. Long before the major theorists of socialism and anarchism had written their big books, the workers had discovered a makeshift ideology that would encompass all three goals – a kind of working-class republicanism.

In 1848 the Republic became a reality in France and revolutions took place all over Europe. By then the spectre haunting the developed world was the working class. The misery documented in

Manchester at the time of Peterloo could now be witnessed in Belgium, northern France, Silesia, the Rhineland and New England. But it was the world's skilled artisans – the weavers, shoemakers and metalworkers – who led the workers' organisations during the great upheaval of 1848.

By then Jean-Claude Romand was out of jail, a reformed character and a broken man, his memoirs a warning to workers not to dabble in revolution. Joseph Benoît became an ardent socialist and remained one until his death. He took part in the revolution of 1848, which in Lyon was a relatively peaceful affair. He would write,

> The workers of Lyon determined the character of all future struggles . . . in branding their own with the immortal slogan, which summed up in a few words the needs and aspirations of modern society. They inscribed on their banner: Live working or die fighting![33]

3. This is the dawn . . .
The Paris Commune, 1871

> The old world crumbles. The night that covers the earth tears back its shroud. The dawn approaches . . . Today, with the triumph of the people, the era of work has begun . . . Brothers the whole world over, our blood is flowing for your freedom; our victory is yours; rise up! This is the dawn . . .
>
> Jules Vallès *L'Insurgé*, 1871[1]

Amukoko, Nigeria, 2005

The man who flags down our van says he's a policeman. His frightened eyes peer through the windscreen and he rattles a sawn-off AK-47 to make his point. The driver pulls a disgusted face, looks pointedly at the gunman's bare feet as if to say 'Come off it' and edges forward. The police mount roadblocks every mile along the dual carriageway that borders this Lagos slum but they don't come in this far.

Amukoko is a sea of shacks and alleyways, long terraces of one-storey huts clustered around improvised concrete 'compounds' sometimes four storeys high. A canal spills through the middle, green with vegetation, filthy with excrement and swarming with mosquitoes. Thanks to this canal, one out of every 25 children skipping barefoot in these streets will die of malaria before the age of ten. Only 5 per cent of Amukoko's homes have running water. 'We call it the ghetto,' says Stephen Oluremi. 'Those who live here only have money just for living'. Three million people live here.

At night they sleep eight or ten to a room, and the overspill can be found in corridors, cupboards and stairwells. In the daytime the passage-ways are teeming with family life: a woman is getting a fire going under a cooking pot; kids race around in states of clothing corresponding to their age. The very young are naked; school-age boys wear ragged shorts; an adolescent might – if his family has had just one life-changing piece of good luck – wear the faded football strip of Liverpool or Juventus bearing the name of a player famous five years ago.

There are very few old people; Amukoko is a place for migrant workers. Young mothers control the streets, dressed in the tribal styles of every part of Nigeria. Hausa women from the north in Muslim scarves fetch water beside Ibo women from the south with bare stomachs and ornate dreadlocks.

Most of the men are out at work or out looking for work. But where do you work if you come from Amukoko? If you are a child you can sell things. Every road junction within half a day's walk is full of kids from Amukoko, offering the neo-junk of a Third World economy: phone cards, cellphone chargers, rip-offs of self-improvement books in English. One boy proffers a fistful of black electrical cables to a van driver stuck in a traffic jam; the driver picks one out and then, with the traffic suddenly unjammed, drives off without paying. The boy's face goes into tearful meltdown but then the adrenalin kicks in and he chases after the van, shouting.

Or you can work as a tailor. This means wandering around Lagos with a small white cushion on your head, balancing a 1950s vintage Singer sewing machine on top. Once in a while your shout for work will coincide with somebody's need for sewing and their ability to pay. The rest of the time you keep your neck gracefully erect and walk the streets.

For all its printed shawls, red-hot coals and football regalia the overwhelming colour in Amukoko is grey. The gutters and the streets are coated in a grey mud that is not really mud but layer upon layer of toxic rubbish – decades-old plastic bags, last year's carpet, yesterday's chicken bones – all ground into a fine dry paste by millions of passing feet. The same grey settles on the roofs and, thanks to coarse detergent, the bleaching sun, and polluted rain the grey seeps into people's clothes.

Tuberculosis, malaria, measles and Aids are the biggest killers. Babies are delivered by traditional birth attendants whom tradition has taught to do lethal things. Serene Nigerian nuns, barricaded into their compounds at night, glide through the streets by day doling out medicine and discouraging condom use.

Amukoko is the classic slum. One billion people live in slums, one sixth of humanity, one third of city dwellers. By 2030, according to the UN, slum dwellers will number two billion. It is easy to dissociate the world of Amukoko from the world of factories and offices, to think of slums as one social reality and the modern workplace as another, but in countries like Nigeria they are inextricably linked.

Less than two miles from the edge of Amukoko is Ikeja, the industrial heart of Lagos. A long straight road bordered by wire fences and a railway takes you past the big names: Guinness, Dunlop, Dulux, Berger Paints, Nigeria Steel and Wire. The men coming out to buy snacks from street vendors look tough, dusty, confident. Ikeja looks like it's in a different century from Amukoko. But the lives of men like Stephen Oluremi straddle these two worlds.[2]

Oluremi works in a metal bashing factory, making aluminium pots for electrical appliances. He is single, in his early twenties with hard hands and scrappy clothing. There are 250 permanent workers where he works and 200 casuals. He is one of the casuals:

> In this country I don't know how they get away with it: the casual works like a staffer but the money is different. You don't have a contract. When you are working you are supposed to collect good money, but for the casuals you are not collecting good money at all. Even though you do the same job as a staffer, you are not paid very well. That is the casual way.

He earns 5,000 naira a month – £21 sterling and about half the going rate for a factory worker in China. The hours are bearable – 7 a.m. to 3 p.m. – and conditions are tough, but he counts himself lucky to be on the production line and not the section where they hand-polish the castings: 'In the "village", where they are polishing, it's very hot. If I worked in that place for just two days I would be sick because they are using all their power, their strength, their everything, to work.'

Like most big factories in Nigeria his workplace is unionised. Nigeria's unions won legal recognition and a compulsory 'check-off system', where the company collects union dues from wage packets, in the 1970s. Though the government has recently made this voluntary, most foreign investors, under scrutiny from NGOs, have not felt inclined to tear up union agreements. In fact they have lavished company benefits on their core workforce. But Oluremi can't get into the core workforce. He's been at the factory four years and, by law, should have been taken on permanently after six months. But he hasn't, and that is his big gripe – against the employers, the other workers and the union.

> People risk their bodies for this work. I am sick – tomorrow I am supposed to go to the medical centre – but if I get signed off sick they will not pay me. If you are a casual and you go for a medical you will not be paid. Even if the doctor gives you three weeks for your illness you will not be paid. The staff will be paid. If the doctor gives you sick leave more than a week, it is tough for you.

The staff with regular contracts earn double what he earns, plus housing and medical benefits, so he lives in the slum, spending half his wages on transport and another quarter on the rented room he shares with another young factory worker. The union leader in his factory is also a senior manager. To get a job here you need to know somebody in the management or the union. So why don't they challenge the union leaders, if they are so dissatisfied?

> People who have worked in the factory a long time are called elders. When the youth are talking, the elders will always be against, so they don't unite. We youths will present candidates; the elders will gather themselves. When the elections take place the casuals will not be there. Only the staff will be at the election, and there are more elders than youth among the staff, so that is how the union overcomes the people.

The Nigerian labour movement lives in wary symbiosis with the recently demilitarised state. It has a heavy presence in foreign-owned industries and the public sector but cannot normally sink roots into the population of a place like Amukoko. The social networks in the slums come together haphazardly around the mosques, the churches, the struggling clinics and the NGOs. Like most workers in the Lagos slums, Oluremi is too busy struggling for survival to think about the wider politics of it all:

> After work, for a man like me, you want to go to school. Once I finish work maybe I'll go to my friend's place, or to the computer school to study. I just have to fight for my life, after I finish work. I have to fight for my own life, just to survive.

It is only in abnormal times that the Nigerian Labour Congress, the main trade union federation, links up with the passions and priorities of the slum dwellers. In 2003 the NLC called a general strike after the government raised the price of petrol. The strike was solid in heavy industry and the oil sector, but when a pro-government union organised a return to work, youth gangs from the Lagos slums attacked the strike-breakers with machetes and erected burning barricades. By nightfall on 7 July 2003 ten protesters had been shot dead by police. In October 2003 the government slashed the price of fuel under the threat of a new general strike and there has been a sullen truce with the unions ever since.

Stephen Oluremi's life is lived across two realities, the lawless slum and the modern workplace. They look like separate worlds but they are products of the same forces: foreign investment, the collapse of agriculture, migration to the cities, corrupt administration and unemployment. The labour movement is entrenched in the official economy but almost incapable of playing a role in the unofficial economy. Its leaders use the strike weapon rarely, because they know it will unleash forces they cannot control.

This is the dilemma for unions across the developing world: how to go beyond the core workforce and organise the poor, the slum dwellers and the casuals without fomenting chaos and drawing down repression. The same situation faced trade unions in Europe and America in the second half of the 19th century, above all in Paris. Here a dictator was trying to democratise, a core workforce was trying to organise and a mass of slum dwellers, pushed to the outskirts of the city, were, like Stephen Oluremi, 'just fighting to survive' . . .

Paris, April 1867

The age of revolution is over. True, there are still some bearded revolutionaries exiled in the bolt-holes of the world but they are haunted men, scarred by failure. The uprisings of 1848 in Vienna, Berlin and Budapest are just a memory. In Paris, ancient alleyways have been replaced with wide boulevards designed to make 1848-style barricades impossible and artillery fire lethal – not that anybody expects this will be needed. Europe is a continent of strong government, new technology and honest work. The age of industrial exhibitions has begun.

In a small hall in Paris, the Bookbinders' Mutual Society is about to elect its delegation to the biggest technology fair ever seen, the Universal Exposition, which has just opened in a palace of glass and iron by the Seine. There is state funding on offer to cover the workers' costs and some in the hall are in favour of taking it. But the man on the platform is against: 'If we want to keep our independence, our power to speak freely about what we see and express our own ideas, we have to reject every kind of patronage and organise the delegation with our own resources.'[3]

Eugène Varlin knows something about resources. He brought the bookbinders out on strike two years before in a fight for the ten-hour day; he raised a massive strike fund; he has fought and won. Varlin is 28 years old, with a halo of black hair and a straggly beard, round face and studious eyes. He's already had a poem written about him and launched a workers' grocery store. He is in all ways a typical member of the mid-century labour movement – highly skilled, self-educated and convinced technology can bring social progress.

He has tried to convince the employers that new technology should mean shorter hours and rising wages:

> The development of industry should result in rising living standards for all. Production is increasing every day due to the increased use of machines; the rich alone cannot sustain consumption. The worker has to become the consumer and, for that, he needs money enough to spend and time enough to enjoy his possessions.[4]

These are not revolutionary ideas; forty years later they will be echoed, almost verbatim, by Henry Ford. And they are not far off the sentiments of the man whose money will back the Universal Expo, Louis-Napoleon, the self-styled Second Emperor of France. He is the man who crushed the revolution of 1848 but he has not ground the Paris slums to brick dust for nothing. France is to have world-class industry and needs a world-class workforce. And, since the age of revolution is over, the Emperor has legalised workers' mutual funds and cooperatives, though their meetings are banned from discussing politics and have to lodge their minute books with the police.

The bookbinders of Paris vote to decline the Emperor's money and send Varlin to the Expo to study the mechanical wonders of the world. All over France skilled workers are electing their delegations: mechanics, shoemakers, hatters, brass-moulders. They converge on the Expo wearing their Sunday best and carrying notebooks.

It begins with the crowned heads of Europe in attendance and a cavalry parade. Inside the exhibition hall every modern wonder is on display – fancy corsets, international weights and measures, fine art – but the star attractions are vast and intricate machines. The Americans bring McCormick's harvester and Morse's telegraph; Krupp, the German steel magnate, presents a 50-ton cannon that can fire 1,000-pound shells; the French unveil a contraption for making hats out of rabbit skin.

In November the exhibition closes and the workers' delegates compile their observations. These are delivered to the Emperor by civil servants in a state of shock. Instead of a poem of praise to mechanisation the reports read like a sustained critique of the mid-19th-century social order. 'Surely,' asks the shoemakers' delegation, 'machines belong to everyone? Thousands of workers have kept them going. Surely it is contrary to justice and equity that they have become a monopoly and a profit to a few individuals?[5]'

The new division of labour is, they maintain, robbing the workers of both their skills and status. But they are not Luddites – all they want is their fair share of progress:

> The system is basically excellent but fails at the top. And though everyone participates in this great productive effort, only a few profit from it. Therefore we must join forces, answering strength with strength and, while respecting the positions that have already been won, gradually replace it with an economic system which will be more profitable to everyone.[6]

The hatters too are ready to sound a sour note. Granted, the new gizmo – which, they joke, can turn a live rabbit into a finished hat – is a true symbol of industrial modernity, but in the factory it has become the symbol of their own worthlessness.

> It is put in a small, badly lit room in the remotest corner of the building and, as this precaution is deemed inadequate, it is boarded up with planks like some supposedly holy image which must be hidden from the sight of the crowd . . . It has become almost like a symbol for the passion, or rather the religion, of every man for himself.[7]

The mechanics' delegation leaves in a state of excitement. Machines like these, they enthuse, could end the need for manual labour altogether. The minds of men whose workaday world is one of grease and metal filings leap forward more than a hundred years to imagine robots: 'Our aim is to get the machines to do all the material work, and to make them in sufficient quantities so that all that will be required will be a few hours supervision each day.'[8]

These reports capture better than any rare daguerreotype the way skilled workers' minds are turning. Self-education, respectability and betterment are the recurrent themes. Their vision of social justice is one of a cooperative society based on new technology. Work, skill and respect will be its core values. Faith in human progress colours the way the mechanics write about the steam locomotive on display. They see it not just as a means of transport but as the basis for a global system of mass communications which,

> by propagating uniform ideas, principles, rights and obligations will hasten the moment when all peoples will finally understand one another, and by throwing off once and for all the subservience that centuries have imposed upon them, and the yoke of capital and ignorance, will at last profit in the widest possible way from the serious advantages that machines offer them.[9]

These engineers, whose only knowledge of the wider world has been learned from borrowed books by gaslight, have gazed at the steam engine and imagined the Internet.

Louis-Napoleon decides that men capable of measuring microns on a lathe and assembling so politely at the greatest show of capitalist power on earth can be trusted not to become a revolutionary mob. Social reform will continue. After all, the age of revolution is over.

'Strikes were productive of great injury . . .': The moderation of skilled workers was not just a French phenomenon. Even where there was more political freedom trade unions were using it responsibly. In America in 1866, still in recovery from the Civil War, iron moulders' leader William Sylvis set up the National Labor Union representing 60,000 workers. 'Strikes,' he concluded, 'were productive of great injury to the labouring classes.'[10] The same attitude would be heard at the founding conference of the British TUC.

Moderation was the watchword in every sphere except one: support for faraway revolutions. In a mass act of psychological displacement, the skilled working class diverted their revolutionary passion towards foreign wars against slavery and oppression. The Lancashire cotton workers had supported the Union side in the

American Civil War, even though it meant starvation; New York workers had turned out in thousands to welcome the Irish nationalist O'Donovan Rossa; the Parisians of Varlin's generation idolised the Italian liberation fighter Garibaldi, the Che Guevara of the 1860s; and trade unions everywhere sympathised with the Poles, whose uprising against Russian domination had been ended by mass executions and deportations.

It was the Polish massacre that set in train the formation of the first cross-border workers' organisation in history. In September 1864 union leaders in London called a public meeting in support of Poland with a delegation from the French mutual societies in attendance. The venue was St Martin's Hall, Long Acre, ironically on a site which is today the premises of the clothing company French Connection.

> At the meeting, which was chock-full (for there is now evidently a revival of the working-classes taking place) . . . it was resolved to found a 'Workingmen's International Association', whose general council is to have its seat in London and is to 'intermediate' between the workers' societies in Germany, Italy, France, and England . . .[11]

The reporter here is Karl Marx, cheekily described in the minutes as the representative of the German working class (his profession is listed as architect). The exiled revolutionary did not speak at the meeting but was soon presiding over a fractious internal conflict between his own supporters and followers of rival revolutionary Pierre Joseph Proudhon. Proudhon was the father of a creed of moderate anarchism whose tenets had a lot in common with the prejudices of skilled trade unionists, namely an obsession with workers' cooperatives and opposition to women's rights.

Proudhon had said that women should not be allowed to work in factories. 'Man is essentially the power of action; woman, the power of fascination,' is one of his sayings that you will not find on many anarchist websites today. In the stateless society he envisaged the family would be the main source of social order, the 'absolute monarchy' of the anarchist system. Sexual freedom for women would cause social collapse; prostitution was the most terrible social vice.

All this went down well with the union men of the 1860s and was adopted as the policy of the International. The French mutual societies were led by Proudhon's supporters. Varlin was the only French delegate to vote against the ban on women at work, telling the International's Geneva congress, 'To condemn female labour is to acknowledge charity and authorise prostitution.'[12] But, like the rest of the International, Varlin remained fanatical about cooperatives.

'You could get yourself a modest meal, but well presented . . .': Cooperatives were the defining idea of the mid-century workers' movement. They could be producer co-ops like the non-profit iron factories Sylvis set up in New York, or consumer co-ops inspired by the shops founded in Lancashire in the 1840s. The principle was that you could opt out of the capitalist system by bulk buying collectively, lending at affordable rates, even running the production process without anybody higher than a foreman. Getting the state to provide capital for cooperatives became the main electoral demand of the workers' movement in Germany under the leadership of Marx's other big rival, Ferdinand Lassalle. The beauty of the cooperative strategy was, as Lassalle put it, 'the means themselves are absolutely imbued with the very nature of the end'. You did not need a revolution to make cooperatives happen; nor was it a pure electoral strategy. You could combine a highly creative social experiment in the here and now with the long, slow campaign for parliamentary representation and state funding.

In Varlin's Paris, cooperatives were an idea whose time had come. One of the biggest sources of resentment among workers was, ironically, the philanthropy they felt was being shoved down their throats by the Emperor. The mechanics' report after the Expo complained there were too many 'soup kitchens, tenements and churches': 'While we fully appreciate the value of these things, we are partisans of freedom and we wish to make it clear that we want to run our own lives, and that all we need is the freedom to do so.'[13]

Alongside resentment there was a persistent worry: that shipping them out and walling them off from the 'Paris of horse racing and love affairs' inevitably exposed the 'respectable' working class to the habits and morals of the slums. Like all skilled workers at the time they harboured a deep abhorrence of beggars, criminals and prostitutes. Marx had called this the lumpenproletariat; on the Paris streets the word was *canaille*, which can mean riff-raff, rabble or just plain bastards, depending how you say it.

Victorine Brocher was a shoemaker's wife from a respectable working class family. Constantly on the brink of penury herself, she joined the International because the doctor treating her baby was a member. By the time the Expo came around she had a view too close for comfort of what life was like for *la canaille*:

> I have seen poor women working twelve or fourteen hours a day for derisory wages, forced to leave elderly parents and young children, holed up for long hours in unwholesome workshops where neither air, nor light nor sunshine ever penetrates . . . On Sunday . . . if her husband is alright he will stay at home after dinner; if he's an alcoholic he will discover that he is the unhappiest man in the world; that he can't stand being at home. He will seek consolation at the local cabaret . . .[14]

For respectable workers like Varlin and Brocher, the cooperative strategy provided reassurance on two fronts: it bought freedom from the charity efforts of the rich and it was an insurance policy against a swift transition to the depths of *la canaille*, where the high ideals of socialism were impossible to maintain. On 19 January 1868 Varlin launched a workers' cooperative cafe called La Marmite (The Stock Pot) with a PR offensive the like of which the Paris restaurant trade had never seen:

> Workers! Consumers! Let's not look for the means to improve our conditions anywhere else but in liberty. Freedom of association, by strengthening our forces will let us emancipate ourselves from the parasitic middlemen who we see, every day, making fortunes out of our shopping budget and to the detriment of our health. Let's join

together, not only to defend our wages but above all our right to a decent meal.[15]

La Marmite served cheap, basic food and – though designed to cater for day labourers in lodging houses – soon became the haunt of Varlin's comrades. One remembered,

> You could get yourself a modest meal, but well presented – and an air of gaiety around the tables. There were a lot of customers. You had to choose what dish you wanted yourself, and write the price down on the bill, then give it – with your money – to the comrade on the till. Generally you did not hang around long and, to make space for others, you left once you'd finished eating. Sometimes, however, some comrades would hang around for longer and chat to each other. We would sing as well . . .[16]

La Marmite became such a legendary venue that, years later, when many Parisian workers washed up as exiles in London's Soho district, they opened a branch there and drowned their sorrows in it nightly.[17] For now, backed by 8,000 subscribers, they opened three more restaurants in Paris and started a credit union.

But things were about to go bad for the revellers at La Marmite. Noting the growing influence of the International and its involvement in strikes all over Europe, the Emperor declared it illegal. The first group of leaders was arrested in December 1867, the second group, including Varlin, three months later. At his trial Varlin told the judges, 'The International is opposed to strikes on principle. It considers them anti-economical. It declared this at Geneva and has declared it everywhere.'[18] He was sentenced to three months in prison along with the rest. With the International out of the way, Louis-Napoleon felt confident enough to move to the next stage of his social reform policy, the legalisation of public meetings. By the time Varlin came out of jail Paris was a changed city.

'Their palace is a slum . . .': When the old alleyways were cleared the workers had been moved to the hills around central Paris. There was an arc of workers' tenement areas running from Batignolles in the north-west, via Montmartre, to Belleville and Menilmontant in the east. The city was now divided into concentric circles: glamour in the centre, then a ring of wide boulevards, then poverty, then the fortifications that marked the city limits. The working population had mushroomed from 1.3 million in 1851 to 1.9 million in 1870, mainly due to immigration.

This was not a factory city; most people worked in small and medium-sized workshops. Tens of thousands of women worked at home, sewing or making paper flowers in order to keep themselves one rung above the underworld of prostitutes and gangsters. Working-class Paris was a world-famous Bohemia full of half-starved dreamers like Louise Michel. A reporter described Michel as 'thirty-six years old, petite, brunette, with a very developed forehead which recedes abruptly . . . her features reveal an extreme severity. She dresses entirely in black.'[19] 'I am in fact tall,' she would retort.

In her head Louise Michel was a poet, novelist and composer. In reality she was a poverty-stricken schoolmistress in Montmartre where, according to prosecutors, 'from her lectern in her spare moments she professed the doctrines of free thought and made her young pupils sing poems she had written, among which was a song entitled "The Avengers"'.[20]

Michel's natural element was not the workplace or the co-op but the slum. She gave free adult literacy classes, organised republican lectures, joined the feminist-led Campaign for Women's Rights. She was a member of the International but, given its position on women, semi-detached. 'And so here is Louise Michel,' she would remember later; ' . . . she is a menace to society, for she has declared a hundred times that everyone should take part in the banquet of life.'[21]

The sparkling ring of boulevards that separated posh Paris from poor Paris was lined with theatres and dance halls. Here young workers could seek solace in drink, dancing and casual sex. This was also an age of live-in lovers; for many young women, moving in with a boyfriend was the only way of avoiding penury. Barred from political activity, workers had created a subculture that fizzed through these dance halls and bars, celebrating their own misfortune with maudlin ballads. There was even a song called 'La Canaille' which, during the last days of the Empire, became a big hit on the cabaret scene.

When Louis-Napoleon lifted the ban on public meetings in June 1868 it was like removing the cork from cheap champagne: the two decades of frustration popped and sprayed. The dance halls, bars and circuses were transformed into a network of political discussion clubs, with thousands in attendance. There were no minutes of the meetings but the Emperor's police were diligent, producing 900 pages of verbatim notes. These tell the story of how *la canaille* became communist.

The first meeting was called at a place called Vaux-Hall. Wasting no time on niceties, the workers joined in the arguments that had been raging inside the International. The event was entitled: 'Work for Women' and there was a massive turnout to hear feminist journalists clash with Proudhon's men. The men were ready with left-wing arguments against women's right to work. Left-wing teacher Gustave Lefrançais asked,

> What does it matter to working women who ply the needle or the burnisher, or who bloody their fingers in fashioning the stems of paper flowers that they are not voters, that they may not administer the property they do not possess, and that they cannot deceive their husbands on an equal basis?[22]

It mattered a lot. The meeting ended with a vote and the vote went against the International. Women should have the right to work, said the majority.

This opened the floodgates. By 6 October the debate had moved on to issues that shocked Proudhon's old guard:

> No law is needed to consecrate the union of a man with a woman. The only sanction this union needs is reciprocal affection. The triumph of this system . . . will mean the beginning of a revolution which will change society completely.[23]

Night after night the workers turned up in thousands. There were 933 meetings during the next two years in 63 venues. Titles ranged from 'Capital and Interest' to 'The Art of Raising Rabbits and Getting an Income of 300 Francs' (the latter designed to confuse the policemen who sat alongside the platform). Documentary evidence suggests that the audiences were largely local and regular. You went to your neighbourhood cabaret, you met your friends, you cheered the incendiary speeches; the next night you would be in the same room drinking and dancing with the same set of people. It was here, amid gaslight and cheap perfume, that the moderate anarchism of Proudhon – sacred among the bookbinders and mechanics – was subjected to relentless criticism by dirt-poor men and women from the slums.

Activists from the International were everywhere in the public meeting movement, but they did not get a free run. In the shadows of Montmartre a different kind of socialism had survived, inspired by yet another bearded hero of 1848 (and another bitter rival of Marx), Auguste Blanqui. Blanqui favoured terror and insurrection, and if the workers weren't up to the job a few good men with guns could do it for them. He had spent half his life in jail and was now in exile. But his followers, who despised co-ops, trade unions and the International, lived a Robin Hood existence in the backstreets, tolerated and sometimes celebrated by *la canaille*. Theophile Ferré, the Blanquist leader in Montmartre, was Louise Michel's platonic lover. He told a public meeting, 'I am enough of a communist to want to *impose* communism.'[24]

In this atmosphere, opposition to women's work was just the first idea to be torn apart. Next came cooperatives. A cooperative bank set up by Proudhon's supporters crashed in the summer of 1868 and the skilled activists who had set up the co-ops now had to rub shoulders in mass meetings with the poor – to whom a shop was still a shop if you owed it money, whether it was a co-op or not.

The next big idea to be challenged was the trade unionist's distaste for strikes. Varlin may have gone down the prison steps protesting his opposition to strikes but within months of his release there were strikes everywhere. During 1869 there was a cotton strike, a wool-carders' strike and a big miners' strike in the Loire with eleven strikers shot dead. Even Paris was hit, when shop assistants in the department stores walked out. 'Up to now,' said one speaker at the public meetings,

> strikes have not enjoyed good results because they have always been partial and not general. All workers should get together and declare that they are no longer willing to work for current wages, then you'll soon see the bosses going after the workers and agreeing to meet their demands.[25]

Now the government began a crackdown on the meetings, arresting the most radical speakers and issuing fines. But venues moved, crowds re-formed, meetings about insurrection were called under ribald titles such as 'The Rise and Fall of the Crinoline in France'.

For Louise Michel, the instinctive rebel, the two years of the public meeting movement had a dreamlike quality. As she walked back from meetings with her fellow teachers '. . . we talked about many things. At other times we were silent, dazzled by the idea of sweeping away the shame of twenty years.[26]

For Varlin the public meeting movement was a revelation. He had argued with Blanquist prisoners during his time in jail, and now, standing alone in the dark corners of the dance halls, he was hearing their ideas shouted out by poverty-stricken workers. In the spring of 1869 he wrote, 'Eight months of public debate have laid bare this strange fact – that the majority of workers actively engaged in the reform movement are communist.'[27]

Louis-Napoleon had tried to bend with the wind but it was blowing too hard. He had pardoned miners arrested during the Loire strike; he had set up voluntary insurance funds for workers. And where was the gratitude? By January 1870 he could console himself with only this: there had been strikes, even the odd disturbance, but no mass demonstrations.

Chance and idiocy intervened. During a trivial argument the Emperor's nephew, a famous philanderer, emptied his revolver into the chest of a radical journalist called Victor Noir. The next day 100,000 people swarmed onto the streets of Paris for the funeral. Louise Michel remembered, 'Almost everyone who turned up at the funeral expected to go home again as members of a republic, or not to go home at all.'[28] A young singer from the Paris cabarets, Rosalie Bordas, was hauled onto a cart by the crowd and belted out 'La Canaille', the words of which had been written as a self-effacing joke but now rang like a declaration of war.

> In the old French city
> There's a race of iron men
> The furnace of their fiery soul
> Has forged to bronze their skin
> Their sons are born on straw
> Their palace is a slum
> That's what we call the riff-raff
> And well, I'm one of 'em.[29]

For Varlin it was a symbolic moment. He knew a crisis was imminent unless he could tame and direct the energies of *la canaille*, and he spent the day of the funeral arguing against Blanquist agitators who wanted the crowd to storm Paris that afternoon.

A week later the miners and steelworkers at the Schneider plant in Le Creusot went on strike. This was the biggest industrial workplace in France and the boss was, to cap it all, the president of the Emperor's tame legislature. Solidarity with the strikers became the main theme in the public meeting halls. Varlin re-formed the Paris branch of the International and persuaded the unions to band together into a federation.

Panicked by strikes, panicked by the funeral of Victor Noir, panicked by a police report that the International had precisely 433,785 French members, Louis-Napoleon called a plebiscite to endorse his right to rule. On 8 May 1870, seven million people voted to back the Emperor, while one and a half million voted against: essentially Montmartre and Belleville were outvoted by the French peasantry, who cared nothing for cabarets or cooperatives. The International, which in reality had more like 70,000 French members mainly recruited during the strikes, was again banned. Varlin fled to Brussels.

If the Second Empire had managed to reform itself faster, Eugène Varlin might have ended his days a respectable trade union leader. Victorine Brocher might have sunk forever into domestic obscurity. Louise Michel might have spent her life teaching Montmartre children to sing subversive songs. But on 19 July 1870 Louis-Napoleon ensured they would all face a different future. He declared war on Prussia.

'All these were hollow phrases now . . .': The pretext for the war was who should take over the Spanish throne; the deeper issue was who should dominate mainland Europe. What happens next is the stuff of school history textbooks: telegrams, generals, dates and battles, dead elephants in the Paris Zoo, dramatic escapes by hot air balloon. The events fit neatly into the five-act structure of a tragedy, though the first half could be mistaken for comic opera.

Act One: the French army marches to the border where it is pushed back by a bigger force with better generals. Act Two: Louis-Napoleon marches to the rescue at the head of a second French army, with 100,000 untrained troops. Act Three: the Prussian army smashes this manoeuvre, the defeated French surrender, the Emperor is taken prisoner.

Forty-eight hours later Victorine Brocher is part of a crowd pushing against a line of police in Paris. They chant, 'It's not just abdication that we want, it's the Republic.' A cavalry officer rides up at the head of his regiment, sabre unsheathed, salutes the crowd and shouts, 'Long live France! Long live the Republic.'

Act Four: the war must go on, say the leaders of the new Republic, and the people agree. The International issues an appeal to the German people: 'The man who unleashed this fratricidal war, who does not know how to die and who you now hold prisoner, does not exist for us. Republican France invites you in the name of justice to withdraw your armies.'[30] The Kaiser declines this invitation and, for many French workers, though they'd initially opposed the war, it becomes a legitimate fight to defend their new political freedom.

Workers flock to join the National Guard, which has been hurriedly reinvented. Louise Michel and Victorine Brocher both sign up. Varlin joins on his return from exile. But the guns are rusty and so are the generals. The Prussian army lays siege to Paris for 100 days and the giant Krupp cannon displayed at the Expo of 1867 is put to use flattening the outskirts of the city. The people starve.

On 27 January 1871 an armistice is signed, allowing Prussia to remove a chunk of territory from the body of France and stage a victory march through Paris. After the parade the Prussian army retreats to the outskirts.

Act Five: the Republic's leaders call elections. The newly elected assembly meets in Versailles. As food begins to arrive in Paris, Victorine Brocher notes that children born out of legal wedlock are given only half the normal ration. 'Poor bastards,' the working women whisper, 'they didn't ask to be born – and this is the Republic?'

The National Guard battalions form a Central Committee to ensure 'the working man' will not be sidelined. Varlin persuades the International to let him join it. The Central Committee calls a demonstration at the Bastille, telling left-wing members of the Guard to wear red ribbons in their buttonholes. Brocher's commanding officer orders her to wear a blue ribbon. She storms off.

> I left the Company and I would never return . . . I went alone to the Bastille demo, it was a giant crowd, highly excited – not the kind of criminals and lowlife you heard [when the Republic was proclaimed]. Everyone was convinced that with a little effort and a lot of luck we could even yet save France . . .[31]

One day merges with the next. Brocher has to watch with horror as her child falls ill and dies. Like the rest of Paris she is living through days of shell-shocked misery.

> My head felt absolutely empty of those grand phrases that are supposed to animate the human mind: God! Fatherland! Republic! All these were hollow phrases now, which could only aggravate our misery and destroy the human race: I needed a new ideal.[32]

The new government can't wait to return to business as usual. It orders all debts run up during the war to be repaid within 48 hours and sends regular troops into Paris to remove the city's cannons. These have been paid for through mass subscriptions by the people, who – as a gesture in case the Prussians tried to remove them – had physically carried 400 guns into the workers' districts for safe keeping. As the regular soldiers form up at 4 a.m. on 18 March 1871 the fog closes round them like a final curtain. But the drama is not over.

'The splendid deliverance of the dawn': A wiry, dark-haired woman runs screaming down the cobbled street that links Montmartre with the boulevard below. It is Louise Michel and she has a rifle hidden under her jacket. The word she's screaming is 'treason'. She's just seen government troops take possession of the guns lined up in the Montmartre cannon park. Drums are beaten in the alleyways and soon Michel returns, accompanied by her boyfriend Ferré and a motley column of armed citizens.

> Montmartre arose . . . In the dawn, which was just breaking, you could hear the tocsin ringing; we went up at the speed of a charge, knowing that at the top there was an army in battle formation. We expected to die for liberty. It was as if we were lifted from the earth . . . Crowds at certain times are the breaking wave of the human ocean. The hill was enveloped in a white light, the splendid deliverance of the dawn.[33]

The regular troops may be in battle formation but they are not in battle mood. It has been raining; their officers have forgotten to bring horses to move the cannon so they have been standing around like idiots for hours. Now a crowd of women is giving them a hard time. 'Between ourselves and the army,' Michel remembered, 'the women threw themselves up against the cannons and guns; the soldiers stood still.'[34] The general in charge of the regulars, Lecomte, orders them to open fire on the crowd, but nothing happens. Instead the regulars break ranks, mingle with the crowd and arrest Lecomte.

Two miles east, in the working class district of Batignolles, Varlin is struggling into his uniform. The Central Committee has been in session until 3.30 a.m. and he is exhausted. Now there are notices on the walls declaring the Central Committee illegal. At first, his troops don't want to leave their barracks but eventually he gets them onto the streets. 'I saw a regiment, about three hundred men, perfectly organised and marching as if they were conducting a review,' reports the local mayor; 'they were led by Varlin.'[35]

At 8.30 a.m. cannonfire echoes across the rooftops of Paris. A National Guard commander in the south is firing blanks to call the workers into action. This is Duval, an ironworker who has served time in jail for membership of the International. 'The district,' a courier reports to the despondent army staff, 'is entirely in the hands of the self-styled General Duval, who is recruiting the local urchins and giving them shovels with which to dig trenches.'[36]

With fraternisation going on everywhere, the French army is pulled out of Paris. Only the Central Committee can replace them as the civil power, but they do not have control; *la canaille* is in control. A mob surrounds the house where General Lecomte is being held and he is dragged away and shot, together with another elderly general famous for massacring workers in 1848, who's made the mistake of coming out of his house to see what's going on.

Victorine Brocher rushes into the streets, arriving at the City Hall in time to see government troops marching off with the money and the archives of the Paris administration. On the barricades members of the National Guard are posing for photographs. In the workers' districts people have decided to get drunk. 'We believed, in fact, that a new era had arrived . . . everyone was in a holiday mood,' Brocher remembers, adding, 'They say the mob is cruel and nasty; I think myself that it is stupid: it is always the poor bird that lets itself get plucked – and this time, really, it behaved stupidly, idiotically.'[37] By nightfall the only authority left in Paris is the Central Committee of the National Guard.

'This is the dawn . . .': The Central Committee, realising it held political power, called elections to a 'Commune' – an elected city council, which Paris had not been allowed to have for 80 years. A week after the rising 230,000 people went to the polls to elect the new Paris Commune. Of the 92 members elected 24 were workers, 17 were members of the International. A few days later the French army attacked Paris and the second siege began, with sporadic fighting outside the city walls throughout April. In early May the army made a breakthrough; two weeks later, in a tacit agreement with the Prussians – who were still camped outside the city – the French army entered Paris. During a bloody week of street fighting both sides took hostages and some were shot. The last stand of the Commune took place at a barricade in Belleville on the rainy Sunday afternoon of 28 May.

Because the Commune left verbatim minutes and plastered the walls of Paris with announcements it has been easy for historians to study its politics. The survivors were fascinated by the story of who did what, day by day, as they tried to work out what went wrong; the old revolutionary leaders trailed their beards over lengthy analytical books about it. The mystery they had to grapple with was: why had the Commune talked so much about socialism but achieved so few social reforms? Why were the most extreme measures proposed by middle-class radicals, not workers? Why did members of the International end up in the minority opposed to the suppression of 'traitors' within the Commune? Eugène Varlin stands at the centre of this debate; he was the best-known man on the Central Committee when it inherited power on 18 March; he was the one who led the resistance to the authoritarian tendency within the Commune; he was minister for war during the last two days.

The beginnings of an answer are to be found in sociology. The skilled, self-educated workers and the working poor of Paris knew each other well, but they lived in overlapping circles with different priorities. The 'respectable' working class, the men of the Expo delegations, had a two thirds majority among working class delegates to the Commune, but the Commune as a whole had a two thirds majority inclined to radical republicanism and Blanquism. Most of the middle class professionals who stayed in Paris to fight were revolutionary romantics, determined to liberate humanity with newspaper articles and

decrees. Their strategy and rhetoric meshed well with the street politics of *la canaille,* which had been learned in dance halls, not trade
union meetings.

So the activists on both sides of this divide focused on work that
mirrored their vision of social justice: the guerrilla fighters went to
the ramparts and the orators made speeches in the Commune; the
social reformers of the International ran committees. But while the
Commune would spend 22 million francs on fighting, it would spend
just 267,000 francs on social reform.

What the Commune achieved politically was scandalous enough
for its enemies. It abolished the 'morality police'; it abolished the
standing army and conscription; it made service in the National Guard
obligatory, together with the election of officers; it pegged the wages
of elected Commune members to those of skilled workers; it decreed
the separation of Church and State, banning prayers and priests from
all state schools.

Against this the economic reforms look puny. The Commune never
touched the money in the Bank of France; no factories were seized
other than those abandoned by their bosses. It wrote off the back rents
accumulated during the siege and declared a two-year moratorium on
debt repayments. It closed pawn shops to new business and forced the
owners to give back every item under 20 francs. It banned night shifts
in bakeries.

Lack of time, lack of money, lack of focus – these are all reasons
why the Commune's social programme dragged behind its political
action. But that tells only half the story.

Power and control are different things. Having seen the power of
the employers melt away, the Parisian workers did not look to seize
political power themselves; instead they looked for ways to control
their own destiny – at home, in relationships, in the workplace, on
the barricades. The social revolution did happen, but it happened in
people's lives and from the bottom up.

'I will not be agitating for the international revolution': Varlin
found liberation where he had always done, in the sober work of

administration. During the first week he fought to dampen expectations. When the Swiss section of the International offered to spread the revolution into the mountains, Varlin disabused them:

> [Varlin said] the dispatches had given us the wrong idea about the situation; that he would not be agitating for the international revolution; that the movement on 18 March had no other aim but municipal elections in Paris, and that this goal had been achieved; that the elections were fixed for the next day, and that once the council was elected the Central Committee would resign and the episode would be over.[38]

His first job for the Commune was to run its finance commission. He secured a credit line with the Bank of France and put himself in charge of feeding 350,000 people. He would walk to work in the morning, impose new taxes on the railway companies before lunch, eat at a cheap cafe and in the afternoon veto requests by National Guard commanders for new dress uniforms. In the evening he would dine with his comrades at La Marmite. When the fighting started he did not rush to the front line or get his photograph taken in military regalia, but carried on his official routine. What that routine achieved is only possible to understand if you look at what was going on in the unofficial sphere.

All over Paris workers were bringing forward schemes to reform society from the bottom up: the stonecutters set up an accident insurance scheme; candlemakers and butchers formed city-wide co-ops. The unions made a list of bright ideas and the Commune's labour committee, run by the International, steadily implemented them: the abolition of fines at work, the eight-hour day, the upward revision of wage rates in state-run factories.

The expulsion of priests from state schools was only the start of the Commune's experiment in education. As Louise Michel had often maintained, primary education under the Empire was 'rubbish'. Now, area by area, local activists tried to implement reforms in the content of classes – teaching, they said, should 'limit itself to known and proven facts springing pure and without alloy from the crucible of human reason'.[39]

Varlin believed that the Commune's function was not to enact socialism but to allow all these social experiments to happen. He believed the arrival of socialism would be dictated by the progress of technology and the self-education of the working class. That was for the future. In the present, he knew what *la canaille* could do and he feared what it would do in the hands of a rabble-rousing republican dictator. Just how keenly he understood the Commune's role as a facilitator of these low-level social reforms and freedoms can be judged by how he acted when they were threatened.

At the end of April, for the first time a professional soldier was made commander-in-chief of the National Guard, and a Committee of Public Safety was set up to crack down on pro-government 'traitors'. By this time Blanqui had been taken prisoner by government troops, but the establishment of this body was an essentially Blanquist move. Every French worker knew the precedent for this: the Terror unleashed by the Jacobins during the French Revolution. Some supported it; others believed it would kill the spirit of the revolution, as it had during the original Terror. Varlin led the opposition. What was the point of forming a dictatorship, he argued, since the whole purpose of revolution was to bring diversity and freedom into workers' lives?

It was only once the French army broke into Paris that Varlin left off the political struggle to keep the Commune democratic and picked up a rifle. In command of the 6th Legion of the National Guard he organised the defence of the Left Bank, retreating across the river to Belleville where, in the final days, after the Blanquist group fell apart, he was named the Commune's last minister for war.

On Friday 26 May he was at his command post on the corner of the rue Haxo, on the eastern edge of Paris, when a mob attacked a column of pro-government hostages, killing 47. Victims included priests, generals and police informers. Varlin ran into the street in civilian clothes and stood on a wall shouting for calm. Together with four other remaining members of the Commune he pleaded for the lives of the hostages to be spared. An eyewitness reported, 'The Communards . . . formed up and made a barrier against the multitude. The mob shouted, they cursed . . . there was even one who cried! They told the Commune to get stuffed!'[40]

'Then,' remembers another witness, 'sombre, grim, crushed, but cold in appearance Varlin returned to the command post, certain that his sweet dream of justice and fraternity was dead.'[41]

On the final day of the Commune, when resistance was confined to three streets, he would lead a last, defiant counter-attack:

> A small phalanx of fifty men, led by Varlin, Ferré, and Gambon, their red scarfs round their waists, their chassepôts slung across their shoulders . . . came out on the boulevard. A gigantic Garibaldian carried an immense red flag in front of them.[42]

'I had never set foot in a public meeting': For Victorine Brocher the Commune provided liberation in the realm of fighting. She and her husband helped set up a unit of demobbed soldiers from north Africa. They moved into the officers' quarters of a former barracks, draping the statues with a red flag. 'Our battalion had no organisation, no uniforms, no equipment, no guns: among us there were Zouaves, Arabs, Turks; my assistant was a Negro, and he was a very nice boy.'[43] At first they lived the high life, with so much food that she was able to start a soup kitchen for the poor in the officers' mess. But the French army's attack on 3 April came as a shock. Not only were they under attack from fellow Frenchmen, but they heard that 'General' Duval and his staff, having been captured, were lined up against a wall and shot.

Brocher took part in sporadic fighting throughout April, at the end of which the unit fought in a major engagement around the strategic fort at Issy, taking massive losses. As she tended the dying, she remembered.

> Despite everything, the mutilated soldiers never offered a word of regret or complaint. They suffered, but they were happy to have retaken the fort; happy to give their lives to create a more just and equitable society. For us the Republic was a magic word, through which we would achieve great things for the benefit of humanity.[44]

It is not clear what Pierre-Joseph Proudhon would have made of Victorine Brocher. His slogan 'Man is action, woman fascination' was from another planet as far as she was concerned.

When the battle moved from the fortifications to the streets, Brocher was cut off from her unit. With twelve companions she headed, as did most of the surviving activists, for the City Hall, intending to make a final stand. At this point she met Louise Michel, who tried unsuccessfully to recruit her to an all-female unit of medics. 'I didn't know her. I knew even less about the women's movement – I had never set foot in a public meeting . . .'[45]

Brocher's group made its way to the barricade in rue Haxo where Varlin's command post was, arriving the day after the shooting of the hostages. By now, the French army was executing anybody captured in a National Guard uniform. So Brocher changed into civilian clothes, had her hair chopped off and gave away her wedding ring and a locket containing her dead child's hair. Together with the remnants of her unit, she prepared to die. As the ammunition ran out, '. . . we stood together, our flag flying, ready for the last battle. There were waifs and strays from every battalion there and some members of the Commune, none of whom I had ever met.'[46]

'Ripped open to her very womb': For Louise Michel, no amount of liberation in the real world would ever be enough; neither the battlefield, the class struggle nor the women's movement could satisfy her creative energy. It poured out into her imagination. If Varlin represents the Commune of the skilled worker and Brocher that of the republican barricade fighter, Louise Michel embodies the revolutionary soul of *la canaille*, with all its tendencies to extremism.

During the siege she had organised the Montmartre Women's Vigilance Committee, terrorising profiteers and organising 'revolutionary requisitioning' to feed the hungry. Now she organised a corps of medics but also fought at various stages as a soldier. 'Equal education and equal trades so that prostitution would not be the only lucrative profession open to a woman – that is what was real in our programme.'[47]

She spent her evenings during the Commune at the church of Saint-Bernard de la Chappelle, but she was not praying. The church, like many others, had been taken over by a workers' debating club. Michel's was called the Revolution Club. These clubs met nightly and, while they had no official power within the Commune, were a means of exercising local control in the neighbourhood. They were also partial to taking votes. On 18 May, the Revolution Club voted for

> The suppression of magistrates and the annihilation of legal codes, with their replacement by a commission of justice. The suppression of religions, the immediate arrest of priests . . . The execution of an important hostage every 24 hours until Citizen Blanqui, an appointed member of the Commune, is freed . . .[48]

This was where the voice of *la canaille* was heard, and Louise Michel was the most prominent of the women who tried to turn its words into action. Having unpadlocked the lives of poverty-stricken women – the kind of women for whom 'honour, virtue and faith were hollow' – the Commune could never control them. It is true that the terrified French authorities conducted a witch-hunt against working-class women, accusing them of setting fire to Paris with petrol in the last days of the Commune; it is also true that women were among the most radical supporters of harsh revolutionary violence.

It was a female medic who instigated the massacre at the rue Haxo, though only men were prosecuted for it. Interviewed straight afterwards the medic said that

> she cared nothing about the social struggle . . . but her sister had been the mistress of a priest who, having got her pregnant, had abandoned her and stolen their savings. 'That's why I came down from the window to see the cassocks; that's why I ripped the beard of a monk who looked like the man who seduced Celine; that's why I shouted *Death*! and why my sleeves are bloody.[49]

Michel revelled in the fact that women of the slums had become the most ardent advocates of revolutionary violence.

> Our male friends are more susceptible to faintheartedness than we women are. A supposedly weak woman knows better than any man how to say: 'It must be done.' She may feel ripped open to her

very womb but she remains unmoved. Without hate, without anger, without pity for herself or others, whether her heart bleeds or not, she can say, 'It must be done.' Such were the women of the Commune.

For Michel, the last days of the Commune were visionary and apocalyptic. Her unit retreated to the cemetery in Montmartre, which was being shelled.

> When I went on reconnaissance it pleased me to walk in the solitude that shells were scouring . . . One shell falling across the trees covered me with flowered branches, which I divided up between two tombs . . . The Commune, surrounded from every direction, had only death on its horizon. It could only be brave, and it was. And in dying it opened wide the door to the future. That was its destiny.[50]

'Guard it like a treasure . . .': The skilled trade union man, the barricade fighter who had never been to a public meeting, the mystic feminist from the backstreets; these were the archetypes who made the Paris Commune. There were 15,000 people like them under arms during the last week and tens of thousands more supporting them. The Women's Union, after a final meeting, took to the streets en masse, led by a female bookbinder who had been the chef at La Marmite. One hundred and twenty women, armed with rifles, fought at a barricade in the Batignolles district until they were wiped out.

Only the scale of shock at seeing workers in control of a major city can explain what happened next. Some 3,000 Parisian workers had been killed in the defence of the city, but once the army regained control, 30,000 were slaughtered, many of them buried in mass graves. In the judicial process that followed thousands more were sentenced to hard labour or transported to prison colonies in the Pacific.

Louise Michel surrendered on 24 May, after the authorities took her mother hostage. She was held in a camp where prisoners were randomly shot each afternoon. In court, she pleaded guilty to fighting for the Commune, 'since above all else the Commune wanted to bring about social revolution, and social revolution is my dearest wish'. As the judge tried to silence her she shouted, 'If you are not cowards, kill me . . .' She was deported to New Caledonia, only returning to Paris after an amnesty in 1880. She was imprisoned again for three years in 1883 following an anarchist demonstration and emigrated to London where, as a supporter of anarchism, she remained isolated within the labour movement. She died in 1905.

When the firing stopped, Victorine Brocher left the barricade on the rue Haxo and hid in a nearby house with her comrades. As soldiers executed the owner, who had been stalling for time, she was lowered out of a rear window, carrying the banner of her regiment. 'Guard it like a treasure,' her comrades told her, 'so that it may fly one more time above the heads of those defending human rights, if ever another revolution should occur.'[51]

She tramped through streets running with blood and littered with corpses, her shorn hair giving her the look of a teenage girl. On reaching her own neighbourhood, terrified shopkeepers looked at her as if she herself were a corpse. She had been condemned to death as a petrol bomber and subsequently confirmed killed. But they had shot somebody else by mistake. She lived in Paris under an assumed identity for months, fleeing to Switzerland on false papers a year later. She too became an anarchist exiled in Brixton and Lausanne. She died in 1922 after writing a book called *Memoirs of a Living Corpse*.

Eugène Varlin wandered away from the last barricade and sat down disconsolately to await arrest. He was recognised and handed over to army troops.

For an hour, a mortal hour, Varlin was dragged through the streets of Montmartre, his hands tied behind his back, under a shower of blows and insults. His young, thoughtful head, that had never harboured other thoughts than of fraternity, slashed open by the sabres, was soon but one mass of blood, of mangled flesh, the eye protruding from the orbit. On reaching the rue des Rosiers, he no longer walked; he was carried. They set him down to shoot him.

The wretches dismembered his corpse with blows of the butt-ends of their muskets.[52]

The age of revolution was over. Normal service in the age of industrial exhibitions would shortly be resumed.

4. Every race worth saving
How American workers invented May Day

> I do not claim any power of prophecy but I can see
> ahead of me an organisation that will cover the globe. It
> will include men and women of every craft, creed and
> color; it will cover every race worth saving.
>
> Uriah Stephens, founder of the Knights of Labor[1]

Basra, Iraq, 2006

Basra was not the ideal place to be celebrating May Day but they
gave it a go. A few hundred union members marched behind red
banners, some bearing the hammer and sickle. Being a trade unionist
in Iraq has always been risky. Under the Ba'ath regime there was a
pro-government union staffed by Saddam Hussein's favourites. In 1987
it announced that 'class structures' had disappeared in Iraq; oil workers
were no longer workers but civil servants and did not need to be in
trade unions. Then Saddam issued Decree 150 banning trade unions
in the public sector.

'Practically three generations have come up since the introduction
of Decree 150 and for all that time had absolutely no real experience
of labour organisation,' says Hassan Juma. He is general secretary of
the Southern Oil Company Union, which he formed 11 days after
Saddam's fall from power.

> In the beginning there were twenty union activists in the Southern
> Oil Company. All of us had suffered under the previous regime.
> When the American troops arrived, the management were not
> convinced of the need to restore a labour union in the oil sector,
> but there was a need for it, amid the chaos that accompanied the
> entrance of the occupation forces.

79

The workers patrolled the installations to prevent looting and foraged for spare parts to keep things going. Their next problem was wages: American contractors had brought with them low-paid Asian workers to repair the wells and pipelines and introduced a wage table for Iraqi workers where the starting salary for a technician with three years' experience was just £18 a month. Demonstrations were a criminal offence in the early days of the occupation.

> . . . nevertheless we had quite a few, against Kellogg Brown & Root and Halliburton, and there was a confrontation when we tried to organise in the Southern refinery. But because they needed the refinery to produce fuel for the military we won the fight for the existing pay levels to be respected there.

Three years on, the union has thousands of members in the oilfields around Basra, and is part of a wider federation, the General Union of Oil Employees. But Juma's problems have multiplied. As well as the occupation – which he bitterly resents – the country has been torn apart by the insurgency and the rise of religious sectarianism. Juma complains, 'Religious warfare is something that America has been promoting and nurturing in Iraqi society. Until the Americans came, we were not involved in the issue of who is Sunni and who is Shiite.' But the union, like all Iraq's trade union federations, claims to stand above religious conflicts.

> In the union there are secularists, Islamists, people linked to one party or another, but they are all working for the interests of labour, not on political platforms. We have had to take the religious issue right out of our labour work: if we had not done that the union would be at each others' throats, because the members are Shia, Sunni and Christian.

With regard to the insurgency the oil workers' union draws a distinction not recognised by the occupying forces. It opposes the Islamists but supports what it calls 'honourable resistance': 'It is part of Iraqi society and has a great deal of support from the workers,' says Juma, 'but terrorists who kill innocent Iraqis in the midst of this are violently opposed by the workforce.'

The oil workers have had to re-learn trade unionism, establishing links with unions in Britain, Germany and America. Only workers over the age of 50 remember the time before Saddam's coup destroyed free trade unions.

> Because of that we focus on younger workers. We try to explain to them the principles of union organisation, union work. There is a sense that there were heroes in our history – though their names are lost – who stood up against BP under British rule. But we don't have the sources, we don't really have anything to read about the history of the labour movement, because from the late sixties, under Saddam, it all became pretty distorted.

Which made May Day 2006 all the more remarkable. With society on the brink of religious civil war and most political parties aligned to some form of ethnic or religious power base, Iraqi unions are among the few forces prepared to advocate a secular and unitary state. During the occupation, union leaders have paid with their lives for this stance. Three days before the march, the body of Hussein Thabet Ali, leader of the health workers' union, was found riddled with bullets and bearing evidence of torture with electric shocks and a power drill. He was not the first and would not be the last; in the power vacuum created by the occupation union leaders have found themselves under attack both from religious fanatics and former Ba'athists out to settle old scores.

But on 1 May 2006 Iraq's trade unions found time to commemorate not just their own martyrs but America's. 'Today,' says the leaflet circulating at the Basra demonstration, 'millions of people stand together for freedom and equality . . . it is the day of solidarity to commemorate the Chicago workers who gave their lives confronting the capitalism a century ago'.[2] For it is a fact, forgotten by many who demonstrate on the first of May but remembered by the oil workers of Basra, that May Day was invented in America in 1886. At the time it too was a country scarred by civil war with a workforce divided by colour, craft and creed. But in the run-up to the first May Day American workers built a huge popular movement dedicated to healing the divide. In those years the small-town

America that today's occupying troops call home was itself a battlefield in the class war. And in the fighting of it, innocent men were about to die . . .

Philadelphia, USA, 1869

The Garment Cutters Association of Philadelphia had, like many American unions, come and gone. Its strikes had failed and its membership was falling. By the night of 9 December 1869 all it had to show for seven years' work was nine active members and the resolution they had before them was to dissolve the union. That was nothing new in the US labour movement. American workers had organised their first strike in 1786 and their first trade union in 1792. By the start of the Civil War in 1861, organised labour had clocked up more than half a century of strikes, boycotts, cooperatives, unionisation drives and even political parties. What they all had in common was that they never lasted.

Before the Civil War American capitalism had a temporary and febrile feel to it too: the industrialists and railway builders were hemmed in, commercially and politically, by the slave owners of the South. The ebb and flow of unions like the Garment Cutters simply reflected the ups and downs of the economy.

But now slavery had been abolished, the South defeated and America's employers were palpably at the start of a new era. This was the beginning of the 30-year transformation of America from a divided, rural ex-colony to the world's number-one industrial power. Uriah Stephens, one of the Philadelphia tailors who met to wind up the union that night, sensed it was time for the workers to raise their game accordingly. Stephens was a Baptist preacher for whom trade unionism was all too narrow in scope, and strikes futile. He took aside six of the tailors and told them, 'I am determined to make an effort to institute something different.'[3]

He formed the Noble and Holy Order of the Knights of Labor. He proclaimed himself Master Workman and handed out the posts with titles such as Venerable Sage, Worthy Foreman and Unknown

Knight to his six loyal followers. A complex initiation rite was outlined, modelled on Freemasonry; the Knights were sworn to total secrecy and mutual aid, codes and special handshakes learned.

This was to be something better than a union: it would be an organisation dedicated to the abolition of wage slavery and the creation of 'harmony between capital and labor'. If today these objectives seem contradictory, to Stephens wage slavery was not the fault of capitalism itself but of monopolies – the land grabbers and financial alchemists of Wall Street. The aim was to change society not through class struggle but cooperatives: consumer co-ops to counteract rip-off shopkeepers, producer co-ops to run workplaces and farms without bosses and middlemen. Where direct action was needed, boycotts rather than strikes were preferred. And above all the crippling effects of skilled elitism were to be left behind: the organisation was thrown open to 'every race worth saving'.

Nevertheless, secrecy was at the heart of the project. Stephens had seen too many lockouts, sackings and blacklisted men to believe a workers' movement could survive without it. Nobody outside the Order was to hear it called by name until ten years after its foundation; it was referred to in print only with five asterisks, code-named the Five Stars. And an asterisk in workers' history is what it would have been if America had remained the same. But the forces unleashed by the end of slavery, the rise of monopoly and the growth of unskilled work were about to turn the economy upside down. By 1886 the Knights of Labor had 700,000 members and was the largest workers' organisation in the world.

The making of a militant: Martin Irons had been fighting, organising, drifting and losing for nearly four decades by the time he discovered the Knights of Labor. Irons typifies the generation of activists who found in the Knights an answer to the question their whole life had failed to provide: how to organise the workforce across the boundaries of skill, sex and colour.

An immigrant from Scotland, Irons was apprenticed to a New York machine shop in the 1840s aged 14. He was a self-educated romantic rebel who clashed not just with his own employers but with those in the rag trade, whose sweatshops infested the city.

> I was very painfully impressed . . . by the discovery of the treat-
> ment meted out to poor women who earned their bread, and some-
> times bread for several children or even a crippled husband, by
> plying their needle from early morning till late at night. In order
> to obtain work at all they were compelled to beg from store to
> store for the privilege of making shirts at five cents apiece . . .
> Often, after a poor weak woman had finished a dozen shirts the
> soulless employer would find fault about a few missed stitches and
> discount half her pay.[4]

Irons vowed 'to be among the first in coming years to help humanise men and debrutalise those that have power over the weak'. Out of his own wages he paid for a lawyer to file thirteen individual lawsuits on behalf of the women against one notorious underpayer, who imme-diately gave in. 'I never had any more complaints,' he recalled. 'This was during my apprenticeship and as my pay was very small my field of operations was necessarily limited.'[5]

At the age of 19, Irons moved to Louisiana, working as a mechanic and a foreman, and then launching a grocery store where 'I had not the heart to refuse credit to the poor who solicited a little indulgence for a few days, or until a pay day that was always coming but never came.' Close to bankruptcy, he drifted back into metalworking in Kentucky, where he organised his first successful strike.

The earliest photograph shows Irons as short, wide-eyed and alert. His long, sandy hair is swept back in the manner of a Confederate cavalry officer; a large moustache droops onto a receding chin. By this time he has been drifting around the Midwest for years, a kind of 1860s rebel without a cause. He leaves St Louis regretfully, after working a year 'with no very startling experiences'. He joins the Oddfellows, a cut-price version of the Freemasons; he joins the Grangers – a radical movement of small farmers dedi-cated to cooperative food production. He avoids fighting in the Civil War, goes back into groceries, makes rope, prospects for lead, all the while 'advocating trades-unionism, eight hours for labor, anti-land monopoly and anti-child-and-woman-labor in the factories'. When he comes into contact with the Knights of Labor, the drifting stops.

> When that beautiful watchword of knighthood, 'An injury to one is the concern of all,' resounded through my life, and when I learned that knighthood embraced every grade of honest toil in its heights and depths – when I learned that it meant broad and comprehensive union for labor on a basis that would counterbalance the power of aggregated and incorporated wealth and give to the creator of wealth a just share of the wealth he creates – then I felt that I had reached a field on which I was ready to spend the remaining energies of my life.[6]

The year was 1884. Up to now the arrival of wiry, fiery Martin Irons had been bad news for uppity foremen and sweatshop owners. Now it was going to be bad news for Jay Gould, America's biggest railway magnate, onto whose payroll Irons had just drifted. But to understand how the Knights captured the imagination of men like this, we first need to know why every other organisation failed.

Working class republicans: Craft unions had two problems: they were based on skill, so rarely organised across different sectors, and they were essentially local, and so could never beat a powerful nation-wide monopoly employer. In the United States during the 1870s, as a recession bit deep into wages and hours, unions were rolled back mill by mill and mine by mine. So the workers turned to politics. The *Iron Moulders Journal* complained:

> Hundreds of the ablest men in the movement have lost hope as to the power and willingness of workingmen to fight capital to the bitter end, through the organisation known as trades unions . . . Hence we find them no longer urging the organisation of labor into Trade and Labor unions but urging organisation for political purposes.[7]

But what kind of politics? At this time, if you were a socialist, you had a choice: you could follow the Marxists, who said trade unionism was important but only as a base camp from which to organise the ascent to power, or you could join the followers of Ferdinand Lassalle, who preached that unions were futile, preferring election campaigns and cooperatives. The debate between the two factions was all the more bitter for being conducted within the same organisation, the Socialist Labor Party (SLP). To follow it properly you would have to speak German, since the party was run by émigrés who, as a point of principle, refused to learn English.

Irons was an SLP member but remained as detached as most non-Germans did from the heavy stuff. When it came to the politics of 'What next?' the socialists had nothing much to say to men like him. Like the majority of militant workers he was at heart a working class republican, dedicated to life, liberty and the pursuit of happiness and convinced that all that stood in the way was the power of Wall Street.

This homespun anti-capitalism was essentially moral, not Marxist. Irons wrote,

> I have never known a strike that might not have been avoided by the simple recognition of the equal rights of man or the application of the elements of reason and common sense ... Strikes are not right; nevertheless they seem necessary as a protest against wrong. It is not right that they should seem necessary. But they are the counter-irritant to a virulent disease.[8]

In 1877, a massive spontaneous strike wave spread across the railway system. It was defeated amid riots, shootings and victimisations. Strikes in the coal mines went the same way: after a show trial, a group of Irish miners known as the Molly Maguires saw their leaders hanged. Suddenly secrecy, which had been a quirky choice for the early Knights of Labor, became a necessity. At this point, with militants reduced to an underground existence, with the left sidelined and the detour into electoral politics a shambles, a man called Terence V. Powderly took control of the Knights of Labor and led them, blinking, into the glare of public action.

* * *

How the Knights of Labor grew: The Order had made slow progress. Whatever its aspirations, it had remained an organisation of skilled white men in Pennsylvania, with fewer than 10,000 members. Powderly, a railwayman, had joined the Knights in 1874. He was a blond-haired, blue-eyed pugilist with a gift for poetry and oratory. 'English novelists take men of Powderly's look for their poets, gondola scullers, philosophers and heroes crossed in love,' enthused one journalist.[9] After opening his mouth once too often in the railway union Powderly was taken aside by one of the founder members of the Knights.

> One evening he invited me into his room, locked the door and told me to kneel down. I thought he wanted me to join him in prayer and refused to kneel until he captured me with a little soft solder by saying I was just the kind of young man he was looking for. He had sounded me, liked my sentiments – such as they were – and desired that I join an order that had for its object the recognition of the rights of all who toiled . . .'[10]

Being a man of talent, he quickly rose through the ranks of the Knights of Labor. After the 1877 strike he realised the Order would go nowhere without a formal constitution and centralised control. He persuaded it to relax secrecy, tone down the ritual and adopt a political programme. At this point Uriah Stephens quit the order and retired from public life.

Powderly wrote a programme that was a mixture of basic reforms and demands to curtail monopoly power. The Knights advocated the eight-hour day and equal pay for equal work, state-backed credit for small business and the creation of cooperatives. Alongside this went a strategic demand – the abolition of monopolies by means of nationalisation of the railways, telegraphs, telephone system and the banks. Though the workers needed to be organised to balance the growing power of big business, arbitration rather than strikes was the preferred method. Strikes, said Powderly, 'cannot change the apprentice system, a strike cannot remove the unjust technicalities in the administration of justice, a strike cannot regulate the laws of supply and demand . . .'[11]

With Powderly in control, the Knights grew by two main methods: recruiting unskilled workers into 'mixed' local assemblies and by allowing existing skilled trade union branches, or even entire unions, to affiliate en masse. For unskilled workers, the mixed assembly was a revelation; the unions' failure in the mining and mill towns had been largely due to their inability to accommodate people from different trades. Now, men from every trade sat beside women workers and, in some states, black workers. By 1880 the Order had 19 local assemblies in Alabama and its newspaper, *The Journal of United Labor*, reported,

> For fidelity to their obligations, strict attendance on all meetings, prompt payment of dues, good conduct and all that goes to make good members and good citizens [Negro members] are not excelled by any other class of men in the Order.[12]

In the South, however, the practice was for organisers to encourage the formation of separate black assemblies. While Powderly publicly banned the exclusion of black members from predominantly white assemblies he privately told them to 'organise colored men by themselves'. But there was resistance, as an organiser from Richmond, Indiana explained:

> It would be plain sailing if we could induce the colored faction to form another assembly but they will not, at least they show no disposition to do, for as one of them observed at a recent meeting: 'This is the only organisation in which we stand on an equal footing with the whites, and it is a big thing, and unless we can work here we will work nowhere.' This equality is what seems to stick in their craw.[13]

For the skilled unions the big attraction of the Knights was that they provided paid organisers who could draw on a national strike fund. And the organisers introduced into the American workers' movement the image of the roving rebel that would stay with it long after Powderly was forgotten. He wrote,

> We walked, daylight and dark. We ate not when we were hungry but when and where we could get it. We shared our homes, tables and beds with each other. I often had two or three Knights of Labor

with me over night. We slept in shanties, ash pits, freight cars or wherever night caught us after our work. Why did we do it? Because it was necessary and we wanted to be of use. . .[14]

Just before it totally abandoned secrecy in 1880 the Order had 28,000 members. By the end of 1884, as a result of its open door and the appeal of its homespun ideology, over 70,000 had joined. It was at this point, quite by accident, that it walked into a battle with Jay Gould, the self-styled Wizard of Wall Street, and made history.

'The great game of speculative finance': The Knights first clashed with Gould in 1883, when the Order called its first ever national strike, among telegraph operators. They lost, but the second round of the battle took place on the railways. Gould owned a whole network of railways in the Midwest, known as the Southwest System, the backbone of which was the line linking Missouri, Kansas and Texas. When Gould cut wages the workers' walked out.

For the Knights to take on Gould in the very heart of his industrial empire was as symbolic as if the employees of News Corp or Google were to walk out today. Gould's railway system was both a transport and an information network. And it was economically crucial not just to America but to the world – because cheap farm produce from the American West was having the same impact on the world market as cheap Chinese electronics have today: keeping world inflation low. As for Gould, he famously boasted he could pay one half of the working class to kill the other half. His biographer wrote of him that 'he bought many things but he never bought a eulogy. He played the great game of speculative finance for all it could be made to yield, without disguise or apology.'[15]

Martin Irons joined the Knights on the eve of the first strike against Gould and became its main organiser in Sedalia, Missouri. The state's labour inspector marvelled at his achievements:

This has been, so far as is known, the first strike that has ever been made where the strikers were thoroughly and systematically organised, and the control and management of it remained in the hands of the organisation. Every movement was directed by the executive committee, and a perfect police system maintained, under which the property of the railroad company and private individuals was fully protected.[16]

At first Gould's tactic was to retreat. He cancelled the pay cut but then began to victimise the strike organisers and locked out the entire workforce. Powderly responded by calling solidarity strikes across the entire Gould system. The Wizard of Wall Street capitulated there and then, promising to go to arbitration in all future disputes.

The news of Gould's defeat resounded like a detonator, not just through the American workforce but in the centres of political power. The *New York Sun* rushed its best investigative journalist into action:

> Five men in this country control the chief interests of 500,000 working men and can at any moment take the means of livelihood from 2,500,000 souls. These men compose the executive board of the Noble Order of the Knights of Labor . . . They can stay the nimble touch of almost every telegraph operator; can shut up most of the mills and factories and can disable the railroads. They can issue an edict against any manufactured goods so as to make their subjects cease buying them and the tradesmen stop selling them. They can array labor against capital, putting labor on the offensive or defensive, for quiet and stubborn self protection or for angry, organised assault, as they will.[17]

With PR like this there was no need to take out advertisements. Within a year the Knights had recruited 600,000 new members, taking the total to over 700,000. They were a mass movement and Powderly a hero across the continent. But Jay Gould was not finished yet.

The call for May Day: While the Knights grew spectacularly, the traditional unions struggled to achieve national coordination. A national Federation, founded in 1881, did little more than pass resolutions. However, one resolution was significant. After the Civil War six states had adopted eight-hour day laws but they were largely ignored in practice. As the labour movement revived in the early 1880s, the eight-hour day became the one legislative demand that united everybody – from the fob-watch-wearing train driver in his Railway Brotherhood to the black farmhand in his Knights of Labour hall.

The 25 delegates who attended the Federation's convention in Chicago 1884, representing only 50,000 workers, were heartened to hear a delegate from the carpenters' union report growing unrest over the eight-hour day. He proposed a novel way forward: to implement the shorter working day 'from below'. 'We want an enactment by the workingmen themselves that on a given day eight hours should constitute a day's work and they should enforce it themselves.'[18] The resolution nominated 1 May 1886, nearly two years away, as the day for the action to begin. It was passed unanimously and buried in the minutes of the convention, along with a lot of other good intentions.

The Federation now approached the Knights, who had also resolved on 'a general refusal to work for more than eight hours'. But the limitations of Terence V. Powderly were becoming all too obvious as he struggled to corral a mass movement exhilarated by strikes into an organisation opposed to them. In the aftermath of the Gould victory, 5,000 lumber workers in Michigan launched a strike that shut down 77 mills, despite the efforts of 150 armed members of the Pinkerton detective agency and the state militia. The majority of strikers were Polish immigrants, most of them recent, and to them the Knights of Labor seemed like a great idea. To a man they joined.

Powderly was now bombarded with letters from local assemblies demanding that the Knights back the strike planned by the union Federation. Alarmed, he told the Order's annual convention,

> The proposition to inaugurate a general strike for the establishment of the shorter-hour plan on the first of May 1886 should be discountenanced by this body. The people most interested in this plan are not as yet educated in the movement, and a strike under such conditions

must prove abortive. The date fixed is not a suitable one; the plan suggested to establish it is not a suitable one.[19]

Until now, Powderly had run the Knights with a mixture of chutzpah and showmanship worthy of the Wizard of Oz; now he was starting to sound like the Cowardly Lion. His next move was worthy of the Scarecrow; he changed the rules so that strikes could be called only with a two-thirds majority in a secret ballot, and only then with the permission of Powderly himself. This backfired. By August 1885 he was complaining that 'over two hundred lockouts have occurred since the employers got the idea that the members of our organisation could not strike without violating the laws of our Order'.

Momentum was developing – both in the unions and among the Knights – for a May Day strike. Meanwhile Jay Gould set sail in his yacht for the West Indies, put two of his railway lines into voluntary insolvency and unleashed a wage cut across the Southwest System.

The Great Southwest Strike: On the last day of February 1886, Martin Irons wired to Powderly, 'Cannot control matters here long. If not settled by 2 o'clock March 1, 1886, must call out Texas and Pacific employees.' Twenty-four hours later, to the screech of train whistles, workers began to down tools all along the Gould railway system. The flashpoints read like a list of Western B-movie locations: Red River, Waco, Fort Worth, Rio Grande . . . It is hard to imagine now that these Texan frontier towns, today strongholds of neocon Republicanism, were once the scene of a mass confrontation between organised labour and corporate America.

Unlike the previous year, this was a strike primarily of unskilled men; the engine drivers continued working – or tried to. So instead of protecting company property, the Knights' tactic this time was to seize it or smash it; there would be no useable trains for the engineers to drive. A Congressional report, compiled in the panicky autumn of that year, describes the strike's momentum:

> On the 3rd March several bridge gangs and all roundhouse men
> at Long View Junction struck. On the 4th March six engines were

disabled at Big Springs roundhouse by a mob of fifty masked men. The miners at the Gordon mines, which belonged to the Texas and Pacific Railway, pulled the coupling pins and notified the trainmen not to come there again until the strike was over. The telegraph operators employed by this company at Fort Worth, with the exception of one man, walked out and great difficulty was experienced by reason thereof.[20]

How did the mild-mannered Knights end up leading a strike in this gun-ridden, violent and literally Wild West corner of the Union? The factors were primarily economic: Gould's railway had, in a just a few years, become a monopoly conglomerate employing machinists, labourers, miners and white-collar telegraphers. When the workers banded together across skill and specialism and seized the railway without any written orders from the Knights, whiskers drooped on Capitol Hill. Washington's political elite were even more depressed when reports poured in of the mass support enjoyed by gun-toting frontier strikers – all the more so because their objectives were minimal: no wage cut, a minimum wage of $1.50 a day, binding arbitration and the reinstatement of a sacked official who had skipped work to attend a meeting.

In the first three weeks of the strike, only freight trains were targeted; passenger services were allowed to run. It is clear from managers' reports that the Knights were exercising workers' control over the trains that ran as well as disabling those they didn't want to move. 'Engine 171 . . . had an air-pump to repair and the committee of the Knights of Labor sent a machinist to do the work. I mention that as illustrating the difficult matter it was to do anything on that date without their consent,' reported the superintendent at Aitchison, Kansas.[21]

On 22 March, engine drivers in the same town found leaflets wedged into their machines:

To ENGINEERS and FIREMEN: Boys, we want you not to run a train out of Aitchison. It is with regret that we call you brothers. If you do, your life will pay the forfeit. Boys we want to throw off the yoke of serfdom and be free men like yourselves. Do not deny us what at that time you prayed for.[22]

The next day, 40 masked men carrying rifles and revolvers seized the repair shops and sabotaged the engines. The pattern of armed seizures, derailments, engine wrecking, machine-belt cutting and organised mayhem continued throughout the Midwest until the end of March, immobilising coal, crops and communications along the commercial spinal cord of America. There had been mass strikes before, but never this violent or effective, and never with so much kudos among the mass of sympathetic bystanders.

A.B. Campbell, adjutant-general of Kansas, tried to explain the mood of the strikers to Congressmen in the aftermath:

> Campbell: There was a good deal of general indignation expressed – feeling against Jay Gould.
>
> Q: Did they mention any particular acts on the part of Mr Gould that were injurious to or against their interests?
>
> Campbell: Nothing but his general grasping nature. The fact that he had acquired great wealth by improper means.[23]

So this was the first big strike against the trend to corporate monopoly. It had achieved a rough system of workers' control, enforced by armed pickets. It was crippling trade throughout the entire US economy. In the cities that formed the major nodes on the rail network, the Knights launched boycotts against anti-union firms. The *Kansas City Journal* was boycotted for its refusal to recognise the printers' union. Any business placing advertisements in it was also boycotted, with protesters forcibly dragging customers out of targeted shops. In De Soto, a few miles west of Kansas City, the entire local clergy supported the strike and were made honorary members of the Order.

> 'A chain of injustices led to the strike,' said a Catholic priest called C.F. O'Leary; 'Among them is the rottenness, injustice and spirit of tyranny that exists on the whole system from Gould down to the lowest official. That is my experience and I have been a close observer . . . It is opposed to the American spirit.'[24]

When the priest defended the use of 'any means that are potent and efficacious' an outraged Congressman asked him if that meant dynamite. 'Even dynamite,' he replied, adding that, since he was not an anarchist, 'I do not believe in using it at random.'

At the end of March, Jay Gould instructed his local representatives to arbitrate and Powderly stepped in to try and engineer a settlement. On 31 March, Irons ordered all the affiliates of District 101 to go back to work, adding, 'Honor demands that those who came out to support you go to work first.' It never happened; Gould's managers refused to re-employ known militants and then withdrew the offer of arbitration. When Powderly ordered Irons to settle the strike on any terms, he refused, and the dispute spiralled out of the control of the Grand Master Workman, who, having 'thirty other strikes and lockouts to look after' returned to the East Coast, leaving Irons in command.

Journalists covering the strike immediately grasped what was at stake in the argument between Irons and Powderly: would America's first mass workers' movement swing towards radicalism or stay within the limits defined by its founders? 'Powderly is a conservative; Irons is a fanatic,' wrote the *Fort Worth Gazeteer*.

> Powderly would bring industrial and social relief by working upon and obliterating the causes of social and industrial ills; Irons would cure the disease by killing the patient. Powderly is a philosopher; Irons is a socialist. Each has a following among the members of the organisation. The men who are for peace stand by Powderly. The incendiaries, anarchists and the ignorant elements sustain Irons. One or two things must happen; the Powderly or Irons faction must triumph and the other submit.[25]

The strike now careered towards its violent conclusion. Irons later denied writing the circular that called for a general strike across the Midwest, but it has the ring of him, and of the global significance the strike was assuming.

> The battle is not for today – the battle is not for tomorrow – but for the trooping generations in the coming ages of the world, for

our children and our children's children. Workmen of the world, marshal yourselves upon the battlefield. Workmen of every trade and clime, into the fray. Gould and his monopolies must go down or your children must be slaves.[26]

On 9 April an armed raid by 40 Knights on the repair shops at Little Rock, Arkansas got into a stand-off with a local posse. The sheriff ordered them to disperse, declaring that he would protect the property of the company even if he fell in his tracks. 'We'll die then,' one of the Knights of Labour is reported to have called out,

> And at that instant they fired a volley. The deputies returned the fire and the firing was kept up until about two hundred shots had been exchanged, when the Knights of Labor finally fell back and were lost to view in the darkness.[27]

On the same day in East St Louis, a crowd of strikers and onlookers clashed with another posse armed with Winchester rifles, who opened fire, killing seven and wounding many more. 'Bloodshed was followed by incendiarism,' the official report noted, as strikers set fire to stranded freight trains.

Mid-April saw the Knights convene a congress in Fort Worth, Texas to consider rubber-stamping Irons's call for a general strike. But the vote went against him. Instead of solidarity strikes Powderly promised financial support. Troops now poured into the strike centres, from the Gulf of Mexico to St Louis. The dispute descended into riot and small-scale guerrilla warfare and simmered down only when a delegation of Congressmen arrived to set up an arbitration panel on 1 May. But by then the rest of America was on fire

The making of a martyr: August Spies was another kind of rebel. Like Irons he had spent his youth drifting across America but was a generation younger – you can see it from his most famous photograph: shorter hair, a more tightly cropped moustache, a brow less romantic and more troubled. By the time it was taken he had plenty of troubles; the photo caption says 'Sentenced to Death'.

Spies' family had left Germany for New York in 1873. His life story

– written on death row in an angry, rambling style – records his first impression of America:

> The factory: the ignominious regulations, the surveillance, the spy system, the servility and lack of manhood among the workers and the arrogant arbitrary behavior of the boss and mamelukes – all this made an impression upon me that I have never been able to divest myself of. At first I could not understand why the workers, among them many old men with bent backs, silently and without a sign of protest bore every insult the caprice of the foreman or boss would heap upon them.[28]

He moved to Chicago on the eve of the big railway strike in 1877.

> The events of that year, the brute force with which the whining and confiding wage-slaves were met on all sides impressed upon me the necessity of like resistance. The latter required organization. Shortly afterwards I joined the 'Lehr & Wehr Verein', an armed organization of the workingmen, numbering then about 1,500 well drilled members.[29]

August Spies' ideas were formed in a parallel world to that of Martin Irons. The list of favourite authors he wrote while awaiting execution reads like a primer in 19th-century determinism and includes not just Karl Marx but Lewis Morgan – who applied Darwinian principles to anthropology – and Henry Buckle, who applied them to history. Irons' radicalism was romantic and rooted in American individualism; Spies' radicalism was rational and, above all, saw individual human beings as the helpless 'bearers' of historic forces.

Spies soon found the Chicago branch of the SLP too moderate. Together with a union organiser named Albert Parsons he broke away and joined the anarchist movement, styling himself a Socialist Revolutionary. Anarchism had come a long way since the Paris Commune: under the influence of the Russian revolutionary Bakunin, it had become more prone to violence, more focused on smashing the capitalist state, more alienated from parliamentary politics and more enamoured with 'propaganda of the deed' – the deed in question ideally involving a stick of dynamite.

Tired of the perennial debate between Marxists, Lassalleans and bomb-obsessed anarchists, Spies outlined a new strategy. To Spies it was obvious that unions, social clubs and discussion circles could at the same time both prepare the workers for political power and wield it. Spies fought for unskilled unionism, workers' militias, the freedom to get drunk and the inevitable march of progress. In a small corner of Chicago he was inventing a whole new philosophy of trade unionism, which was to gain broad support within the international labour movement during its great stride forward before 1914. Known within anarchist circles as the Chicago Idea, it became known to history as anarcho-syndicalism.

Spies was as dismissive of the eight-hour day as Powderly, though for different reasons. 'To accede the point that capitalists have the right to eight hours of our labor,' he wrote, '. . . is a virtual concession that the wage system is right.'[30] But he could recognise the beginnings of a mass trade union movement when he saw one. He became the leading light in the left-wing agitation for a general strike on May Day. 'The month of May,' wrote Spies in his newspaper, *Workers' Times,* 'may bring many a thing about which nobody dreams of today.'[31]

Two big strategies, one little guy: Chicago workers approached 1 May 1886 with two strategies and two organisations competing for their loyalty. On one side were the Knights, rooted in the romanticism and republicanism that had sustained American progress for a century. On the other side was nascent anarcho-syndicalism, a product of Marxism, anarchism and migration. What was it like to be an ordinary worker faced with this battle of ideas? In a word, confusing. Thanks to Abraham Bisno, a young Jewish tailor from Lithuania who left a typescript account of his early years in the Chicago rag trade, we have a worm's eye view. Bisno had arrived as a refugee from the Russian pogroms in 1882. Herded into a makeshift Chicago ghetto, his people feared to venture downtown where Irish kids would stone them and pull their beards. They were sucked into the eight-hours movement by accident.

We knew nothing of that movement; but it was in the atmosphere and it seemed to have crossed the border of our settlement, because in the months of February and March [1886] there was quite a lot of dissatisfaction among our people about the prices paid for work.[32]

One sunny April day a rumour spread that there was to be a meeting at a local hall. Nobody owned up to calling it and the crowd had to bribe the manager to open the door. By the end of it they had resolved to strike, picket and to 'break the heads' of anybody who refused to join in. It was an outworkers' strike, drawing in workshop owners as well as tailors. As he looked back on these events in the 1920s, Bisno, by now a veteran trade union leader, was puzzled:

> Nobody knew who called the first meeting, nor did anyone know who called on the Knights of Labor to send us a delegation . . . None of us knew that an organisation had to have a chairman, a secretary, rules of order, a mode of proceeding by which one man will get the floor while the other man will have to sit quietly and wait until he is through – all that was unbeknown to us. When we went on strike we didn't have a vote. When we agreed to join the Knights of Labor we didn't have a vote . . . As I think it over now after so many years have elapsed I am satisfied there must have been someone who did, with premeditation and intent, help to spread that the meeting was to be held . . .

The Knights clearly had some wily and dedicated activists. But soon the Jewish tailors discovered the downside of the Order: all negotiations were handled by full-time Knights of Labor officials, none of whom were Jewish, Lithuanian or tailors. And the Lithuanians, unable to dream of eight hours, were happy to settle for ten. The Knights of Labor 'ridiculed us', says Bisno.

A mass meeting was called. Many of the strikers were now literally starving, and some homeless. At that meeting 'a man was invited to speak to us in the German language and he made a wonderful speech', Bisno recalls. He spoke in simple German and 'since Yiddish is only a dialect of German I understood every word'. The speaker told them that the more industry developed the more important the working man became, that they were involved in a class struggle and while he wished them good luck in the strike for regular hours, 'this was only a minor effort and that the real effort to be made by us was to destroy root and branch the present capitalist order of things'. The speaker was August Spies, and the effect on Bisno – who having survived pogroms in the old country was now spending all his wages in Chicago's brothels – was electric:

> On that night when I went home I was aflame; the whole argu-
> ment struck me like lightning and went all through me. I had heard
> ideas that I had never heard before in my life and they seemed to
> express the very thoughts that were in my inner consciousness. He's
> right, I thought . . .

On the last two weekends in April the competing strands of the Chicago labour movement, divided almost completely along ethnic lines, performed their final rehearsals for the big day. First the American-born and Irish lined up behind the banners of the Knights of Labor and the craft unions; the themes were moderation and temperance. Then the anarchist-led Central Labor Union called its members to the streets in a separate demonstration; 5,000 marched, 25,000 went to the rally at the end. Not a single banner from the Knights or the official unions was present; 'there was scarcely an American, Irishman, Scandinavian or Scotchman among them', reported the *Chicago Tribune*.[33]

A contingent of German furniture workers led the march, a thousand strong, followed by the International Union of Carpenters and Joiners 'with Bohemian Turners Band'. The German bakers, the Bohemian lumber shovers, the metalworkers union 'with Lassalle Band', butchers, cabinetmakers, 'progressive German cigarmakers', saddlers and typographers marched. The march was in ranks, eight abreast, led by red flags and kept together by twenty-five mounted marshals. Among the many blood-curdling slogans and red flags, the motto 'Workingmen Arm!' would have topped any list of slogans calculated to give Powderly and his followers a heart attack. And it was not just rhetorical. The *Workers' Times* thundered,

> In this hour we call upon the workers to arm themselves. We have but one life to lose. Defend it with every means at your disposal. In this connection we should like to caution those working men who have armed themselves to hide their arms for the present so that they cannot be stolen from them by a minion of order, as has happened repeatedly.[34]

May Day 1886 was a Saturday, a workday. On this, the very first May Day protest in the history of the global movement, 340,000 workers across America joined the strike for the eight-hour day. A further 100,000 had already won a cut in hours. Chicago was the centre of the action, with 60,000 on strike and 80,000 joining a march down Michigan Avenue. According to *Bradstreet's* magazine, 45,000 Chicago workers had won shorter hours by the end of the first week in May.

Though it was a mass movement, it was about tiny, separate disputes. Abraham Bisno's strike was reaching its climax that week as the tailors resolved to march into the city centre to try and bring out the big clothing factories in solidarity. On 5 May, a Wednesday, 'about six hundred of us . . . walked in a body downtown'.

> When we crossed the Van Buren Street bridge, something happened that we had not expected to happen at all, namely patrol wagons came in on us from all sides of the city in large numbers; hundreds, probably thousands of policemen were unloaded in very short order . . . every policeman had a billy and they began to chase us and beat us unmercifully . . . none of us were arrested, none of us had time to do anything that would warrant an arrest. We simply were there, but a great many of us were beaten up very badly and we ran for our lives.[35]

The battered Lithuanians searched for answers. Was there something about America they had missed, some unwritten code, something they should have asked about before setting off? One man produced a German newspaper which solved the puzzle: on the Monday, Chicago police had opened fire on pickets outside the McCormick

Harvester Works, killing several. On the Tuesday, a protest meeting in the city's Haymarket Square had been called, the leaflet for it headed 'Revenge'. As the meeting had wound towards its close, with a mere 200 in the crowd, the police advanced. A bomb was thrown, killing seven policemen. More police and at least four demonstrators had been killed when the police opened fire on the crowd.

The speaker on the picket line at the McCormick Works had been August Spies. The author of the leaflet was August Spies. The man on the platform just before the bomb was thrown was August Spies. The same August Spies who had addressed the tailors' meeting only days before. Only now did the tailors realise that all demonstrations had been banned. This event would go down in history as the Haymarket Massacre but, in their ghetto isolation, it had passed Bisno and his colleagues by.

The martyrs: The Haymarket Massacre punctured the balloon, not only of the eight-hour movement and the anarchists, but of the Knights of Labor too. On the night of the Massacre, at an executive meeting in St Louis, Powderly summarily ordered the end of the Southwest strike. In Chicago, Bisno's strike collapsed.

> Picketing became absolutely impossible . . . the attitude of the police was practically the same as if the city was under martial law. Labor unions were raided, broken up, their property confiscated, the police used their clubs freely.[36]

The Knights' newspaper in Chicago printed on its front page, in capital letters,

> Let it be understood by the world that the Knights of Labor have no affiliation, association, sympathy or respect for the band of cowardly murderers, cutthroats and robbers known as anarchists. They sneak through the country like midnight assassins, stirring up the passions of ignorant foreigners, unfurling the red flag of anarchy and causing riot and bloodshed. Parsons, Spies, Fielden, Most and all their followers, sympathizers, aiders and abettors should be summarily dealt with![37]

In due course, that is exactly what happened. A show trial was held. The prosecution case was that the eight defendants – Spies and Parsons the most prominent – were guilty of murder by inciting the violence. It was accepted they had not lifted a finger on the day itself. The jury was hand-picked to ensure a guilty verdict and five of the men received the death sentence.

Spies and Parsons had effectively squandered their most important discovery: that mass trade unionism could form the basis not just of a fight for hours and wages, but of the fight for a new society. They had squandered it by walking into a trap set for them by their own rhetoric, their fascination with dynamite and their impatience. In the process they gave the excuse for a counter-offensive that was, by the year's end, to wipe out most of the shorter-hours deals won in the run-up to May Day.

Meanwhile Martin Irons was a defeated, sacked and soon to be broken individual. He was the last person to take the witness stand at the Congressional inquiry in St Louis, just seven days after the Haymarket Massacre. The Congressional report would describe him as a 'dangerous if not pernicious man'. His inquisitors surveyed him 'much as the owner of a good terrier looks at a rat in a steel trap', but he would defy them, playing cat and mouse with his interrogators, stonewalling every attempt to link the strike call with the widespread violence and sabotage, hinting the strike had Wall Street backing but defying demands to name names. He concluded, mournfully, 'I am not in favour of strikes and was in hopes that I could make this the last strike . . . Had this strike terminated in favour of the Knights of Labor I should have worked hereafter to make it the last strike.'[38]

Irons's wife had died during the strike and he had been forced to sell his furniture. Shortly afterwards he was jailed for vagrancy. He was blacklisted and never worked again. In the movement he became a whipping-boy as recriminations over the Southwest strike haunted the Order. Irons dropped out of the movement, ending his days in Bruceville, Texas, where the labour leader Eugene Debs discovered him in 1899: 'He bore the traces of poverty and broken health but . . . when he spoke of socialism he seemed transfigured and all the smouldering fires within his soul blazed from his sunken eyes once more'.[39]

In October 1886 August Spies and his comrades prepared to die. Taking the witness stand Spies spoke for hours, calmly and from notes. His death-row autobiography reads as bitter, rambling and confused, yet his speech from the dock was the very opposite. He must have known it would echo around the global labour movement as there was already an international campaign for clemency for the five condemned men. From the dock, Spies addressed not the workers but the employers, with a prediction of their inevitable doom:

> You, gentlemen, are the revolutionists! You rebel against the effects of social conditions which have tossed you, by the fair hand of fortune, into a magnificent paradise. Without inquiring, you imagine that no one else has a right in that place. You insist that you are the chosen ones, the sole proprietors. The forces that tossed you into the paradise, the industrial forces, are still at work. They are growing more active and intense from day to day. Their tendency is to elevate all mankind to the same level, to have all humanity share in the paradise you now monopolize. You, in your blindness, think you can stop the tidal wave of civilization, and human emancipation by placing a few policemen, a few Gatling guns, and some regiments of militia on the shore – you think you can frighten the rising waves back into the unfathomable depths, whence they have risen, by erecting a few gallows in the perspective. You, who oppose the natural course of things, you are the real revolutionists. *You* and *you* alone are the conspirators and destructionists![40]

Spies and Parsons, together with two others, were hanged on 11 November 1887, (the fifth condemned man committed suicide in his cell). 'There will be a time,' Spies shouted from the gallows 'when our silence will be more powerful than the voices you strangle today.' That time was not long in coming. In 1893 the governor of Illinois pardoned the three surviving convicts, declaring the whole trial unfair. By then, as we will see, the ideas of August Spies were helping to drive a global upsurge in trade unionism.

In 1914 Terence Powderly, who had now become a senior official in the US Immigration Bureau, hopped off a train in Pennsylvania to talk to a gang of railway workers. 'I just wanted to learn how much they knew of the lessons that come filtering down through the years.' He wrote,

Inquiry concerning the strike of 1877, the telegraphers' strike of 1883, the Southwest strike of 1886, elicited no information. Then I asked if they had ever heard of a man named Martin Irons, but the blood of that martyr wasn't known to these members of the present day church ... I finally got round to my own name, and though all of them had heard the name, they had lost track of the man or what he stood for ...[41]

5. A great big union grand
Unskilled unionism goes global, 1889–1912

> We want all the workers in the world to organise
> Into a great big union grand
> And when we all united stand
> The world for the workers we'll demand
> > Joe Hill 'What We Want', 1913[1]

Canary Wharf, London, 2004

The woman holding the leaflets clutches them tight against her duffel coat. At street level, Canary Wharf is a like a wind tunnel. The small group of activists in high-visibility bibs are dwarfed by the skyscraping headquarters of investment banks: Morgan Stanley, Lehman Brothers, Barclays and tonight's target, HSBC. The activists are not supposed to be here; this is the new financial heart of London and even the public space is privately owned by the development company. They know they can be thrown off the street.

By day, Canary Wharf teems with men and women in suits; the average salary here is £60,000. During business hours upwards of 80,000 people come and go, surrounded by glass, steel and sky, and the picturesque waterways that used to be London's main docks. By night, it is deserted, except for security guards, cleaners and this small group of leafleters organised by the TGWU and the East London Community Organisation.

Those the leaflet is meant for arrive in small groups, by bus. They are the cleaners who sluice the toilets, dust the desks, swab the telephone mouthpieces with antiseptic wipes and empty brown apple cores from thousands of wastebaskets. They are almost all migrants – not from the settled Caribbean and Asian communities of inner London but from among the new arrivals: Somalis, Nigerians, Sierra Leonese, Kurds, Iraqis, Afghans, Colombians, Bolivians, Cubans, Spanish and Portuguese.

Benedita Goncalves, a Portuguese cleaning supervisor at a major bank, describes the way the cleaners are treated by the office workers:

> The cleaners clean the rubbish and we are like rubbish for them – apart from some who work at night and start to know us and sometimes say, 'Good evening.' For the rest we are no one. We are rats, we come in the night.

Migrant cleaners always talk about being 'looked through' by office workers who don't see them as people, let alone workmates. In most cases they work for sub-contractors and are not part of the core workforce. Cleaners also say they are always the first to be accused of stealing if something goes missing, but their recurring problem is an absence of respect. Says Benedita,

> I started my battle in the first week I was there because the management was horrible. They showed lack of respect to the employees. Everything you did was wrong. They sent people home for no reason – just because they didn't need them. Another thing is the shouting, calling names, saying, 'You are crap; you are no one.' Something like that happened with me and so I started my battle against them.

For Juan Rodriguez the biggest issue is contracts, or the lack of them. When he started work as a cleaner at News International six years ago, he says nobody knew what the official hours, wages or even status were. Now their employer, a cleaning contractor, has tried to get them to sign individual contracts but they have refused. 'One hundred per cent,' he says, 'even the ones not in the union.' For Juan the problem is 'respect *and* money' – respect first but with the cleaners earning on average £200–300 a week, money comes a close second:

> Management harass the staff, blackmail the staff – and worst thing is, which is very, very sad, people with no documents are afraid to make comments. Some of them are even against us – the ones who are afraid of the union.

Martin Wright, a black British cleaner at the Royal London Hospital, echoes the complaint. After three years of organising he's managed to get the hourly pay raised from £5.50 to £7.50 an hour and the contract taken in-house so the cleaning managers have to answer to the hospital managers. But there are still problems: he's having to deal with constant tensions between workers from Nigeria, Ghana and Somalia. 'Martin Luther King is my hero and I tell them we are all brothers and sisters; all our ancestors came from Africa.' Juan and Benedita have both encountered similar conflicts. Juan says,

> Some people, because they come from a background where there is civil war, they still have in their mind just to kill! One guy, working with us came into the room and said to another guy, 'If you were in my country I shoot you,' and we said (we were all shocked), 'What are you talking about?' And everybody in the room realised this guy, in his head, was still in the civil war.

When I ask them how they overcome these divisions, the word they all use is patience. 'You have to be patient and very understanding with everybody,' says Juan. 'Try to learn from each one their background and then explain the difference between your country and their country.' He says Africans are harder to organise than the rest, Latin Americans the easiest because they have a left-wing tradition.

'One guy from Cuba thought he's gonna be shot for joining,' says Benedita, laughing.

'Yeah, we had a Cuban and he said that too, but he joined the union,' Juan retorts. Benedita is optimistic:

> In the beginning it's difficult, but you start to know each other. We are coming together from all parts of the world but we come together because someone wants to make our life not easy. That means we must be together to fight against this and not fight each other – against injustice.

I ask Juan if he knows there was a major strike at News International, which publishes *The Times* and the *Sun,* and that it was a famous strike. 'Long, long ago, way back, I heard that, yes,' he says. His mouth drops open wide as I tell him the story of the year-long Wapping strike of 1986, when the power of the print unions was broken. In fact it opens nearly as wide as my own mouth did back then when I saw a bunch of highly paid and supposedly 'aristocratic' printers turn over a truck at the main gates and set it on fire.

'This information you are telling me is very powerful information,' he nods, still stunned. Up to now this unassuming Spaniard with broken English had no idea he was trying to organise a union in the very place the union movement suffered a symbolic and shattering defeat.

The cleaners, by their own admission, know nothing about the history of east London; many are still struggling with the geography. But the organising team knows all too well the irony of what they're doing at Canary Wharf. Their union was born here; it grew by recruiting unskilled workers who the unions at the time believed were too ignorant to be organised. And the strike that started it all began within yards of where the HSBC skyscraper stands today. It is small compensation to the activists, stamping their feet to keep warm as midnight approaches, but they are treading in the footsteps of Tom Mann.

London, 1889

Tom Mann has been blacklisted as an engineer and is so poor he's had to sell his violin; Victor Griffuelhes is a shoemaker trudging the lanes of southern France in search of work; Bill Haywood is a cowboy in Nevada; Eduardo Gilimon is wandering through the slums of Buenos Aires preaching the non-existence of God; James Connolly is an embittered British soldier in Ireland. The year is 1889 and working class history is at a turning point. Between now and the outbreak of the First World War, the labour movement will go global, creating mass trade unions and popularising a new 'union way of life'. But the men who will make this happen are in 1889 anonymous loners on the fringes of the workforce.

Over the next twenty years their names will become well known in the tabloid newspapers and police stations of the world. They will cross continents and oceans in pursuit of a twofold dream: trade unions for unskilled workers and international solidarity between them. The idea is known to history as syndicalism and is rough and ready, like the unplaned wood of the railway boxcars it is born in – and it will infuriate socialist intellectuals.

But why will it spread so fast? The answer lies in the giant transformation under way in business and politics in 1889. It can be summed up as the three Ms. Monopoly – the rise of heavy industry has created a few big companies which can swallow up the rest; these are companies with absolute power over suppliers, the workforce and even the politicians who are supposed to regulate them. Management – the generation of businessmen that will build the Eiffel Tower and the *Titanic* need scientific methods to run the workplace. They need control over it and at the same time harmony within it. They have started to think scientifically about ways to manage people at work. Militarism – the industrial powers are engaged in the scramble for colonies that will lead to war in 1914; everywhere nationalism is solidifying. Military face-offs and minor wars give warning of the storm ahead.

This is how globalisation looks the first time around; it is not the same as today's version. By 1889 a global system of trade, transport and exchangeable currencies has been created, making international solidarity between workers in different countries a practical question instead of just a high ideal. New Zealand wool makes shawls to keep the heads of British mill girls warm; Chinese migrants undercut the wages of white Dutchmen in the gold mines of South Africa; beef from Argentina ends up in the spaghetti of a Bolognese engineer. And there is mass migration. From Sydney to Seattle workers are on the move, not just from the farm to the factory but across land and sea. The footloose syndicalist agitators will always find an audience in the steerage class of ocean-going ships, or in the cattle trucks of trains.

Traditional trade unionism, born in a century of small strikes, small firms and local economics, cannot cope with this new world of giant things. Its power against monopoly is non-existent; scientific management is undermining its control over training and wage rates; and the vast mass of working people have no way into – indeed see no point to – trade unions.

A small core of activists has struggled to keep alive the principles of anarchism and socialism but it's an uphill struggle. 'Marxist ranters' pay fleeting visits to the Salford streets that had throbbed with republicanism at the time of Peterloo but the reception is now hostile. Robert Roberts, who grew up there in this period, remembers:

> We were battling, they told us (from a vinegar barrel borrowed from our corner shop) to cast off our chains and win a whole world. Most people passed by; a few stood to listen but not for long: the problem of the 'proletariat' they felt, had little to do with them.[2]

The 'class struggle', Roberts will recall acidly, is something that goes on within the working class: between the skilled, the semi-skilled, the unskilled, the unemployed and the irretrievably drunk. Sociologists are struck by this layer cake of misery, above all in that glittering central hub of global trade, the London docks. It is the mass strike there that will change everything.

'Labour of the humbler kind': This is how men were recruited to work in the London docks in 1889.

> We are driven into a shed, iron-barred from end to end, outside of which a foreman or contractor walks up and down with the air of a dealer in a cattlemarket, picking and choosing from a crowd of men, who, in their eagerness to obtain employment, trample each other under foot, and where like beasts they fight for the chances of a day's work.[3]

If that system seems haphazard now, to the employers then it looked like the height of labour market flexibility. The sea is unpredictable, as are harvests, as is trade, so the docker's income should be as unpredictable – that was the theory.

They were paid by the hour at minimal rates, employed a day at a time. Beatrice Webb, a social reformer, tramped the streets of London's

East End jotting down notes about the misery they lived in, less than a mile from the financial district.

> Go to the docks in the early morning. Permanent men respectable, sober, clean. Casuals low-looking, bestial, content with their own condition. Watch brutal fight and struggle: then sudden dissolution of the crowd with coarse jokes and loud laugh. Look of utter indifference on their faces; among them one or two who have fallen from better things – their abject misery . . . If a man weary of ennui and of an empty stomach drops off to sleep, his companions will promptly search his pockets for the haphazard penny.[4]

Webb did not stop at recording the poverty, drunkenness and despair. She plunged into this world, getting herself jobs in the sweatshops where the dockers' daughters worked, and shocked polite society by publishing the diary she kept. Some facts, however, were too brutal to be included:

> I omitted the references in my diary to the prevalence of incest in one-room tenements. The fact that some of my workmates . . . could chaff each other about having babies by their fathers and brothers was a gruesome example of the effect of debased social environment on personal character and family life . . . To put it bluntly, sexual promiscuity and even sexual perversion are almost unavoidable among men and women of average character and intelligence crowded into the one room tenement of the slum areas.[5]

It was not just middle class reformers who found the East End workforce hopeless and disgusting. A socialist docker told Webb that his workmates were 'incapable of organisation'. So the strike, when it happened, was a shock to everybody except Tom Mann.

Mann was already in his thirties. He was a skilled engineer convinced that the existing trade unions were both incapable of surviving industrial modernisation and useless for organising unskilled workers. While others constructed theories to explain the situation, Mann burned to set it right. 'The average unionist of today,' he wrote, in a pamphlet addressed to the average unionist, 'is a man with a fossilized intellect.'[6]

It was the hot, late summer when trouble broke out. It was a pathetically irrelevant dispute over pay rates on a single ship. The men involved laid siege to the nearest union office they could find and pleaded for help. The man they found was Ben Tillett and he sent for his mates Tom Mann and John Burns, both socialists who had been grumbling about union inactivity on the docks for months. Together they set about pulling the whole of east London out on strike.

The docks had their own notorious class system: above the docker ranked the stevedore, who acted as a makeshift gangmaster. Better than the stevedore was the waterman – entitled to wear a ludicrous pink uniform while surviving on next to nothing. At the bottom of the pile were the women, who Webb described as 'the Chinamen of the East End' – the slaves. In normal times you were lucky if you could persuade members of these urban castes to drink in the same pub together, but these were not normal times. Within a week 30,000 dockers were joined on strike by an equal number from 'allied trades'.

Mann, Tillett and Burns set up a strike committee in a cafe. Mann had the job of standing at the doorway with his leg jammed across it, holding back a crowd of thousands queuing for strike pay. These were mean fist-fighters who had never been on strike and who would rob each other without hesitation. There was a large contingent of Irish migrants and a smattering of every other nation on earth. The image of Mann holding thousands of them at the door impressed journalists at the time. Stripped to the waist, sweating into his waxed moustache, cracking jokes and throwing friendly punches at the heads of those who didn't get the jokes, he became an instant celebrity.

There was a mass meeting every day, then the strikers would set off in an orderly procession around the banking district. The smart office workers of the Square Mile preferred their poor 'deserving' and the dockers, with their liking for drink and violence, expected a hostile reception. So they staged tableaux and carried effigies to provide a visual sociology lesson for those who had not read the works of Beatrice Webb. They carried effigies of a 'docker's cat', which was thin, and a 'bosses' cat' which was fat; likewise the docker's child and the bosses' child, depicted by rag dolls on sticks. The watermen wore their pink uniforms.

Tillett recalls collecting 'pennies, sixpences and shillings, from the clerks and City workers, who were touched perhaps to the point of sacrifice by the emblem of poverty and starvation carried in our procession'. The Salvation Army – sternly anti-socialist but a potent force in its east London homeland – had no option but to support the strike. The Catholic Church also weighed in.

What tipped the balance was Australia. The powerful Australian unions used the issue of the London strike to inflame animosity against the English upper classes. First came £2,000, then £15,000; even the government of Queensland chipped in. By the end of the strike a total of £30,000 – at least £2.7 million in today's money – had been wired via the Australian dockers' union.[7] This was more than half the total cash collected during the strike. It was a potent symbol for all concerned. Sixty thousand London dock strikers were now joined on strike by another 60,000 of their drinking buddies and daughters from the rat-infested streets along the waterfront.

'Dockmen, lightermen, bargemen, cement workers, carmen, iron-workers and even factory girls are coming out. If it goes on a few days longer,' wrote a London evening paper, 'all London will be on holiday. The great machine by which five millions of people are fed and clothed will come to a dead stop, and what is to be the end of it all? The proverbial small spark has kindled a great fire which threatens to envelop the whole metropolis.'[8]

On 28 August the strike committee issued a manifesto calling for a general strike across London – for the workers to officially and purpose-fully pull the plug on the 'great machine'. The call was withdrawn a day later for fear of losing public sympathy. A few days later, following the intervention of City bankers, shipowners and a Catholic cardinal, the dockers won. History records that they won the 'docker's tanner' – sixpence an hour instead of five. But they had won much more. Burns wrote,

> Labour of the humbler kind has shown its capacity to organise itself; its solidarity; its ability. The labourer has learned that combination

can lead him to anything and everything . . . Conquering himself, he has learned that he can conquer the world of capital whose generals have been the most ruthless of his oppressors.[9]

To Beatrice Webb, the emergence of solidarity in the East End was 'a new thought . . . modifying my generalisation on dock life'. It dawned on a whole layer of middle class do-gooders that workers might not have to wait for betterment to be handed down through legislation and lectures. The same thought also dawned on tens of thousands of unskilled workers who rushed to join trade unions. The railway union grew from nothing to 65,000 in a year; the bricklayers' union doubled in size, the shoemakers tripled; the miners formed a national federation. The movement was labelled New Unionism. Its aim was to draw the unskilled workers into industry-wide unions that would cut across the petty job descriptions that, in the strike, had been made to look irrelevant.

Tom Mann – the making of a syndicalist: Tom Mann's life perfectly illustrates the torpid state of the British labour movement before unskilled unionism took off. As a teenager he spends three nights a week at college, one night at Bible class, one night at a temperance meeting and Sunday night at church. 'No one, as yet,' he remembers, 'was advocating socialism.' He becomes an agitator against alcohol and eating meat. Armed with these principles he moves to London as a skilled engineer, adding astronomy to his hobbies after being given the job of dissecting a meteorite for the British Museum.

The atmosphere of the engineering factory then is like the atmosphere of a software company or design studio now – a world of relaxed innovation and the tecchie obsessions of meticulous men. Mann works personally alongside George Westinghouse, the inventor of the hydraulic brake, and Peter Brotherhood, the inventor of the torpedo engine. This is how he describes the atmosphere at Brotherhood's factory in Clerkenwell, a place that today is London's 'Silicon Alley':

The foreman was a fine, intelligent man, broadminded and tolerant; but there seemed to be nothing to talk about at mealtimes or on any other occasion but work, government orders, patents just launched or expected, prospects of greater trade for engineers, the mechanical progress of the world as it affected engineers. No talk here of social problems; but every man was in [the union] . . .[10]

Beyond the dead calm and social peace of the engineering shop the world is a troubled place. Mann is a regular at the Salvation Army, where unemployment is blamed on drink: but London is in the grip of a long economic depression and even clean-living workers are being sacked. So Mann catches a boat to New York and works in a Brooklyn factory for three months. In 1884, the same year as the US unions start the fight for the eight-hour day, Mann returns to England and moves a resolution in his union branch for the same objective. He loses – five for, 75 against.

He becomes a minor figure in the socialist pulpits of the time and graduates to organising marches for the unemployed. After he recites Shelley's *Rise Like Lions* at a demonstration in Trafalgar Square a riot breaks out. By this time he owns 'a fairly good collection of books, a violin and a telescope'.

Before the dock strike, the British labour movement was dominated by men like Tom Mann – self-taught, proud of their skills and in control of their work environment, more at home with socialist painters and philosophers than with 'labour of the humbler kind'. After the strike, that changed completely – as this description of the Trade Union Congress in 1890 shows.

Physically, the 'old' unionists were much bigger than the new . . . A great number of them looked like respectable city gentlemen; wore very good coats, large watch chains, and high hats and in many cases were of such splendid build and proportions that they presented an aldermanic, not to say a magisterial form and dignity. Amongst the new delegates not a single one wore a tall hat. They looked workmen; they were workmen.[11]

All over the world 'labour of the humbler kind' was getting organised. If the Paris Commune had closed the door on the era of street revolutions, the dock strike had opened an era of workplace revolutions. The trade union itself could become a mini-commune: training and educating workers for self-government. Mann and his comrades had discovered this could be done in practice but, as ever, it was left to the French to turn it into a theory.

Victor Griffuelhes – the union way of life: When Victor Griffuelhes hit the road to look for work as a shoemaker he was just another French teenager taking his chances in a society on the move. When he arrived in Paris in 1893 the only organisation he had ever been in was a cobblers' social club. But a life of intermittent work, hungry Fridays, dreams and seething anger pulled this gaunt, shock-haired, deep-eyed youngster into the union movement.

> A workman I was; having lived through multiple deprivation and found it extremely hard to make a living, I desired to put an end to it. A wage-earner I was; having submitted to the bosses, I ardently wished to escape from exploitation. But these desires and these wishes could only be achieved through continual struggle alongside men caught in the same trap. So I joined the union, to fight against the bosses, the direct instrument of my servitude; and against the state, the natural defender – because the beneficiary – of the bosses. It was from the union that I got my will to struggle and it was there that my ideas began to sort themselves out.[12]

The French workers' movement was already being transformed. Socialist clubs and parties, which were tiny in London, were big in Paris. The skilled unions were beginning to reach out to unskilled workers. There was a system of labour exchanges funded by the government but – thanks to anarchists who had taken them over – they had become radical night schools and organising centres. Now the movement was gripped by a longing and a passion for something it had never had: a mass strike like the one in London.

Since 1888 a carpenter called Joseph Tortelier – who had been in jail with Louise Michel – had toured the meeting halls of Paris delivering a speech with a single theme: 'Revolution Through General Strike!'

Now he converted Fernand Pelloutier, the leader of the labour exchange movement, who in turn converted a journalist called Aristide Briand, and together they wrote a pamphlet called *Revolution Through General Strike*. Briand was to be prime minister of France ten times; he was to win the Nobel Peace Prize and write the law that made France a secular state. But in the fervid atmosphere of the 1890s his imagination ran towards revolution. He designed a plan for a general strike that would take five years to prepare and 400 million francs to finance. After 15 days it would bring the capitalist order to its knees.

> Instead of a traditional revolution, pitting 30,000 insurgents against 200,000 soldiers . . . the general strike would put in the field: here 200,000 workmen against 10,000 soldiers; there 10,000 against 500; elsewhere . . . 1,000 or 1,200 against a squad of gendarmes. Do you see the difference? And what resources for the strikers! All transport stopped, all the street lights dimmed, all the supplies to the great cities blocked . . .[13]

Victor Griffuelhes joined the shoemaker's union in 1896, the year *Revolution Through General Strike* was being passed from hand to hand in the rough cafes of Paris. The fervour was fuelled by two big changes in French life which were gathering speed: the radicalisation of politics and the mechanisation of industry.

The Dreyfus Case, over anti-Semitism in the army, had split French politics down the middle and the liberals saw the workers as their natural allies. They enacted big reforms: the eight-hour day in the public sector, compulsory arbitration in labour disputes, recognition of trade unions as legal entities. The price they demanded from the workers was cooperation. In 1899 Alexander Millerand became the first socialist politician in the world to enter the government of a nation state.

In industry, France had lagged behind the general acceleration in the rest of the world. A visiting union member from England described a typical workshop:

> Discipline is by no means of a cast iron character. If Maurice or
> Jules have a sudden idea which they wish to communicate to Henri

at the other end of the shop, they go at once, without looking round to see where the foreman is, or pretending to go on business. A good quarter of an hour is lost each morning in shaking hands and passing salutation with comrades in all parts of the factory . . . The workman has the utmost freedom in the workshop, and any attempt to limit this freedom is resented as deeply as an attack on the economic position of wages and hours.[14]

Now, in the 1890s, Maurice and Jules had to put up with massive modernisation. Even Victor Griffuelhes the shoemaker had to cope with mechanisation.

The response of an entire generation to these changes was to reject parliamentary politics, even the idea of parties, and rely on the unions alone to change the world. They called it syndicalism, after the French word for trade union. Instead of politics, parties, theories and alliances with enlightened liberals, the workers would fall back on what Griffuelhes called the 'union way of life':

From solidarity or from slavery, whichever you prefer, syndicalism was born from all these things. It was shaped by the methods of struggle, whose character was shaped by workers' action. And I repeat this on purpose: this action was not driven by vague formulas and theoretical assertions. It did not follow a plan drawn up in advance. I can't emphasise this enough: it was just what we did on one day, joined up with what we'd done the day before.[15]

A General Confederation of Labour (CGT) was formed, with committees to link up the different trades. In 1899, when the liberals formed a government, everybody knew things could go only one of two ways: either a rapid dose of reform would bring the workers alongside the government in alliance against the right; or the union movement would take on the government in a burst of strike action. In fact both things happened, one after the other.

A strike wave gripped France. Days lost to strikes rose from 1.2 million in 1898 to 3.5 million in 1900 and 3.7 in 1901. In 1902 the CGT agreed to merge with the labour exchange movement – and by then Victor Griffuelhes was the CGT's leader. Suddenly, he was everywhere – zipping from one end of France to another, organising strikes and whipping up protest. It was as if a French version of Tom Mann had appeared but on performance-enhancing drugs.

The crucial aspect of Griffuelhes' syndicalism was that it was overtly 'revolutionary'. Tom Mann, sitting in a garret with his violin, books and telescope, might have allowed himself the occasional sober reverie about insurrection but for Griffuelhes revolution was no dream; it was his sole intention. Unions and labour exchanges were to be 'gymnasiums' toning the muscles of the workers' movement not just for the seizure of industry – which everyone thought would be a pushover – but for the exercise of power.

The great attraction of syndicalism, as against the intellectual creeds of socialism and anarchism, was its roots in the working class and the sense it made to militant workers. Syndicalist leaders might get shouted down at street-corner meetings, but at least they belonged on those street corners. The great disadvantage of syndicalism was this: if you did not buy the whole prospectus and wanted the union simply to represent you at work it could look like a con trick. We know today that Griffuelhes was secretly meeting the violence-obsessed philosopher Georges Sorel but the union's members knew nothing of the influence anarchist intellectuals had among the inner core.

Though syndicalism dominates the history of the French working class before 1914, the CGT never organised more than a small minority of workers. Since most of the workers, most of the time, want their unions to be concerned with wages, hours and conditions, syndicalism's biggest problem – even during its heyday – was its inability to launch and win mass strikes. For a movement obsessed with the general strike as a tactic, this was quite a disadvantage. The whole problem came to a head during the run-up to May Day 1906.

Limoges – the Red City: 'At night, huge flames, several metres high, shot up, close together, from the oven where the porcelain was baked. These flames in the night gave Limoges the allure of an enormous forge from which came the wonder so sought after at that time by the two Americas.'[16] The wonder was porcelain. For a century it had been produced in the craft potteries of Europe but the world now wanted it by the shipload. The American businessman Theodore Haviland had mastered a way of mass-producing it. His factory confirmed Limoges' status as a global centre of excellence for ceramics, and his workforce confirmed it as a global centre of syndicalism. Soon, syndicalism too would be the wonder of the two Americas.

If you look on eBay you can still find the stunningly delicate dishes decorated with flowers and birds made by workers who lived the 'union way of life'. The patterns were put on by transfer, not painted by hand. As mechanisation replaced skill, thousands of women had replaced men in the factories. At Theodore Haviland's works there were 5,740 men, 2,400 women and 1,528 children. The factory used modern production methods. It would have been classed a model factory but for one thing: the propensity of foremen to rape the women workers.

The medieval 'right of first night' is known in France as the *droit de cuissage*, literally the 'right to get between thighs'. Notorious supervisors throughout the factory assumed they had that right. In 1905 the owners of the thighs decided they'd had enough. Marcel Body, a child at the time, remembered:

> I was 11 in 1905, when the workers from the Céramiques de Limoges went on strike and took to the streets. Contingents of thousands of demonstrators booed the bosses, and one afternoon, just as we were about to leave school, we heard an immense clamour: the 'Internationale' sung by thousands of voices.[17]

On 25 March 1905 a foreman called Penaud sacked three workers at the Haviland factory. He was notorious for groping women workers as they passed down a corridor near his office and of sacking those who would not have sex with him. After a short walkout the sacked women were reinstated, but on 30 March the local paper reported,

> A small dispute, which was quickly resolved, burst out again on Tuesday at the factory of Mr Theodore Haviland, in the paint workshop. Yesterday, new difficulties emerged and all the painters downed

tools. They demand, it appears, the sacking of their foreman. The strikers held a meeting in the evening at the Labour Exchange.[18]

This was bad news for Penaud, and for Haviland, because in Limoges the union way of life was predominant. There was a women's porcelain union which had struck three times the previous year.

Now the entire factory came out on strike, together with a factory belonging to Haviland's brother Charles. There the problem was another foreman, accused of victimising workers for their anti-clericalism. The wider issue of who controlled the factories was now at stake. Sensing this the Ceramic Federation – an alliance of porcelain employers – announced that unless the strikes at Haviland were ended Limoges' entire workforce would be locked out. On 14 April, 19 out of 32 factories locked their gates. As one newspaper put it, the aim was 'to stop the workers and the unions from getting mixed up in the running and oversight of industry'.[19] Suddenly the strike was a national story and, in a curious reversal, Foreman Penaud, with his wandering hands, had become a Dreyfus for the political right in France.

At this point there were 40,000 union members in Limoges. The labour exchange became the focal point for a daily round of support activities for the locked-out workers. Since Haviland had seized their social security fund the workers were reliant on donations, and vast amounts of money were collected from across the city and the region.

After Haviland raised the American flag over his factory, the workers burned his car to a cinder. A bomb was discovered on his doorstep and this brought the army into Limoges. On 17 April the inevitable clash took place. Marcel Body takes up the story:

> There was the loud roar of a cavalry charge, which came hurtling down . . . past the front of the school, swords in the air. At the same time, the demonstrators climbed the embankment bordering the route to Aixe, and hurled onto the road whatever they could lay their hands on. Others broke up the embankment to release huge stones to throw at the horses. A silence fell, we could leave. I run and arrive at the impressive barricades. It is unreal. How could men erect such obstacles in such a short space of time with their bare hands?

A few days later in a public park, soldiers opened fire on a rowdy gathering of strikers, killing 20-year-old potter Camille Vardelle and wounding scores of others. They jabbed at workers hiding in the bushes with their bayonets, Marcel Body remembered, displaying 'a barely believable anger'. The next day, 30,000 people assembled at Vardelle's funeral. The syndicalist agitator 'Citizeness Sorge', sent to the city by Griffuelhes, impressed on the workers the significance of what had happened:

> Wherever I go, to the north, the south, the east, the west, the centre
> – in France and abroad – it's the same complaint I hear on the lips
> of working wives and mothers: we are victims of the lubricity of
> our bosses and their foremen. It is above all the women I salute – you
> who were not frightened to turn your chests against the bayonets.
> Your attitude proves you know all too well what it means to be a
> proletarian woman.[20]

The violence sent shock waves into the most tranquil corners of everyday life. Body remembered how he immediately wrote and circulated an essay for his schoolmates about the killing of Vardelle. At another school the children presented a petition to the headmaster demanding an end to corporal punishment. On the blackboard somebody had scrawled, 'Long Live the Revolution!'

On 24 April, Haviland submitted a short letter to the local press: 'In order to end the difficult situation in Limoges I am opening my factory on Tuesday, without the services of Monsieur Penaud.'[21]

The crisis of syndicalism: The Limoges strike was not an isolated flare-up. Between 1902 and 1907 waves of strikes broke relentlessly across France. There were national strikes of miners and building workers; there were city-wide strikes as in Limoges. There were bitter strikes in small towns like the metalworking bastion of Hennebont. There was sporadic violence.

The CGT launched a campaign for the eight-hour day and a giant piece of sailcloth was draped across the front of the Paris labour exchange painted with the slogan, 'After 1 May 1906 we will work only eight hours.' Syndicalism, which had initially regarded partial strikes as a waste of energy, now swung round to the view that they could be stepping stones to the 'great day'.

As for the character of the strike that the CGT now planned, there was no room for ambiguity.

> The general strike is not as a simple act of folding your arms; it means transferring the social wealth developed by the corporations to the unions, for the good of all. This general strike, or revolution, may be violent or peaceful depending on the level of resistance. All the productive energy of society will be put under the control of workers' organisations.[22]

In the space of a decade Griffuelhes had created a superbly effective form of trade unionism; with minimal dues-paying and bureaucracy the militant workers could, every so often, unleash a lean, mean striking machine. What is more, they did it not just in an atmosphere of repression but of stolid refusal to negotiate; only in the years 1905 and 1906 did the number of strikes ended by negotiation rise above 10 per cent. Nine out of ten strikes simply finished without any formal contact across the table: either you lost and went back to work or, as with Haviland, the boss opened the factory gates and upped the wages. Sixty per cent ended this way, with victory for the unions.[23]

But now, as the workers forced employers to cut their hours, hike their pay and slam the door on priapic foremen, an unforeseen moderation descended on the unions. It was impossible to coordinate uprisings like that in Limoges towards one orderly stoppage of work on 1 May 1906, let alone a stoppage that would, according to the syndicalist doctrine, put an end to capitalism.

May Day 1906 was consequently a damp squib. A massive miners' strike broke out in early April, sparked by the death of 1,100 men in a pit disaster. The miners of the Pas-de-Calais region took on regiment after regiment of troops sent in to quell the strike. The CGT embroiled itself to the hilt, spreading the strike to the glass and steel-making industries. But the strike was defeated amid blood, mud and bayonets.

Minister of the Interior, Georges Clemenceau now took personal charge of stopping the May Day strike and, in a masterly piece of spin, he fabricated a plot between die-hard nostalgics for Napoleon Bonaparte and the CGT. Griffuelhes secured an emergency meeting with Clemenceau only to be told, 'We are on the opposite sides of the barricade and the best thing now is for each of us to take his place.'[24] On the eve of May Day, Clemenceau had Griffuelhes and the entire CGT leadership arrested on treason charges. These would be thrown out of court just a few weeks later but the union leaders spent May Day in jail. Though the Paris building workers had answered the strike call, in most other places it simply did not happen.

Undaunted, the CGT congress that year passed a document that would become legendary in the history of trade unions, the Charter of Amiens. In it, Griffuelhes laid out a blueprint that would be copied from Chile to China: total separation of the unions from politics, total commitment to the abolition of capitalism, total determination to fight for a revolutionary general strike, total belief in the power of unions to run industry on their own.

> Syndicalism prepares complete emancipation, which can only be fulfilled by expropriation of the capitalists; it advocates as a method of action the general strike; and it considers that the union, today a resistance group, will be, in the future, a group for production and redistribution, the basis of social reorganization.[25]

That is how it would get rid of capitalist monopoly and scientific management. How it planned to fight militarism, was equally clear: '. . . to educate the workers so that in the case of war between the powers, the workers will answer the declaration of war by declaring the revolutionary general strike.'[26]

But in 1914, when it actually came to war, these principles would be smashed just as easily as a piece of fine Limoges porcelain.

Buenos Aires – 'the scum of European scoundrelism': Though his flock was facing poverty and starvation, the place they were heading threatened something even worse and the Catholic Archbishop of Cashel, Ireland was determined to save them.

Buenos Aires is a most cosmopolitan city into which the Revolution of '48 has brought the scum of European scoundrelism. I most solemnly conjure my poorer countrymen, as they value their happiness hereafter, never to set foot on the Argentine Republic however tempted to do so they may be by offers of a passage or an assurance of comfortable homes.[27]

The warning went unheeded. When 2,000 Irish builders, farmers, their wives and children swarmed down the gangplanks into Buenos Aires docks on 16 February 1889 they were swept into a life of mayhem and despair lit only by the twin fires of anarchism and Marxism. On the very same day 1,000 Italian migrants had been dumped there by a rival shipping company and thousands more were on their way: peasants from Italy and Spain, Jews from Russia and Poland. The unlucky ones would be deposited in the middle of the pampas to be tenant farmers. If the land was workable, some of their children would survive the first winter. The rest would remain at the Immigrants' Hotel in Buenos Aires.

Men, women and children, whose blanched faces told of sickness, hunger and exhaustion after the fatigues of the journey had to sleep as best they might on the flags of the courtyard. Children ran around naked. To say they were treated like cattle would not be true, for the owner of cattle would at least provide them with food and drink, but these poor people were left to live or die unaided by the officials who are paid to look after them.[28]

That is how, ship by ship, the Argentine working class was made: 85,000 people a year arrived in the decade to 1889, and by the first decade of the 20th century they would be coming at twice that rate. The population, which had doubled to 4 million, would double again by 1914. And the migration was not just one way; about a third of those on the ships berthed in Buenos Aires harbour were 'swallows', seasonal migrants following the harvest from southern Europe to Latin America and back again. They came because Argentina, like Brazil and Uruguay, had more land than people and there was a world market for its food. That meant higher wages.

But Argentina was not the United States; this was an economy dominated by big landowners and rough merchant capitalists who had no time for management theory or philanthropy. As the tide of migrant labour started to depress wages after 1889, the door between the world of the poverty-stricken tenements and the glitzy hotels was slammed shut, destroying any vestiges of social mobility. The cliques of anarchist and socialist émigrés who had skulked around Buenos Aires since the Paris Commune suddenly realised that a new social force had arrived on their doorstep – the proletariat, and it was mightily disillusioned.

In the hat factory of Dell'Acqua & Ci'a:

> hundreds of women, youths and very young children are working. When they are taken on at this establishment, the workers have to leave a cash deposit – to pay the fines that will be levied from them, to pay a doctor in case of illness, and as a guarantee that they will not leave the factory without giving eight days' notice – on pain of losing the lump sum . . . At the same establishment many young girls are working a fifty-hour week for 50 cents.[29]

The hat makers were among the first to strike. Eduardo Gilimón, an anarchist migrant from Barcelona, remembered:

> All the troubles attendant on the tough, seaport way of life, life without joy, life without excitement, life confined within the stingy rooms of an improvised city – these were heaped on top of the normal difficulties that people faced just making a living, which were growing day by day . . . the wealth of the elite gave life to a ferocious class hatred.[30]

This was a peculiar workforce which was concentrated in transport and agribusiness instead of large factories. It was populated by builders, ranch hands, dockers, seamstresses and sailors – the classic demographic of the syndicalist movement. There had been no time for craft trade unions to form, and nobody had to lecture the Argentine workers against the charade of parliamentary politics because they were not invited to take part. A man could lose himself in the passageways of Buenos Aires, so the city became a bolt hole for anarchist refugees, swelling the ranks of the agitators and ensuring that the labour movement would have the same distinct anarchist influence that could be found in southern Italy and Catalonia.

In May 1901, the Argentine Labour Federation (FOA) was launched, bringing together 27 local trade unions known as resistance societies. At this point it included both socialists and anarchists, but at its second congress the socialists, always in a minority, walked out. Now there were just 6,000 workers in the federation but strikes were breaking out regardless. In July 1902, first the stevedores at Buenos Aires docks went on strike, followed by the porters at the central fruit market. A rash of smaller strikes erupted, including solidarity action by railway workers. These were not revolutionary strikes; the stevedores simply wanted the weight of the average produce sack reduced from a backbreaking 100 kilograms to 65. The fruit porters wanted payment by the 'quarter day' to be replaced by full or half days. These were virtually the same grievances that had sparked the original London docks dispute.

Both strikes ended in victory, but at this point the Argentine government panicked. It declared a state of emergency and put thousands of troops onto the streets. In November 1902 it rushed through the Residency Law, giving it the power to deport anarchists and strike organisers born outside Argentina. The Residency Law provoked a political general strike, which ended with mass arrests, more strikes and the further radicalisation of the unions. By 1905 the federation had changed its name to the Labour Federation of the Argentine Region (FORA) signifying rejection of the very concept of the Argentine state. The constitution it passed that year makes the CGT's Charter of Amiens sound tame. It pledged to teach every member of the unions

> the economic and philosophical principles of anarchist communism. This education, by preventing them from concentrating merely on achieving the eight-hour day, will emancipate them completely and consequently lead to the hoped-for social revolution.[31]

The year 1907 would be the peak of the pre-war strike wave, with 170,000 workers involved in 231 disputes. The dripping humidity, the excited political arguments in Italian, Catalan and Yiddish echoing across tenement courtyards, together with the total absence of social mobility all served to create in the cities of the Argentine seaboard an air of inevitability about revolution. When cart drivers struck in the city of Rosario, the entire railway network of the country was shut by a solidarity strike. When marines were sent in to rough up some strikers in Bahia Blanca, engineering workers walked out across the country. Argentina had not seen national solidarity strikes before, still less among workers who were classed in the anarcho-communist handbook as privileged. Gilimón remembers:

> Those who reduced the 'social question' to the problem of poverty
> – thinking that only hunger can drive people to acts of resistance
> were, without doubt, surprised by these strikes by railworkers and
> engineers. Driven by a spirit of solidarity, they never wavered despite
> the risk the strike posed to their own relatively favourable situation.
> This laid the basis for another social movement of even greater
> significance: the rent strike.[32]

The streets of Buenos Aires, once you left the grand thoroughfares, were by 1907 the scene of major social grievances. Eduardo Wilde, a doctor, describes life inside the *conventillos*:

> A *conventillo* – as they call these tenements that house everyone from
> beggars to small businessmen – has a door out to the courtyard, a
> window and nothing more. It's a room four metres square and
> contains the following: it is a bedroom for the man, woman and
> the 'nippers' – as they say in slang, the 'nippers' being five or six
> completely filthy kids. In addition it serves as kitchen, pantry, play-
> ground for the children, a place to deposit excrement – at least
> temporarily. It is a rubbish pile, a pile of dirty clothes (and clean
> clothes if they've got any), a kennel, bathroom, a larder, a place for
> the oil lamp or candle to burn at night. In summary, each room is
> a hellhole where four, five or more people are living in defiance of
> all the rules of hygiene, society and good taste. In fact, if you had

tried to design a place that broke all the rules of public hygiene, you could not have done it better than the men who built the *conventillos*.[33]

Conditions like these existed in the slums of every city on earth; mass revolutionary anarchism did not. Up against a morbid and invasive Catholicism, anarchists from southern Europe had always tried to create alternative institutions in working class districts – schools, clubs and cooperative shops. So it was in the streets and not the workplaces that in September 1907 the showdown took place.

> One bright morning, the inhabitants of one *conventillo* resolved not to pay their rent until it was reduced. This resolution was treated as a joke by half the population but the joking soon stopped. From *conventillo* to *conventillo* the idea of not paying rent spread, and in a few days the whole proletarian population had heard of the strike. The *conventillos* became clubs. There were street demonstrations in all areas, which the police could not prevent, and with an admirable spirit of organisation, committees and subcommittees were set up in all areas of the capital.[34]

The strike spread to the other main cities, with committees set up to run it and press forward their demands. These were a 30 per cent reduction in rent, a clean-up of the *conventillos*, the abolition of deposits and advance rents, and no eviction of strikers. As with the Limoges strike, children took part spontaneously in the revolt.

> Three hundred boys and girls of all ages marched through the streets of La Boca holding up brooms 'to sweep out the tenements'. When the demonstration arrived at a *conventillo* it merged with another contingent of young people, and merged with it to great public applause.[35]

The strike lasted three months and was ended, once again, by the brutal deployment of troops – sometimes hundreds at a time into individual courtyards. Hundreds of rent strikers were deported back to Europe. But trouble would soon start again.

Industrial workers of the world: Things were looking bad for Big Bill Haywood. He had been kidnapped, dragged across the state line and put in a cell for a year. Now, in the 90-degree heat of a courtroom in Boise, Idaho it seemed like all America's press had come to see him hanged. All around the walls of the courtroom hung the panama hats of famous detectives and politicians and the owners of the hats looked unnervingly pleased with themselves. It was June 1907 and the press were billing it as the 'greatest trial of modern times', at issue the 'struggle between capital and labor'. Haywood knew what to expect; he was already the veteran of a twenty-year war between the unions and the mine owners of the Rocky Mountains. And the men he organised were tough, damaged men.

> The miners worked twelve hours a day in the mills and smelters and mines. In the midst of sickening, deadly fumes of arsenic. Arsenic poisons. It paralyzes arms and legs. It causes the teeth to fall out, the hair to fall off. Weird-looking men worked in the mines: gaunt, their faces sunken in, their eyelashes and eyebrows off, a green aspect to their skin.[36]

Officially Haywood was in charge of handling the dues of 27,000 unruly brawlers and adventurers; unofficially he was the human giant in charge of a violent strike campaign. He wasn't called Big Bill for nothing, standing six feet tall with heavy jowls and a big stomach. He had lost an eye in childhood, but preferred an empty socket to a glass replacement.

His battlefield had been the hard-rock mining towns of the western USA, stretching from the Canadian to the Mexican border, towns with names like Telluride, Goldfield and Leadville. Dynamite, sabotage, bribery and murder were the methods used on both sides. The miners' union blew sky-high the biggest silver processor in the world; they blew sky-high thirteen strike-breakers together with the railway station they were waiting at. And in December 1905 a union organiser named Harry Orchard planted a bomb outside the home of Frank Steuenberg blowing him sky-high too; Steuenberg had retired as Idaho's governor five years earlier but miners had long memories.

Governors throughout the Rockies had called in Federal troops, declared martial law and deployed machine guns in the wooden streets. They had corralled striking miners in 'bullpens' – rough and ready concentration camps. It was Steuenberg who declared, 'We have taken the monster by the throat and we are going to choke the life out of it. No halfway measures will be adopted.' And now Haywood was on trial for Steuenberg's murder because Orchard, having found Jesus, had turned state's witness and named him as accessory.

The jury was stuffed with God-fearing Idaho farmers. The fact that Haywood had been arrested, stark naked, in bed with his sister-in-law and in possession of a 'big revolver' did not improve his chances. Spies from the Pinkerton detective agency had infiltrated the defence team. All the union had going for it was the verbal skill of its lawyer Clarence Darrow.

Darrow would later become known as the 20th century's greatest criminal lawyer, but at this point he was nobody. He could see that, in the eyes of the jury, Haywood was already a dead man so he gave them a lecture about trade unions, global in its scope.

> I want to say to you, gentlemen of the jury, you Idaho farmers removed from the trade unions, removed from the men who work in industrial affairs, I want to say that if it had not been for the trade unions of the world, for the trade unions of England, for the trade unions of Europe, the trade unions of America, you today would be serfs of Europe, instead of free men.[37]

There was a prickly silence broken only by the wives of Idaho politicians fainting as Darrow delivered his last-ditch defence:

> I don't mean to tell this jury that labor organizations do no wrong. I know them too well for that . . . But I am here to say that in a great cause these labor organizations, despised and weak and outlawed as they generally are, have stood for the poor, they have stood for the weak, they have stood for every human law that was ever placed

upon the statute books. I don't care how many crimes these weak, rough, rugged, unlettered men committed, who often know no other power but the brute force of their strong right arm . . . I know their cause is just.[38]

If Haywood had been hanged, that speech would have gone down as a classic piece of courtroom chicanery, but something had happened in the twenty years since the Haymarket trial. The global union movement's refusal to be led by intellectuals and its dogged championship of the poor had captured the imagination of ordinary people, even in the literal backwoods of America. The jury returned the verdict: 'Not guilty.'

In mining camps all along the Rocky Mountains dynamite held ready for retaliation was now set off 'by the ton', just for kicks. Haywood recalled:

In Goldfield, when I went there later, they showed me the dents that had been made in the mahogany bars in the saloons by the hobnails of the boys who had danced to celebrate their joy at my release. There is no way of estimating how much whisky was drunk for the occasion.[39]

Bill Haywood, who had used his time in prison to do some thinking, skipped out of the dock like a man reborn.

Even before his arrest, Big Bill Haywood had begun to broaden his horizons. In June 1905 the miners' union set up a wider organisation, the Industrial Workers of the World. In setting up the IWW, Haywood had been scratching at the same problem as Mann and Griffuelhes, the gulf between unskilled workers and official unions, but in America the problem was acute. The official unions, grouped in the American Federation of Labor, were closed to unskilled workers – and that meant black people, women and the millions of foreign migrants who were changing the face of America. The AFL, said Haywood,

does not represent the working class. There are organisations that are . . . affiliated with the AFL which in their constitution and bylaws prohibit the initiation of a colored man; that prohibit [the initiation] of foreigners. What we want to establish at this time is a labor organisation that will open wide its doors to every man that earns his livelihood, either by his brain or muscle.[40]

Haywood had a striking, saloon-bar way of explaining this in the mining camps. He would raise his hand and spread out his fingers. 'The AFL organises like this . . .' And he would list the different crafts and grades, finger by finger. Then he would clench his fist and shout, 'The IWW organises like this.' But to wield the fist east of the Rockies the miners needed allies in the cities, so they roped in a motley coalition of socialists and anarchists, together with the brewers' union, to launch the IWW. For Elizabeth Gurley Flynn, a 16-year-old New Yorker, the attraction was irresistible.

> The [socialist] leaders were, if you will pardon me for saying so, professors, lawyers, doctors, minister, and middle-aged and older people, and we felt a desire to have something more militant, more progressive and more youthful and so we flocked into the new organization, the IWW.[41]

The membership, Flynn remembers, was drawn from two distinct social groups: east of Chicago it was foreigners working as unskilled labour in the factories; in the west it was English-speaking cowboys, miners, sailors and lumberjacks. What they had in common was their lack of roots. And out of these rootless foreigners and rootless Americans the IWW formed a movement that rooted itself permanently in the American imagination.

They were known as the 'Wobblies'; the origin of the nickname is disputed, but try saying IWW with a deep mid-European accent. Their slogan was 'One big union': solidarity across colour, craft and continent, embodied in a single organisation with 'industrial departments' for workers in each branch of the economy. It was the same idea that had fired up the Knights of Labor but it was now mingled with the conscious anarchism of the foreigners and subconsicous anarchism of the mountain men. During the year Haywood spent in jail, the Wobblies registered two firsts for the American working class: the first commune, formed in Goldfield, Nevada, and the first sit-down strike, staged in the low, sleek buildings at General Electric's showpiece plant in Schenectady. 'Never in the industrial world did organization effect a more magical change in releasing pent energy,' proclaimed General Electric's handbook issued that year – they meant the production process, but it could just as well have been said about the Wobblies.[42]

Haywood's first act on his release was to purge the organisation, by now 60,000 strong, of socialist intellectuals. Over the next four years the IWW lit a fire in the undergrowth of working America. Like the syndicalists in France they believed that 'by organizing industrially we are forming the structure of the new society within the shell of the old'.[43]

The Wobblies brought the 'union way of life' to America and mixed it with that archetypal image of the American dream, the wandering loner. They took the spontaneous communism of the 'jungle' – the migrant worker's transit camp – and organised it so that, in some states, no man without a membership card could drink from the collective coffee pot. To men case-hardened by work they added a further layer of political hardening. 'You could use direct action anywhere, even in jail,' remembers building worker Jack Miller.

> They put a bunch of IWWs on the rock pile and told them to break rocks. They broke one big one and passed the pieces around as souvenirs. Then they broke the handles off the sledges and threw them over the fence. That ended the rock breaking . . .[44]

Miller wrote that if he had not become a Wobbly, he would have been a criminal. Having left behind religion there was no hell he could be threatened with. But there is a clear echo of millenarian religion in the way he describes life on the road as a Wobbly:

> We were not making a new building in the shell of the old, not a new city, not a new country – we were building a new world. What greater task, what greater inspiration could there be than that we workers were the only ones who could do this?

The attraction of the IWW's message was that it worked just as well with the tired, poor and huddled masses arriving by the boatload at Ellis Island, New York as it did with the frontiersmen of the West – and it gave the migrants, for the first time, an idea of what their future in America could be.

The IWW was of course a world organisation only in the way the baseball World Series is – fundamentally American but with powerful 'little leagues' in countries where the idea took root. It had 6,000 members in Canada within a year of formation and, by 1907, a small presence in Australia. Wobbly 'clubs' were founded in New South Wales by itinerant miners who had worked in the Rockies. By 1909 the Australian Wobblies found themselves in the middle of the first major union confrontation of the century on that continent. And it is here that Tom Mann comes back into the story.

Broken Hill Australia – Tom Mann's grave: The grave has been freshly dug in a landscape that could only be either the moon or the Australian outback. Three policemen uniformed like English bobbies but wearing white helmets against the heat are posing for the camera on a mound of earth. One is holding a rifle. There is a cross made of sticks and, spelled out in foot-high letters made from stones, 'Tom Mann'. To add insult to injury, the lifelong teetotaller's final resting place is topped-off with a beer bottle. If he had really been dead, Tom Mann would surely have been spinning in his grave. But he was alive and kicking, and the photo, preserved in Australian government archives, was just propaganda.[45] The strike at Broken Hill was becoming nasty.

Tom Mann arrived in Broken Hill on 30 September 1908, at the request of the Combined Unions Committee to help them fight a 12.5 per cent wage cut imposed by the town's mining company, Broken Hill Proprietory. Union membership was patchy and divided along craft lines. The existence of a sailors' union branch 300 miles north of the nearest port testified to the state of flux and fragmentation in this raucous boom town. Mann set about solidifying things.

We opened the campaign with special meetings at union branches, to which members of other unions were invited. Stress was laid on the need for solidarity. There were also meetings for women at hours to suit their convenience, and street corner meetings to get in touch with those sections not likely to turn up at indoor meetings . . . A few weeks of such efforts brought about so complete a change that it soon became difficult to find any qualified person outside the unions.[46]

Next, Mann went to Port Pirie, where BHP smelted the metal. The smelters worked eight hours a day, seven days a week. The job involved dragging heavy loads of ore in wagons and tipping them into the furnace. There were no health and safety regulations, no union and no holidays: 'the strongest could not endure the work for more than a year, then becoming-utterly incapacitated'. Mann knew that the dispute at Broken Hill would fail unless the smelters joined in. 'I saw easily enough that the first thing to do was arouse in them sufficient self-respect so that they would be ashamed of the conditions they were quietly tolerating.'[47] The first mass meeting of the smelters heard Mann enthusiastically until it came to the suggestion of swapping a seven-day week for six. But after two more weeks of agitation, 'we obtained a 98 per cent organisation and unanimity in the demand for the six-day week'.

After a failed attempt at arbitration the strike began, lasting five months and drawing hundreds of armed police into Broken Hill. For Mann it was a life-changing experience because for the best part of two decades since the London docks strike he had been involved primarily in politics rather than direct action. In London he had been described by Frederick Engels as a 'nice sincere fellow . . . without backbone'. He had helped launch the British Labour Party. Then, after travelling to South Africa and New Zealand, he found himself a job organising the Australian Labor Party. If he had really had no back-bone, he would have been sitting in Parliament by April 1909. Instead he was sitting in a prison cell after the police moved in to stop the miners' regular parade around Broken Hill. 'For ten minutes there was as lively a time as I had ever experienced and I was in the middle of it,' he remembered later.

He was bailed on condition that he take no further part in the strike, but since Broken Hill stood on the state line between South Australia and New South Wales the miners' solution was to organise a train, with 4,000 people on it, to the border fence. Mann stood on one side of it and spoke, the crowd the other. After that, effectively banished from Broken Hill, he had to watch from the sidelines as the strike petered out into a messy compromise. But Mann himself, after nearly twenty years as a quiet consolidator of the labour movement, was revitalised.

> I realised more clearly the need for perfecting industrial organisa-
> tion. It was plain to me that economic organisation was indispen-
> sable for the achievement of economic freedom. The policy of the
> various Labour Parties gave no promise in this direction, nor did
> the super-adding of political activities to the extant type of trade
> union organisation.[48]

At this point a pamphlet dropped through the letter box of Mann's house on the banks of the Yarra river in Melbourne. It was 'Socialism Made Easy', written on the banks of the Hudson in New York by a Wobbly activist called James Connolly. Connolly would become famous in world history for leading the 1916 Easter Rising in Dublin, but at this time his efforts were focused on syndicalism. The pamphlet was a poetic, quasi-religious celebration of syndicalism's origins among self-taught workers. 'The fight for the conquest of the political state,' wrote Connolly, 'is not the battle, it is only the echo of the battle. The real battle is the battle being fought out every day for the power to control industry.'

> The power of this idea . . . cannot be over-estimated. It invests
> the sordid details of the daily incidents of the class struggle with
> a new and beautiful meaning, and presents them in their true
> light as skirmishes between the two opposing armies of light and
> darkness.[49]

By the end of 1909 Mann was lecturing the union branches of South Australia and Victoria on the experience of syndicalism in France, Italy and Spain. By February 1910 he was on a boat back to England.

As he stepped onto the quayside at London's Victoria Dock on 10 May 1910 his first words to the group of waiting socialists were, 'Let's go and see the men of direct action.' He set off for Paris on 30 May, on a two-week tour during which he spoke to all the leaders of the CGT and addressed several meetings. By this time Griffuelhes had been forced to stand down from the leadership and replaced by the more moderate Leon Jouhaux. Mann set up a regular correspondence with Griffuelhes's supporters and then returned to Britain.

By July 1910 he was ready with the first issue of a new paper, *The Industrial Syndicalist*. This contains a single article, by Mann himself, explaining the rise of monopolies, the perils of craft unions in the face of them, the tactical difference between the Wobblies and the CGT and a plan to reorganise the British unions along syndicalist lines.

> Unite! Was Marx's advice long ago, but we have never thoroughly acted upon it. Now is the time to do it and we will do it right here in England. We will lead them a devil of a dance and show whether or not there is life and courage in the workers of the British Isles.[50]

Whatever might have been said about his political backbone, there was nothing wrong with Mann's political antennae: the summer of 1910 marks the beginning of a wave of mass strikes across the world. By the time it ended, though it was not listed in any current dictionary, syndicalism had become the number-one topic in the press. According to one breathless business magazine it threatened to 'bring the world face to face with the greatest crisis of modern civilization – perhaps any civilisation'.[51]

The Great Unrest: The period known as the Great Unrest began in Barcelona. In 1909 the Spanish government had called up reservists to put down a rising in Morocco. On 25 July Workers' Solidarity, a syndicalist committee representing 112 local trade unions called for a general strike in the Catalan capital. It was a near-total stoppage, stunning anarchist veterans like Anselmo Lorenzo. 'What is happening here is amazing. A social revolution has broken out in Barcelona and it has been started by the people. No one has instigated it. No one has led it. Neither Liberals, nor Catalan Nationalists, nor Republicans, nor Socialists, nor Anarchists.'[52]

The strike turned into an armed riot which lasted a week. Seventy churches and monasteries were destroyed by the anarchist-inspired workers, who associated the Catholic Church so completely with the rule of the Spanish upper class that some broke open the graves of monks and nuns and dragged their bodies through the streets. Troops from outside the city arrived, and by the time it was over, what is known as the Tragic Week had seen eight soldiers and at least 104 workers killed.

On 2 August 1909 the main Swedish trade union federation called manufacturing and transport workers out on strike; 300,000 obeyed the call and struck solidly for a month. In contrast to the Spanish strike, the unions in Sweden maintained total order. The strike failed and thousands of workers were locked out.

May 1910 saw an attempted general strike in Argentina. Timed to coincide with, and to sabotage, the centenary of national independence, it was prevented by mass arrests and the imposition of military rule. Gangs of patriotic youths raided union offices and set fire to radical printshops. Hundreds of union activists were killed, thousands put in jail and Argentina passed a law specifically aimed at preventing anarchists from migrating there.

In September 1910 miners at the South Wales collieries belonging to the Cambrian Combine launched a strike to reinstate 800 locked-out men. Big Bill Haywood, in the middle of a European tour, was taken to meet the strikers by followers of Tom Mann. He made his usual speech, raising five outstretched fingers and then a fist.

I told them of the methods that we adopted in the West, where every man employed in and around the mine belongs to the same organization; where, when we went on strike, the mine closed down. They thought that that was a very excellent system.[53]

Thirty thousand miners picketed, hurled rocks at the managers and for a few days took over the mining town of Tonypandy, before being dispersed by troops. The strike itself lasted a year and was defeated, but the miners – until then utterly conservative and devoted to passive unionism – now provided scores of activists for Tom Mann's syndicalist movement.

In October 1910 the French railway workers went on strike. It was the nearest France ever came, pre-war, to the kind of general strike the syndicalists imagined. The government, however, was now run by an expert on general strikes, Aristide Briand. As socialist dreamer in the 1890s he had laid out the plan for a general strike; as a parliamentary liberal on the eve of world war he called in troops to break the strike. But after three days Briand had to resort to calling up the entire railway workforce as army conscripts to end the action. Bill Hayward was present there too, and later regaled a gleeful New York audience with tales of sabotage.

The Big Apple itself had already been swept up in the great unrest. When 150 women shirtmakers were sacked at the Triangle Shirt Waist Factory in Manhattan in July 1909, a meeting had been called with Samuel Gompers, king of craft trade unions and master of moderation, in attendance. He was giving a speech about the injustice of it all when at the back of the hall a young Jewish seamstress stood up. She spoke fast, in Yiddish, and said she was tired of talking and would like to propose a general strike of the whole garment trade. Union organiser Alice Henry recounts what happened next:

> From every waist-making factory in New York and Brooklyn, the girls poured forth, filling the narrow streets of the East Side, crowding the headquarters at Clinton Hall, and overflowing into twenty-four smaller halls in the vicinity. It was like a mighty army, rising in the night and demanding to be heard.[54]

In 1911 it was Britain's turn to be rocked by mass strike action: there was a general strike in Liverpool and a mass strike of seamen and dockers throughout Britain and Ireland, with James Connolly whipping up action on the waterfront in Dublin and Belfast. In

South Africa the Wobblies pulled tramway workers out on strike; in Broken Hill the miners struck again. In Spain, metalworkers in Bilbao launched a general strike, provoking a solidarity strike in Barcelona.

The years 1911–13 were to be the high-water mark of syndicalism – not because syndicalist unions led the strikes but, on the contrary, because they were now being called by traditional union federations, their ranks swelled by tens of thousands of unskilled workers who had forced their way in.

So what did syndicalism achieve in its heyday? It brought unskilled workers into the unions so that, in Britain, Ireland, Australia, France, Argentina and to an extent the United States the labour movement today visibly bears the hallmark of the organisations created then. It led mass strikes and sparked general strikes, but rarely of the kind imagined by syndicalist theory – strikes that spilled over into insurrections threatening the state. Those that did threaten the social order were easily dealt with by troops, disproving the revolutionary mathematics of Pelloutier and Briand, who had assumed that troops could not break a general strike. Nor did they ever seize and run the workplaces – except in frontier towns like Goldfield, Nevada; the control they exercised was over communities and the self-education of the working class. Despite all this, they achieved one thing that could not easily be undone: they implanted the union way of life deep in factories, streets and apartment blocks. They proved it could take root in places the old trade unionists had given up for dead. They did this by uniting the rough economic realities that dominated workers' lives with their dreams. And nowhere did they do it better than in Lawrence, Massachusetts. The strike that electrified New England at the height of the Great Unrest stands as a symbol of all the changes syndicalism had wrought within the labour movement in the run-up to the First World War.

The 'Bread and Roses' strike: Fred Beal was fifteen when he first began living the union way of life. He was working in a woollen mill on the banks of the river Merrimack. The state had passed a law cutting the working week from 56 to 54 hours. The work was hard and dreary so the 40,000 mill workers of Lawrence, Massachusetts would normally have welcomed the move, but the employers had announced a pay cut to match it. As he shuffled out of the mill into the biting January cold, Beal noticed a man on a soapbox, shouting.

> He declared with emphasis that we, the textile workers, were wage slaves and that all the mill owners were slave drivers as bad and as brutal as Simon Legree of *Uncle Tom's Cabin*. This was news to me as I always thought that only coloured people could be slaves . . . The Irish workers did not like the speaker; the Italians did. The Irish cupped their hands to their mouths and made strange noises every time the Italians applauded and yelled: 'Ef ye don't loike this countr-r-y go back where ye come f-r-rom![55]

This was what the Wobblies were up against. Lawrence was a textile town but not a union town. There were people from 25 nationalities working in the woollen mills. It was the classic American melting pot of first-generation migrants, too poor and full of optimism to be bothered with a strike; too busy making ends meet in cramped tenements full of consumptive kids. When it came to payday, Beal remembers, the armed guard wheeled a box full of pay checks 'just like any other Friday' to the front of the waiting queue.

> There was much chattering in different languages and much gesticulation. I stood with Gyp halfway along the line. When the great moment came, the first ones nervously opened their envelopes and found that the company had deducted two hours pay. They looked silly, embarrassed and uncertain what to do. Milling around they waited for someone to start something. They didn't have long to wait . . .[56]

It was an Italian worker who stood up and shouted 'Strike! Strike!' waving his hands in the air like a cheerleader. A Syrian worker threw the switch for the plant's electricity and the machinery clanked to a stop.

Then all hell broke loose in the spinning room ... Gears were smashed and belts cut. The Italians had long sharp knives and with one zip the belts dangled helplessly on the pulleys. Lefty Louie and I went from frame to frame breaking 'ends' while Tony smashed windows ... We piled out into Canal Street, singing and shouting. It was snowing.[57]

Within days, virtually the entire unskilled workforce of the city was on strike. Since the AFL had declared the dispute 'unjustified' and urged them back to work, they turned to the Wobblies. The employers turned to Harvard University, home of the local militia, whose students 'rather enjoyed going down there to have a fling at those people'.[58]

First they used fire hoses on the strikers. The strikers flung back chunks of ice. As the strike escalated, police used bullets and bayonets, killing an Italian woman and a Syrian boy. The IWW's two organisers in the strike, Ettor and Giovannitti, were charged with being 'accessories to murder' because of their role in organising the picketing, and martial law was declared. A local schoolmaster was arrested while ineptly trying to plant dynamite in Ettor's office. At this point the IWW sent Gurley Flynn and Haywood to run the strike.

Over half the workforce were women between the ages of 14 and 18. The work was so hard and the benefits so pitiful, that 'pregnant women worked at the machines until a few hours before their babies were born. Sometimes a baby came right there in the mill, between the looms'.[59] Among the immigrant communities there was opposition to women attending strike meetings, so Haywood organised additional daily meetings for the women and children. 'It was amazing,' remembers Gurley Flynn,

how this native-born American, who had worked primarily among English-speaking men, quickly adapted his way of speaking to the foreign-born, to the women and to the children. They all understood his down-to-earth language, which was a lesson to all of us ... They roared with laughter and applause when he said 'The AFL organises like this' separating his fingers ...[60]

It was women strikers who dreamed up the slogan that, daubed onto a placard in the middle of a freezing New England winter, summed up what syndicalism had brought to the labour movement: 'We Want Bread And Roses Too.'

As the strike wore on, and became more violent, the Wobblies organised to move the strikers' children out to New York. The liberal and socialist intelligentsia queued up to take them in, so there were not enough to go round. But the first contingent to arrive, in the chill of mid-February, shocked the journalists waiting at Grand Central Station. Most were wearing threadbare summer clothes and were starving and filthy.

Determined to end this washing of their city's literally dirty linen in public, the Lawrence authorities violently arrested the next contingent of children, together with their parents, as they stood at the railway station waiting for a train. This caused outrage even among opponents of the strike and led to a hearing on Capitol Hill. Fifty teenage strikers went to Washington to show their bruises and pay slips to the House Rules Committee. Asked why they had left school young, a 15-year-old boy said, 'We had to have bread and it was hard to get.' Asked why they had gone on strike, another answered, 'The stomach telephoned to the head: I cannot stand molasses any longer for butter, and bananas for meat.'

On 1 March 1912, eight weeks after the pay cut, the wool industry bosses announced a 7.5 per cent pay increase in 33 cities across the USA: 125,000 workers got a pay rise. By 14 March the Lawrence strike was settled. There were wage increases from 5 to 20 per cent, increased overtime pay and reinstatement of all those sacked during the strike. As new strikes now kicked off in the mill towns along the Merrimack, the Lawrence workers turned to the task of freeing Ettor and Giovannitti. The two were acquitted, but not before the town had shut down in a one-day general strike.

As is still the case in the United States, it took a special tragedy to open the eyes of journalists to the poverty that was right there in front of them. The Lawrence strike did that, prompting a change of view about the 'social question' in editorial offices and inspiring some of the finest 'new journalism' of the period. Ray Stannard Baker, who covered the strike for the *American Magazine* left this haunting description, which sums up how far the workers' movement had come from the filth and ignorance of the London docks.

It is the first strike I ever saw which sang. I shall not soon forget the curious lift, the strange sudden fire of the mingled nationalities at the strike meetings when they broke into the universal language of song. And not only at meetings did they sing, but in the soup houses and in the streets. I saw one group of women strikers who were peeling potatoes at a relief station suddenly break into the swing of the *Internationale*. They have a whole book of songs fitted to familiar tunes – *The Eight Hour Song, The Banner of Labor, Workers Shall the Masters Rule Us?* But the favourite of all was the *Internationale*.[61]

6. Wars between brothers

How German workers tried to stop the war

> Wars between nations, as we have learned to our cost, are
> terrible; civil wars – as we have likewise experienced – are
> more cruel: but wars between brothers are the most abom-
> inable of all.[1]
>
> Philipp Scheidemann, 1929

Huanuni, Bolivia, 2006

The line of trucks and tankers runs like a white scar across the alti-
plano; the blockade lies two miles ahead along a road spattered by
rain, strewn with plastic bottles, corn husks and a couple of hundred
stranded vehicles. Even from here you can feel the thud of the dynamite.

The tin miners of Huanuni have set up a road block. It's not any
old road; at 4,000 metres above sea level it's the main north–south
artery across the Andes. The miners have commandeered a police
station and a toll booth, dumping a tipper-load of earth onto the road.
The approaches are strewn with hundreds of small boulders, arranged
into neat, impassable V shapes. Although there are only about 200
pickets huddled in the lee of adobe huts, there are plenty more camped
out in the village up the hill. Given the miners' reputation, they don't
really need physical force. The truckers bow to moral force and sit
around resignedly. Just to make sure though, every ten minutes a lighted
stick of dynamite is lobbed into the road.

Their demands are simple and have nothing to do with mining.
They want 55 extra teaching posts to be created in Huanuni's schools.
They want more money for secondary education and vocational
training. 'Education is all we've got,' says Marisol Huaylla, a member

of the miners 'civic committee'. She's a grey-haired community leader and explains patiently: 'Our children need education, otherwise they will end up like us.' She's wearing the baseball cap of the main trade union federation, COB. The B is formed by the face of Che Guevara.

I find Roberto Chavez, general secretary of the Miners Federation of Bolivia, huddled with his lieutenants in the middle of the road, keeping an eye on the dynamite throwers. The government will give in, he thinks, but it's not the end.

At least we've made them feel this pressure, with roadblocks, and if the government doesn't give us satisfactory answers we will come out again. We're talking about education here, for our children! And not only for Huanuni but for the rest of the country.

Most of the younger men are wearing dark blue overalls in a high-tech design bearing a company logo. Thanks to Chinese demand the price of tin has bounced back, boosting the workforce in the commercial mines. There are also cooperative miners on the picket. They don't wear overalls but have printed bomber jackets denoting which seam or shaft they work in, and Roberto Chavez is keen to make sure I see the distinction. The unionised miners, schooled in Marxism, regard the cooperativists as 'petit bourgeois'. To the union men it is better to get agreed wages, conditions and a contract from a US mining company than go digging around yourself like a scavenger. The cooperative miners, in turn, call the company men 'neo-liberals' because they work for a capitalist and not themselves. The rivalries are real – six months later the two groups will fight each other with dynamite, leaving twelve men dead – but they come together on days like this, united by bigger necessities.

Lighting and lobbing a stick of dynamite is done carefully, even by those who have used the two nights on the picket line to take on board large quantities of home-made alcohol. The onlookers stand a good ten metres away and the *dynamitero* throws the lighted charge with a graceful underarm motion; there is no backswing. It does not fizz like in the movies, but eventually there is a loud thump. It does not echo either. The endless plain damps the sound down and the rain soon dissolves the cloud of black smoke.

By nightfall negotiations have started and at 9 p.m. there is agreement. The Huanuni authorities will create 28 new teaching posts, and the government has promised 3,000 new teachers nationwide. I leave the blockade, speeding along the deserted road towards Huanuni, the entire scene becoming a speck against the magnificent Andean plain, the peaks and the thunderclouds . . .

The pithead of the Dolores mine is just a line of single-storey sheds bricked into the mountainside. There's a first aid post, a police cell and then the barred gate, decorated with plastic flowers, which leads to the mine itself. It is always open – they work a three-shift system, seven days a week. There are no bosses here. This is a cooperative mine, and Sabino Fabrica, head of safety for the Co-operative Miners' Federation, explains what makes 4,000 miners in the district risk their lives in such places:

> We work in poor conditions, and if we don't work we don't eat. That's our system. Sadly they've left us very little. They've exploited us, and our cooperatives are full of people looking for work. The transnational companies took everything, and the cooperatives survive on what's left in the deep interior of the mines.

Absence of bosses is one thing. Absence of ventilation, machinery, electricity and safety standards is another. This mine, a modern industrial complex 20 years ago, is now worked entirely by hand.

They straggle down in teams of four. The only required equipment is a helmet, a light, a belt and battery pack – which Sabino makes us pay for at the shop next to the pithead. You need wellington boots against the acid mud and rubber gloves for the climbing. There are no overalls; the uniform of a cooperative tin miner is a bandanna (for when the fumes get bad), a tattered football shirt and tracksuit bottoms. Each miner carries a grey sack about 60 centimetres square: going down it holds tobacco, water and coca leaves; coming up it will hold up to seven kilos of tin. What seven kilos of tin feels like, when you have carried it up 400 metres of slimy wooden ladders, you can tell from veins jutting from the foreheads of the men, and women, staggering out of the mine gate.

When it was a state-run industry there were no women miners. Twenty years of unemployment eroded the taboo, says Roxana Estrella Mercado, the leader of the women's commission:

> In the past, they didn't let the women down the mines because there was a myth here in Bolivia, like they have in other countries, that women make you lose the minerals, the seams inside the mines. But nowadays there is great want here in this district as the tin has been exhausted outside the mines, in the rivers and down the mountainsides. It's finished, and we are so desperate that we now have to go inside the mines in order to extract what's left. At first it was just one or two women. Now we are many.

The ladders get busy not long after the natural light disappears. It's a two-way system – as one team strains its way up another is descending, almost at a run. The young lads show off by going front-first. 'Good evening, comrades' is the routine greeting, with an added breathless joke if you bump into your mates.

After the first two ladder descents there is a plank across a ravine then two more sets of ladders. Now you are 40 metres down, though at 4,000 metres above sea level this is all relative. When it was owned by a company there must have been another, more official, way in because the roadway is head height and at least two metres wide. It has been driven expertly for more than a mile and a half into the mountainside. But that entrance has been lost, along with the cutting machinery, the underground railway and electrical power. Now, though a ventilation pipe runs down one wall and two thick cables down the other, there is neither air nor power coming in. If things go wrong there will be no pneumatic drills, no stretcher teams or respirators. You rely on your comrades, and on Tio.

Tio sits in a broad alcove under a pile of little plastic bottles, streamers, candle wax and coca leaves. A miner is bending close to Tio's head, whispering while he lights a cigarette. He spikes the cigarette on Tio's fang, then lights another one – puffing a few times to get it going – and fixes it onto a horn. By the time he's finished there are five glowing Marlboros, making a pentangle. Lit by the miner's headlamp, Tio's face is impassively ferocious: red cheeks, black eyes, flared nostrils. The miners come to sprinkle water and coca leaves, the two basic sources of energy down the mine, to appease this Quechua deity. But he's a tricky devil, this Tio. Two miners a month are killed down here.

After Tio, it is a long, grim walk to the tin workings. Your world becomes the circle of silver mud in front of you, lit by a 40-watt bulb. Suddenly the road turns downward and the temperature rises ten degrees; a thick, nauseating sulphur smell signals you are near the tin. A sweating, scrawny Quechua man crawls out of a hole in the floor near Sabino's feet. The tunnel he has come up from is vertical and has no ladders, only footholds. It is hot and putrid and spirals down like an Escher puzzle. The miners climbing behind him are old men. 'There's no tin down there today, we couldn't find it,' they complain. Their cheeks are bulging with a day's worth of coca leaves; they've been working eight hours and their water's finished. They lean exhausted against the rock walls to take a breather. Then they set off for the exit at a sprint, in single file. One has a picture of Che Guevara stencilled on his helmet.

'When the mines were closed we moved to the tropics and lived in shanty towns. But it was hard to adapt to that life and we had to return,' says Sabino Fabrica. 'You see, we have no alternative but to work with tin. It's our life.'

The main street of Huanuni is bleak. The backstreets are dusty alley-ways leading to the river and the colour of the river is somewhere between shit and silver. Young boys pick over the debris of cans and plastic bottles at the water's edge. A queue of squinting people waits patiently outside the Cooperative Miners' Federation office. The co-op subsidises a weekly visit by an ophthalmologist. He works for nothing and there is a lot to do. Something around here, poor diet or what's in the river, is giving large numbers of people trouble with their sight.

Further along the valley women in bowler hats and shawls, the traditional Quechua outfit, pan for metallic silt from mountain streams. These women are the lowest link in the value chain of the global tin market. Roxana says,

The woman miner has to do everything. She has to be housewife, doctor, washerwoman, cook, teacher. Look after the children, take care of them when they're sick, wash their clothes, cook their meals. And then she has to work. She keeps no hours. She can't say, 'I'll work today and take tomorrow off.' No, she'll work till the job is done.

The only thing in Huanuni that is not bleak is the workers' movement. It provides the eye doctor; it fights for more teachers for the local schools. On Saturday afternoons its members slide-tackle each other on gritty football pitches, or give a brisk rendition of 'Bandiera Rossa' at the brass-band hall. There is a miners' radio station, a miners' TV station and a choir – though, says my guide apologetically, it sings 'mainly tragic songs'. Twenty years of economic decline have left it a bitterly divided movement – unions versus co-ops – but the cultural institutions keep things together.

The miners of Huanuni have created a world within a world. To see it now is to glimpse Germany 100 years ago, then the global heartland of the labour movement. German workers too made themselves a world within a world, an alternative lifestyle of comradeship, committees, brass bands and choirs. And it too was ripped apart by forces larger than it could comprehend.

Germany, 1905

Picture yourself, a typical German worker, on Saturday 4 August 1905. You are at work in a Hamburg engineering factory. You are male, in your mid-twenties. It's getting towards the end of your shift and the weekend's near. You haven't shaved for six days and, as you pass your mate on the way to the lavatory, you give him a 'beard polish' – rubbing your stubble into his face until his eyes water. In the lavatories, there are a couple of comrades skiving off and whispering about strikes (it's been a year of strikes – from St Petersburg to Chicago). While you are at the urinal somebody creeps up behind you, grabs both ends of your moustache, and gives them a painful tug. Wincing, you hear your mate's distinctive laugh echo down the corridor.

Inside the factory everything is regulated by law: the hours, the wages, the fines you have to pay if you make mistakes, the compulsory overtime. But soon the bell rings and the week is over. Your mate claps you on the shoulder and you run together for the train: there's no horseplay now because you're on your own time, not the bosses'. What do you talk about? Who knows, but this is what you tell the sociologists when they get you on your own:

> The future state advocated by social democracy will come, must come. I think the future socialist state, a new epoch in human culture, will – like all the preceding systems – need time to develop. I hope I am right, but I think history is moving faster than it did in earlier times. In our era modern technology . . . has hit us like a tidal wave. That's what always creates a new way of life: it makes the class issues clearer, and draws the battle lines in the class struggle.[2]

Maybe your mate is a pessimist. Maybe he's been reading reports of this year's trade union conference, where the idea of a general strike was voted 'undiscussable' on grounds of cost, and confides,

> Despite it all I lose hope sometimes. Man, whether you're a social democrat, trade unionist or both, abandon all hope. Why? The fault lies with the trade union leaders. The day-to-day issues which they have to keep a grip on stop them seeing the strategic ones and make the final goal seem like Utopia. They look at everything like penny-pinching businessmen, worried about the cost. They look in the till and say, 'It's going to cost too much.'[3]

At six o'clock, bathed and shaved, you arrive at the Workers' Gym. You sign in and get changed. Like work, it's men only here and there is a lot of muscle on display. Somebody throws you a copy of the *Workers' Gymnastic Times*. Another bourgeois gym has come over to the workers' federation. 'It's crumbling!' – the sing-song slogan gets parroted around the hall as the lads strip off.

You line up with the others in your team; there are nine of you and a squad leader. At the front is the instructor. He's a tough nut, a former sergeant, but fair. And he's up for election soon, so if the men don't like him they can always boot him out. He shouts out the greeting: 'Hail Freedom!' Sixty voices echo back. Then he barks out the instructions and you perform the exercises in unison.

A year in the army has toughened you. Nobody talks about it but you've all been through the same ordeal during national service – getting your head kicked in by corporals in the barracks, getting your buttons cut off for leaving one undone, being generally humiliated. In the Workers' Gym discipline is strict but comradeship is everything. Sometimes, say the editors of the *Workers' Gymnastic Times*, there's too much comradeship:

> The gymnastic exercises are hardly finished before one goes to the bar just as fast as possible to pass a few hours as a genuine beer philistine. In a few minutes the room, normally not very large, is so heavy with smoke . . . that one is no longer able to recognise those who are present. [4]

You move on to the local pub where everyone is waiting. Some you know from work, others from the party. It is thick with smoke but the garden is lush this time of year and packed with comrades. The talk again is of strikes and general strikes. There are disputes everywhere; by the end of the year one in three union members will have been on strike. And with Hamburg City Council voting to halve the number of councillors the 'working class section' is allowed to pick, some want to invoke the policy of the political mass strike. But nobody wants a 'Latin, pseudo-revolutionary putsch' – syndicalism here is a dirty word.

Towards the end of the evening the singing starts. The older men start with the socialist favourite 'Who Hammers Brass and Stone?' but the youngsters prefer 'We Are The Petrol Bombers' and, when everybody is drunk enough, you belt it out:

> It's burning in the cities
> So bright and frank and free,

It's burning in the villages
From sheer necessity.
Even the army's blazing.
We're dumbstruck, it's amazing.
There's insubordination.
There's blinding conflagration.
Petrol here, petrol there,
Petrol everywhere.
Landlord, fill the tankards full!
Three cheers for petroleum![5]

If you stop to think about it, and a couple of litres of St Pauli can make you thoughtful, the beauty is in the double meaning. It's supposed to be about the women petrol bombers of the Paris Commune, but it's got layers and layers of irony. No Prussian cop believes the Social Democratic Party would resort to wanton violence. The 'petrol' here is knowledge and, thanks to the SPD's libraries and night schools, it's burning brightly all over Germany. And then of course there is the punchline – the petrol is really the beer you're drinking, the oil that keeps the machinery of the labour movement running smoothly every night in thousands of pubs like this. 'We Are the Petrol Bombers' is a song you sing with a cruel, knowing smile playing at the corners of your eyes. Just like the practical jokes at work and the words 'comrade' or 'future-state', no outsider can really understand it. Nor are they entitled to – and that's its purpose.

Next morning your head is sore but it's a big day: the social democratic singers' festival in a park near the city centre. All the workers' choirs from Hamburg and surrounding towns have turned up: the Tanners, Equality of Eimsbüttel, their big rivals the Eimsbüttel Male Voice Choir, the Glassmakers of Ottensen, Freedom of Langenfelde, the Funsters of Barmstedt, the Saint Pauli Song Circle of 1883 . . . and that's just the first shift![6]

There are carousels for the kids, tents doing a roaring trade in 'breakfast beer', a cycling demonstration by the Red Falcons. As you wander round looking for that girl you fancy, the band plays the festival march,

'True and Firm!' Then the conductor sets off a miniature cannon as a signal to keep the noise down, but it's no good.

> The clanging of glasses and the jumbled noise of voices rolled out from the beer concession tents; playing children, for whom the art of singing is a triviality, pushed their way through the lines of listeners; here a young girl talks loudly and loosely about her sweetheart who, up front in all his singer's glory, adorns the podium; there a wife chatters with another about household matters – and above all of that waves of musical sound flow indistinctly . . .[7]

Spotting your girl with a group of comrades from Socialist Youth you invite yourself to sit down with them. It's a mixed group and there's no shyness here, and none of that religious guilt you're supposed to feel while you are courting. You've had *Woman and Socialism* read out to you by your branch secretary and you know passages off by heart.

> In the new society woman will be entirely independent, both socially and economically. She will not be subjected to even a trace of domination and exploitation, but will be free and man's equal, and mistress of her own lot . . . In the choice of love she is as free and unhampered as man. She woos or is wooed, and enters into a union prompted by no other considerations but her own feelings.[8]

True, all the SPD's choirs are men only, and the union branch, and the factory, and the gym – but in the party everybody's equal. Or just about.

The landlord is staggering over with an armful of tankards. 'Long may he live!' you shout together. When the band launches into 'Moonlight on the Alster' you sing along, drowning out the performance. Another feeble cannon shot sounds and everybody laughs. You're living in the most militarised society on earth, where every man can handle a rifle, but wars are something that happened in the last century.

Later, a few of you wander off into the park. Your girl is pretty frosty but you know she's a member of the party's rambling club the Friends of Nature, so you try the perennial line: 'Let's go for a walk'. Arm in arm, you stroll alongside the river. The factories in the distance are black and silent. The birds are singing. You wonder aloud if either of you will live to see see the future-state.

You sit down on a grassy bank together, amid caterpillars and bees, and your girlfriend reads to you from *Friends of Nature* magazine.

We are but a minuscule part of the matter that has been constantly in motion for millions of years and for which nothing changes but the form. Whoever lives with such thoughts cannot doubt the final victory of enlightenment and truth, he cannot doubt that freedom and equality will be achieved through great effort by working people on behalf of all producers. [9]

For now, as the sun begins to set, your fingers intertwine . . .

A world within a world: Life was like this for millions of German workers in the approach to the First World War. With half a million members in 1905, rising to a million on the eve of war, the Social Democratic Party was just the core of the wider workers' movement; 2.5 million were in the unions – a quarter of the workforce.

It was a world within a world. You could live in it literally from the cradle to the grave; there were workers' crèches and workers' cremation clubs. It was above all a world of self-help. Though the party had 4,000 branches it was through affiliated clubs that workers lived their lives. They kept meticulous records. There were 2,818 workers' singing clubs by 1913, with an average membership of 30. Nine out of ten choir members were party members and registered subscribers to one of 90 daily party newspapers. As well as the Workers' Choir or the Workers' Gym, there was the Workers' Library, the Workers' Theatre Group. Once the law barring women from politics was relaxed there were women's branches of the party – and one in five choirs admitted women by 1914.

The politics of the SPD were in theory orthodox Marxist. The very word 'workers' at the front of something as innocuous as a swimming club was there to signal that. You got your Marxism from books written by the party's old guard – *Knowledge is Power, Women and Socialism, Socialism, Utopian and Scientific* – you could borrow them from one of the party's 1,147 libraries. Lending surveys tell us that a young metalworker in his twenties would have most likely been reading a novel by Emile Zola. Pulp fiction was purged relentlessly from social democratic libraries.

Though the party's intellectuals were obsessed with politics and the bureaucrats worried perennially about all the singing, cycling and late-night country walks, culture was what cemented the workers to the party. Through the SPD workers could gain access to the 'progressive' bits of high culture, but consume them separately, on their own terms and in defiance of a police state that still claimed the right to invade their meetings and censor their newspapers.

If this mass socialist culture looks a lot like the union way of life syndicalism built in America and France that is because it was part of the same general phenomenon: mass trade unionism, a radicalised workforce and the rise of mass consumption. But to the people on that Hamburg meadow in 1905 the achievements of syndicalism looked like the puny product of chaotic Latin minds. The German workers' movement had not been built by improvisation; nor was it something that waxed and waned with strike waves or economic downturns. The disciplined party model was the key to its success. Though the unions were strong, they had an auxiliary role – the 'economic struggle' as outlined in the party programme.

The SPD knew the empire, with its Kaiser, its three-class system of voting and powerless parliament, had to be overthrown. But it was not a revolutionary party. It was geared to the slow, meticulous work of convincing the working class to vote socialist in the elections. And it was getting there.

Even while it was banned, individual candidates had managed to poll 7 per cent of the vote. Unbanned in 1890, that jumped to 20 per cent. In 1903 the SPD shocked the world by winning three million votes. In 1907 tactical voting halved its parliamentary presence, but in 1912 it would score 4.25 million votes and become the biggest party in the Reichstag, albeit a Reichstag that had no power over the Kaiser's ministers.

The rise of a mass workers' movement in Germany was part of a global phenomenon; that it took the form of a strict, self-contained

Marxist party was the product of national circumstances. But it did not look that way. The German socialist party became the leading force in the global workers' movement. Aspiring socialist leaders adopted both its Marxism and its realpolitik – though never with the same success – and built parties on this model in Italy, Poland, Sweden, Belgium and the Netherlands.

The success of the mass party model in Germany would shape the global workers' movement for the next 100 years; the export of that model to Russia – whose working class had grown without the benefit of libraries, glee clubs and free trade unions – would have far deeper consequences. As for Germany, what it meant was this: once the workers' movement split, the discipline, masculine culture and Marxist certainty that pervaded the lives of 'party soldiers' would become a destructive force and the strongest workers' movement in the world would suffer the most massive defeat.

'Events have overwhelmed us': Oskar Hippe's first job was stacking coal into a wagon at a coking plant near Merseburg in Saxony. One day, with the press running too fast, the 14-year-old Hippe had had enough. He stopped work and let the coal fall onto the floor while he had a rest. The foreman chased him round the workshop. 'Next to the rapid press there was a mound of nut coal . . . I defended myself by bombarding him with the coal . . . The next day, I was sacked.'[10] At a loss, his father shipped him off to Leipzig, where it was thought his brother, a building worker and SPD activist, might exert some civilising influence. Hippe, however, had already spent three years secretly reading Marxist pamphlets in the family hayloft.

Toni Sender was a stenographer in a metal company in Frankfurt who had left home at thirteen, swapping middle class home comforts for the freedom and low pay of white-collar work. She set up an office workers' union and in 1910 led a contingent of typists and filing clerks in their first demonstration.

It was then that we made our first acquaintance with the old Prussian police truncheon . . . scores of armed policemen stopped us and immediately began to beat us up. 'What have we done? Is the street forbidden to the tax-paying citizen,' I dared to ask. The answer was a rain of blows . . .[11]

Swearing a secret oath of vengeance they set out to educate themselves.

With a small group of friends I talked with the librarian in the labour library and thus came into contact with books on socialism. It was difficult stuff to comprehend. We needed time for this complicated study, so we decided to meet in the park in the early morning before office hours to read and study together.[12]

She joined the SPD reluctantly; its meeting halls were 'unaesthetic' and its public speakers dull. After a few months of party activism in Frankfurt she moved to Paris, rising through the ranks of the French socialist party and becoming a lecturer at its night school.

Hippe and Sender were part of the generation reared on German socialism's rhetoric of peace and internationalism. What happened next would leave them horrified and disorientated. In June 1914 a Bosnian student assassinated the heir to the Austrian throne. Austria blamed Serbia; Russia warned Austria to leave Serbia alone; Germany told Russia to keep out of the crisis; France told Germany to stop threatening Russia; Britain, allied to France, warned everyone not to compromise the neutrality of Belgium. This slide from a blissful European summer to the brink of war took just four weeks. World war, always seen as a theoretical possibility rather than a material threat, was now a week away.

Everybody knew what the SPD would do in the event of war: oppose it. They knew they might not be able to stop a war but were confident that European socialist parties would act as a cross-border anti-war movement. On Saturday 25 July an emergency edition of the SPD paper carried the leadership's appeal for mass demonstrations to stop the war:

The class-conscious proletariat of Germany raises a fiery protest in the name of humanity and culture against the criminal activities of the warmongers . . . No drop of a German soldier's blood must be sacrificed to the Austrian despots' lust for power . . . Comrades we call upon you to express immediately in mass meetings the unshakeable will for peace of the class-conscious proletariat.[13]

Workers went onto the streets all over Germany. On Tuesday 28 July, 150,000 workers massed in the centre of Leipzig. Oskar Hippe was among them.

I marched with my brother, my sister Ottilie and many comrades from the Leutzch branch of the party in a great procession through the town, with red flags and banners and shouting slogans against the war . . . The next day the newspapers reported that similar demonstrations had taken place in all the larger towns and industrial areas.[14]

By then all the main figures of European socialism were meeting in Brussels. The Austrian leader Victor Adler opened the meeting with a depressing announcement: mobilisation had begun, martial law was in force and the Austrian party could do nothing. That night thousands of workers packed Brussels' biggest meeting hall for an anti-war rally. They cheered as French socialist leader Jean Jaurès put his arm around the shoulders of Hugo Haase, the SPD's parliamentary firebrand. Two days later Russia mobilised. On his return to Paris, Jaurès was assassinated. By 2 August Germany was at war. Hippe remembers: 'It was one of the greatest disappointments I have ever experienced . . . In the evening of 3 August a whole bunch of comrades turned up at the flat, all confused, disappointment written clearly on their faces.'[15]

They were not the only ones. In Paris on 26 July the CGT newspaper had blazed, 'Workers must answer any declaration of war by a revolutionary general strike.' The next day there had been a massive anti-war march. But by 4 August, the day war was declared, the leaders of French syndicalism had swung behind the country's war effort, using the capitulation of the German party as an excuse.

The SPD members in the German Reichstag had voted unanimously for the Kaiser's war budget; the French socialists had no option but to enter a 'sacred union' to defend their own country. The CGT paper announced simply, 'Events have overwhelmed us.' The activists who turned up on the first morning of the war ready for a general strike had 'tears in their eyes. Nobody was prepared for anything of this order. Defeated, disappointed, morally broken, we dispersed.'[16] Within weeks, Victor Griffuelhes, the former syndicalist firebrand, was on a government train to Bordeaux, evacuated from Paris together with ministers and civil servants as the Germans advanced. Having capitulated to war rhetoric he now capitulated to the argument that union leaders would be 'safer' if they were as far away from the actual fighting as possible.

Toni Sender remembers the impact of the German party's vote for war: 'The fourth of August brought a terrible blow. The German Socialists had voted the war credits! Everything seemed to collapse. How could they?'[17] The answer to that was, in the first place, that they had no strategy to stop the war. Second, the SPD leaders were acutely sensitive to the charge of being traitors: the Kaiser had called them 'fellows without a country' and they had replied with the promise that they would 'never leave the Fatherland in the lurch'. Thirdly, they believed the party would be fatally isolated if it opposed the war and its roots within German society torn up. This, rather than any patriotic swing among the party membership itself, led them to vote for the Kaiser's war budget on 4 August 1914. And to avoid breaking party ranks the anti-war MPs voted with the majority.

Further disorientation was to follow: the SPD leaders had convinced themselves that this would be a defensive war. 'We in Germany,' wrote one, 'had the duty to defend ourselves from Tzarism, had to fulfill the task of protecting the country of the most highly developed social democracy from the menacing enslavement by Russia . . . A Germany enslaved by the Tzar would have meant setting back for decades the socialist movement of the whole world, not only the German.'[18] They had no inkling the German army would invade Belgium, violating its neutrality and killing the notion of a defensive war. Having voted for war the SPD leaders were admitted to the inner circle around the Kaiser's government, where they stayed for four years, increasingly isolated from the workers and, crucially, losing their feel for the mood among them.

★   ★   ★

'Life had taught them . . .': In the spring of 1915 Toni Sender slipped across the Swiss border to take part in the first international anti-war conference since hostilities erupted. She came back with a pacifist manifesto in her toilet bag, which she had printed and then distributed in large numbers on the streets of Frankfurt from beneath a long cape. She formed an anti-war group of women workers.

> We met every fortnight. I gave a short report of the news the author-
> ities did not see fit to print. Most of these women were the wives
> of soldiers. Their loved ones were in the trenches. At home they
> endured near famine. Some of them were working in munitions
> factories. They had become emancipated and independent. Within
> a short period life had taught them what nobody had explained to
> them before.

War work was drawing women into munitions factories all across the world. Almost overnight a new sociology was taking shape in facto-ries from Clydeside to the Danube: a core of skilled, male trade union-ists alongside an unskilled mass of women and youths, with the women enjoying unprecedented levels of personal freedom. The official trade unions, full square behind the war effort, refused to lift a finger to either defend the privileged status of the skilled men or protect the unskilled workers from exploitation. So an unofficial network of union shop stewards, known in German as *obleute* or 'confidential men', did the basic work of organising.

In April 1916 Oskar Hippe arrived at a Berlin train station. He had come to work with his brother-in-law in a munitions factory and, as was the fashion, was sporting a tie in patriotic colours. 'The first thing that happened,' he remembers, 'was that my sister took off my tie and threw it onto the rails under the train.'[20] The munitions factory had 100 per cent trade union membership and there was vague unrest among Oskar's workmates; a lot of whispering in the toilets.

> On the eve of 1 May 1916 my brother-in-law told me that we
> would not go to work the next day, since the workforce would all
> be joining an anti-war demonstration on the Potsdamer Platz. We

went there at the specified time. Ten thousand workers had gathered in the square, and Karl Liebknecht spoke to them from the platform of the Potsdam local station.[21]

Liebknecht was an SPD deputy in the Reichstag who had voted grudgingly for the war in August 1914 but switched to open opposition by November. He had been called up for military service and then expelled from the SPD in January 1916. As a serving soldier, he knew what he was about to say would land him in jail but he also knew that its impact would be massive. The crowd marched out of the factories in total silence, telling bystanders 'Keep your tongue between your teeth' in symbolic protest at the press censorship of Liebknecht's speeches. Liebknecht told them,

> Poor and unfortunate German soldier . . . the sufferings that he endures are past description. About him everywhere shells and bombs sow death and destruction. His wife and children at home are suffering want and hardship; she looks about her and finds her children crying for bread . . . everyone must keep his or her tongue between the teeth, for the war profiteers must make money out of the want and misery of the wives and their husband soldiers at the front.[22]

As the crowd cheered him he shouted, 'Do not shout for me, shout rather, "We will have no more war. We will have peace – now!"' At this point the police attacked. Hippe remembers: 'For a time the demonstrators put up resistance and many policemen were knocked off their horses.' As the demonstration was dispersed Liebknecht was arrested, but the street fighting continued into the evening, with Hippe forced at one point to jump into the River Spree to avoid the police horses.

> On the following day scarcely any work was done at the factory: the toilets were turned into discussion rooms. Foremen and managers did not dare to put a stop to the discussions. The shop stewards declared that the demonstration had been a complete success . . . I soon became a delegate to secret meetings.[23]

Liebknecht was on the far left wing of the SPD and had, with the Polish socialist Rosa Luxemburg, formed the Spartacus League, a secret network of revolutionary communists. But his speech, trial and imprisonment in 1916 caused a wider split in the SPD. In January 1917 the Independent Social Democratic Party of Germany (USPD) was formed. Its leaders were 20 left-wing Reichstag deputies but its core activists were shop stewards. Liebknecht's supporters also joined, but maintained a separate Spartacist faction. Though many in the USPD saw themselves as simply upholding the original principles of German social democracy, there were new forces at work. This was a party of women workers like Toni Sender and youngsters like Oskar Hippe, and their whole world was changing, not just their political allegiance.

The starvation rations of the winter of 1917 boosted the USPD's membership to 120,000, and in January 1918 the shop stewards launched a strike for an end to the war, better food and shorter hours. Up to 300,000 munitions workers struck for ten days but were defeated. Hippe was sacked and conscripted. He joined the German military just in time to see it disintegrate.

'Up for the red dawn of a new day!': The Imperial German Navy was supposed to be the Kaiser's strategic weapon but after an inconclusive battle against the British at Jutland in 1916 it was holed up in its ports in the Baltic and the North Sea. In the age of steel the crew of a battleship had to be drawn from skilled workers but the senior officers were relics of Prussian feudalism. Thus the two ends of the German social spectrum were compelled to live alongside each other below decks. 'It does not matter whether you are worked to death or not,' the captain of the dreadnought *Rheinland* told a deputation of engineers, 'the principal thing is that the ship is in fighting trim. Sailors are a minor matter; we can always get as many as we want.'[24]

In October 1918, as the Kaiser began to plead for 'peace with honour', the naval high command decided to stage a great Wagnerian finale to the war, a suicidal foray against the British navy: 'No secret was made of it. The officers . . . revelled all night. They spoke of the death ride of the fleet . . .'[25] But on the ships and in the ports the sailors whispered to each other, 'Long live Liebknecht!' And while the man himself was still in prison, he was by now no longer the only left-wing symbol of resistance. The Russian Revolution had happened; workers' councils, known as soviets, had replaced both Tsar and parliament. Jan Valtin, a sailor's son in Bremen, remembers how the news was heard first-hand from navy deserters:

> Once a sailor returning from Petrograd was our guest . . . he stood in the corner of the living room and told about the victory of the Bolsheviki and the first workers' government in the world. He drank great quantities of black, unsugared coffee and talked until he was hoarse. The room was full of people. They kept coming and going. They asked questions, shook their heads, argued, and many eyes shone.[26]

The mutiny of the Imperial German Navy has been portrayed as a spontaneous act by demoralised and starving men but it was in fact planned by highly organised sailors sympathetic to the USPD. A revolutionary committee and a cell structure were in place for more than a year before the rising. Ernst Schneider, a naval rating, remembers how, in the summer of 1917, they pulled off a secret meeting in a Wilhelmshaven dance hall:

> The dance hall was filled with sailors, girls and a few civilians. The orchestra had left the stage during the interval when suddenly the great curtain of the stage fell, and shouts were heard: 'Stay where you are, do not move!' Then, from behind the curtain was heard a loud voice, impressive and convincing: 'We are on the eve of decisive occurrences. There will be at last no more war, no more oppression of the toiling and bleeding masses. Our day is coming.'[27]

It came on 3 November 1918. The fleet set sail for its 'death ride' but a meeting of ships' delegates the night before had issued the order to mutiny. 'When control has been gained, hoist the red flag in the maintop or gaff. Up for the red dawn of a new day!' By nightfall the fleet was back in port and the sailors were in control. Jan Valtin remembers:

That night I saw the mutinous sailors roll into Bremen on caravans of commandeered trucks – red flags and machine guns mounted on the trucks . . . The population was in the streets. From all sides masses of humanity, a sea of swinging, pushing bodies and distorted faces were moving toward the centre of town. Many of the workers were armed with guns, with bayonets and with hammers.[28]

The SPD's leaders, now part of the Kaiser's war cabinet, sent a party tough guy called Gustav Noske to order an end to the mutiny, but the sailors started fanning out to the rest of Germany.

'The people have triumphed . . .': Oskar Hippe had suffered all the usual brutalities of the German conscript – bullied on the parade ground, beaten up in the barracks – but the war had only weeks left to run and, as his unit moved up to the front line, he could sense morale crumbling.

A lieutenant-colonel made a short speech and told us that we were going to defend bridges behind the front line. We marched through the town to the station; it was more like a demonstration. From the train came continuous shouts against the war: 'Equal rations, equal pay, then the war can stay away!'[29]

They were ordered to board a train to the front but without ammunition. As it began to leave the station it was riddled with bullets by a unit that had already mutinied and was hiding further along the track. Deployed to the front line at Mons, his unit then came under attack from British troops.

In this situation we called for a retreat so that we should not be captured. This was on our own initiative. We called on the two companies lying to the right and left to join us. It was not far to the station where a train stood with steam up . . .[30]

Far away in Frankfurt, on the morning of 8 November Toni Sender's USPD group decided it was time to act. They called all the city's shop stewards to a meeting in a sympathetic pub. There was already a buzz in the town as she left work: 'I had reached the main station when I saw a crowd. Sailors! They had come from Kiel. Their blue blouses seemed a symbol. I rushed to meet them . . .' It was the start of a frantic evening. Sender went with a USPD delegation to the local barracks where they organised a soldiers' committee and freed those who had been jailed for insubordination. Then, pushing her way through the heaving streets, she arrived at the shop stewards' meeting. They called a general strike in Frankfurt for the next morning and prepared to elect a workers' council. At this point they learned that a parallel mass meeting of soldiers was taking place down the road. She remembers:

> In the first hours of the revolution we encountered what was to prove to be its main handicap, the Soldiers' Councils. The soldiers to a large extent were completely untrained politically. What they demanded was the end of the war with as little disturbance as possible . . .[31]

The local USPD leader was sent to talk to the soldiers' meeting. Meanwhile Sender, together with four shop stewards, set off to arrest Frankfurt's police chief, who – with workers marching on the streets, workers' councils forming and prisons unlocked – was asleep in bed. 'Could there be a better illustration,' she remembered wryly, 'of how aloof this caste was from the life of the people?'[32]

By this time the mayor of Frankfurt had declared his support for the workers' and soldiers' councils and Sender got to work writing a leaflet declaring a republic. Then it was dawn, and that was it. While the Kaiser was still mulling over his abdication, the workers and soldiers of Frankfurt were not only in control but had effected an orderly transfer of the existing civil power. The mayor, the new police chief, the government press bureau and the local newspapers all pledged loyalty to a republic that did not yet exist. The south German region of Bavaria had gone even further and declared a separate workers' republic.

On 9 November the Kaiser abdicated. In Berlin it was still quiet but in the factories the workers' restraint was about to snap. They had worked the first two hours of the morning shift until the breakfast break. After that, remembers shop stewards' leader Richard Müller, it became lively.

> The factories emptied unbelievably quickly. The roads filled with enormous masses of people. From the outskirts, where the biggest factories were, big demonstrations converged on the city centre. That it was not a peaceful demonstration you could see from the many pistols, rifles and hand grenades, which were visible everywhere.[33]

Karl Liebknecht, recently released from jail, was lifted to a balcony on the Kaiser's palace, from which he addressed a crowd of more than 100,000. In the Reichstag the SPD leaders were sitting in the canteen, despondent; the soup was thin and in addition the place had been occupied by armed workers. Suddenly a group of demonstrators rushed in and dragged Philip Scheidemann, the only manual worker among the socialist ministers, to the balcony. Scheidemann was part of the generation which had built the SPD from a secret organisation to a mass movement. Unlike the lawyers and bureaucrats who had come to dominate the party leadership, he was seen as 'one of us'. Now someone informed him that Karl Liebknecht was about to proclaim a workers' republic just a few streets away. The problems of the soup paled into insignificance. Scheidemann, aghast at the imminent triumph of Bolshevism, had a rush of political blood to the head.

> I was already standing at the window. Many thousands of poor folk were trying to wave their hats and caps. The shouts of the crowds sounded like a mighty chorus. Then there was silence. I only said a few words which were received with tremendous cheering . . . The Emperor has abdicated. He and his friends have decamped. The people have triumphed over them all along the line. [Ebert, the SPD leader] will form a Labour Government to which all the socialist parties will belong.'[34]

On his return to the canteen, Scheidemann remembers: 'Ebert's face turned livid with wrath when he heard what I had done. He banged his fist on the table and yelled at me, "Is it true . . . You have no right to proclaim the Republic."' Clearly Frankfurt's police chief was not the only person out of touch with reality. Scheidemann's move – to set up a joint government of the SPD and USPD – saved Germany from a socialist revolution along Russian lines, but it could not have worked had the majority of workers not remained loyal and receptive to the politics of the SPD.

Scheidemann had been pulling hard on the levers of control inside the Berlin factories that week and his memoirs show they were still in working order:

> The heads of the SPD were having a bad time with the political rankers and unskilled workmen of the radical factions in the factories. Again and again they had to restore them to reason, thereby bringing on their heads the charge of being funks and blacklegs. They bore everything like well disciplined, class conscious working men and did their duty and their job.[35]

The armistice was signed on 11 November. Elections were set for 19 January. Meanwhile the workers' and soldiers' councils effectively had to run Germany, but in parallel with the government rather than replacing it. That was the crucial difference between Germany and Russia.

Armed force was fragmented, with detachments of sailors taking possession of the main barracks, socialist lawyers assuming the role of police chiefs and only elite regiments of the army staying intact. Sensing the rising anger among those workers who backed the left, the SPD issued a call for unity entitled 'No War Between Brothers'. But later Scheidemann would write, 'Wars between brothers are the most abominable of all. Such a war had now to be fought out for years in Germany among the working masses.'[36]

'From the dregs of the German Labour movement . . .': When Oskar Hippe's unit made it back to their home town of Halle near Leipzig he demobbed and deloused himself and set off for Berlin to link up with Liebknecht. Toni Sender was to experience the first days of the revolution as a makeshift civil servant in Frankfurt, organising the evacuation of troops from the Rhineland and feeding the local population. Shortly it dawned on her that all the people who had previously opposed democracy were now calling for elections as fast as possible.

> All the reactionaries saw their chance to escape fundamental change and shouted Election! Democracy! The majority socialists (the right wing) were not prepared for revolutionary changes and were perfectly satisfied to have only parliamentary government. The soldiers, weary and desiring only to get back home again and lead a normal life, joined them . . . The USPD had, during the entire period of the war, been cut off from public opinion, and all its activity had been prohibited. We had to reach the masses before a fundamental decision was taken.[37]

Oskar Hippe saw things differently. In the world of the demobbed teenage soldier of December 1918 there were as many forces pulling to the left as to the right. To Hippe the strategy was clear. A final clash with the remnants of Prussian militarism was imminent and must bring all power to the workers' and soldiers' councils. After that Germany would link up with Russia and the global revolution would unfold. Ernst Schneider's sailors on the Baltic coast, for example, were in no mood to hang around and were trying to establish direct radio contact with the Russian fleet: 'For the purpose of ensuring permanent communications with Kronstadt, several hundred fully armed sailors were sent by the Revolutionary Committee to occupy the wireless station at Nauen, near Berlin.'[38]

It was this detachment which, having failed to capture the radio station, installed itself in the centre of Berlin as the People's Marine Division. Meanwhile the SPD leaders were also preparing their supporters for battle, as Scheidemann recalls: 'They had been politically and industrially educated in contrast to the radicals, whom the communists recruited from the dregs of the German labour movement that had been torn asunder in 1914.'[39]

The first clash came at the National Congress of Workers' and

Soldiers' Councils. In the eyes of men like Hippe and Schneider, parading outside as members of the Red Soldiers' League, it should have cancelled the elections and taken control of Germany. But it voted decisively not to. Some of the soldiers pointed loaded rifles at Leibknecht when, during a speech to the congress, he argued that 'counter-revolution is in our midst'.

Hippe remembers that, at this stage, 'we regarded [the National Congress] as the most important instrument for working towards a socialist republic . . . Liebknecht was quite clear that we had to win the majority in the committees if we were to reach the stage of the socialist revolution.'[40] But events overtook that strategy. A Republican Soldiers' Corps was formed, consisting of SPD members, which sporadically ran into demonstrations by the Red Soldiers' League. Shots were fired. Faced with a power vacuum, the SPD gave permission to the army generals to recruit *Freikorps* – paramilitary units composed of right-wing ex-servicemen and students. Posters appeared all over Berlin with the words 'Kill Leibknecht'.

Now Liebknecht and Luxemburg split from the USPD and formed the Communist Party (KPD).[41] Its leaders were revolutionary veterans from the Second International stiffened by advice from Moscow. At the founding congress Leibknecht argued that the time for seizing power was in the future, but he was defeated here as well. Young soldiers and sailors like Hippe and Schneider were in no mood for moderation; they wanted revolution. One of the leaders would remember:

> The air of Berlin was filled with revolutionary tension . . . The delegates, who represented the unorganized masses who had just come to us through action alone, by action and for action, could not understand that a new action, easily foreseeable, could end not in victory but a setback.[42]

The spark for action was the sacking of Berlin's police chief, a member of the USPD. Hundreds of thousands took to the streets in protest. The USPD leaders, together with the shop stewards, decided the time had come to break with the government and form one of their own.

This was designed as a purely ministerial manoeuvre but for Oskar Hippe it seemed like the signal for the final battle.

The six days of fighting known to history as the Spartacus Rising ended, inevitably, with massive bloodshed and defeat. The government deployed social democratic soldiers alongside the right-wing *Freikorps*. The left stormed the SPD's printworks. Liebknecht and Luxemburg were arrested by a *Freikorps* unit and, on 15 January 1919, murdered. Their bodies were thrown into a canal. All over Germany the left and right of the workers' movement were shooting at each other. Schnieder remembers the scene in the North Sea ports:

> By this time, fighting was going on in the streets and at the barricades throughout Wilhelmshaven. Heavy losses were inflicted on the reactionaries, who fought in close column. A hail of hand grenades descended upon them from the roofs and windows of the houses, and their shouts of 'Ebert! Scheidemann!' were drowned by those of the revolutionaries 'Liebknecht! Luxemburg!'[43]

'War between brothers' was now the central reality in the workers' movement. Its outcome would shape not only German history but world history.

'This is the new man . . .': It was only years later, when the books came out — the memoirs and novels by former soldiers — that people began to understand what had happened to them during four years of fighting. This was 'a generation destroyed by war, even though it might have escaped the shells'.[44] The violent split in the workers' movement completed that process of destruction. The pre-war idyll of social democracy, the world within a world, was not just divided, it was gone.

The fascist writer Ernst Jünger would remember the young soldiers in the trenches, men totally acclimatised to a world of high technology and violence, 'ruthless toward themselves and others':

> I am overcome with recognition: this is the new man, the storm pioneer, the elite of Central Europe. A whole new race, smart, strong

and filled with will. What reveals itself here as a vision that will tomorrow be the axis around which life revolves still faster and faster . . . The war is not the end but the prelude to violence . . . The war is a great school and the new man will bear our stamp.[45]

The left shared this intuition − that war had created a new sociology of work, a rebellious spirit and a new psychological type, the 'authoritarian rebel'. Anti-Nazi screenwriter Carl Zuckmayer described a generation in recovery from post-combat trauma: 'We are the ones whose lives began with the knowledge of the ultimate and greatest things of earthly existence − of the most terrible, the mortal abandonment of man; and the highest, comradeship.'[46] What Nazism managed to create out of this new human material is well known. How it impacted on the German workers' movement can be traced through the lives of men like Hippe, Schneider and Valtin − and women like Toni Sender.

By the mid-1920s the German workers' movement was not just politically split but sociologically riven. The USPD split in half, some going back to the old SPD, some to the communists. As a result the KPD became the biggest communist party outside Russia. Most of the KPD's members were young male manual workers like Oskar Hippe; only 17 per cent were women. Meanwhile the SPD saw the blue-collar portion of its membership begin to fall away. White-collar workers like Toni Sender flocked to it, particularly women.

With hindsight we can see Toni Sender and Oskar Hippe as symbols of two 'types' which had emerged from the trauma of the war: the educated white-collar socialist, committed to parliamentary democracy and prepared to defend it through mass action where needed; and the self-educated manual worker, committed to a soviet republic and spoiling for a fight. History now pitched these two cohorts into action, sometimes with each other, sometimes against each other.

Three critical events would restore the authority of the SPD leaders and, ultimately, order. First, in March 1920, came a military coup known as the Kapp Putsch. The SPD leadership first tried to suppress it with regular troops but these refused to fight so they turned to the trade union leaders to request something that, only ten years before, would have had them choking on their *Weissbier*, a general strike. The strike was solid. After 48 hours the coup was paralysed.

With the Kapp Putsch defeated, the KPD, together with many left-wingers in the SPD, refused to stand down. In the coal mining region of the Ruhr battalions of armed workers temporarily took control. But the political impact of the general strike was to restore the credibility of the SPD leaders, above all the union officials who had delivered what they had spent their entire careers deriding, the political mass strike.

The second crisis came in March 1921 and found Oskar Hippe right at the centre of the storm. In the Saxony state elections of 1921 the KPD had polled 204,000 votes, beating the combined returns of both social democrat parties. Hippe's home town of Merseburg was not only a KPD stronghold; an even more extreme left party had influence at the massive Leuna chemical works there. On the orders of the Communist International, a general strike and uprising was launched throughout Saxony, known with hindsight as the March Madness.

Armed groups of workers toured the region, blowing up police stations and railway bridges. They engaged the police and *Freikorps* in full-scale battles until eventually, forced onto the defensive, Hippe together with 3,000 miners and chemical workers made a final stand inside the Leuna factory.

> We did not know that no one apart from ourselves in the Leuna works was putting up any more resistance. The police attack began the following evening . . . There were areas in the Leuna works containing high explosives. Our leaders, who had counted on our opponents not using heavy guns, had to provide a suitable answer to this attack. On the very first day our mechanics had started building a train . . .[47]

But even the armoured train could only delay defeat; they were captured and imprisoned inside a nitrate silo. 'Every day civilians came into the silo, accompanied by policemen . . . If they met anyone who was known to them as a communist, then the individual concerned was put up against a wall and shot.'[48]

These scenes took place a full two years after the revolution was supposed to be over, and in the heart of Europe's most industrialised country. Years later, Hippe would place on record his gratitude that the SPD-led police battalion that eventually removed him from the silo 'never overreached itself'. In the 'war between brothers' all you could hope for now was fair treatment as a POW.

'An explosion was due . . .': Picture yourself, once again, as a typical German worker in Hamburg, but now in 1923. The third and decisive crisis of the postwar era is under way. Hitler's Beer-Hall Putsch in Bavaria has been defeated but his National Socialist German Workers' Party is now a political force and well on its way to a million votes. But Communism is stronger: half a million workers marched on the KPD's demonstration on May Day 1923, headed by 25,000 members of its uniformed militia. All the focus is on preparation for the clash that everyone can see is coming. The French army has occupied the Ruhr and the workers' movement is coordinating passive resistance to the occupation. There is hyperinflation: in 1905 you might have earned two marks a day, now you earn 17 billion. Unemployment will rocket from 6 to 29 per cent within 12 months. The country is being run by presidential decree, not parliament. The SPD is being pushed to the left. It is the ruling party in the regional governments of Saxony and Thuringia and the communists are about to take a historic step; they will join the socialists in regional coalition governments. In response, the army is getting ready to invade these two regions. Meanwhile the communists have an elaborate secret plan for armed uprisings once the crisis comes to a head.

There is, of course, no longer a 'typical German worker'. Working-class brains are reeling from the experience of hyperinflation and foreign occupation, but there are two political tribes and they will react very differently when the crisis comes.

Jan Valtin had run away to sea on the day the Baltic Fleet's last barricade fell, in January 1919. He arrived back in Hamburg in 1923, world weary at the age of 19 and the epitome of the post-war New Man.

> I pitched into party work with a high fervour. Nothing mattered outside the communist offensive . . . I went from ship to ship, from wharf to wharf in fulfillment of party duty. And in the evenings there were meetings and discussion circles and political courses to attend which rarely broke up before midnight. I had no thought of clothes, amusements or girls. I felt myself a living wheel in the party machine. I grew leaner, harder and was supremely happy.[49]

'I was class conscious because class-consciousness had been a family tradition,' he remembers. But the consciousness takes a different form: the 'world within a world' created by the communists was created in the image of the New Man, the 'hard, lean' barricade fighter, ruthless with himself and others. Valtin became an underground courier for the communist leaders, rubbing shoulders with Russian military advisers drafted in to supervise the revolution and acquiring a taste for the romance of secrecy that would last a lifetime. Toni Sender, on the other side of the social divide within the movement, remembers a 'terrific tension' on the streets. 'Crowds of people milled about without aim or purpose. It seemed as if they sensed that something was about to happen and they wanted to be there when it did.'[50]

> An explosion was due. It came in the form of demands for a general strike. Why did its proponents want to involve the entire working class in a political general strike? None of them could answer this question – they themselves did not know . . . A valve had to be opened. They thought a general strike would change the entire situation.[51]

In Frankfurt a united action committee was formed to fight a factory closure and to mobilise support for the beleaguered socialist governments in Saxony and Thuringia. Sender remembers:

> Everything was wrecked by the obstinacy of the communists. The unions opposed the general strike on principle, but they were ready

to take part in a limited demonstration strike in order to save the situation . . . on the next day only a partial strike began. It showed that the Communists influenced a large part of the unemployed, but only as small part of the employed. After two days it was decided to resume work.[52]

Now the army moved in to depose the regional socialist governments. Sender rushed to Saxony in time to witness the paralysis of the labour movement there. The communists called for a general strike. A big conference of trade union delegates was called but refused even to vote on the general strike. Frantic telegrams between Moscow and Berlin resulted in the last-minute cancellation of the communist uprisings.

But nobody told Jan Valtin. His telegraph did not arrive. In Hamburg there were 1,700 workers in the communist militia. They began the insurrection as planned, at midnight on 23 October. There was no general strike and the local SPD branches knew nothing about the plan for an uprising. Valtin was in the working class suburb of Eimsbüttel, whose socialist male-voice choirs had been the pride of the seafaring city in 1905. His job was to assault the police station with hand grenades and secure the weapons there. By dawn

Communists were marching into Hamburg from all outlying communities. Then came two shrill whistles – the signal for assault . . . I
leaped down four flights of stairs into a hall already crowded with
armed partisans. Perhaps one in five had a rifle, one in four a pistol,
and the rest carried hammers and spiked clubs . . .[53]

Tens of thousands of social democratic workers woke up that morning to bewildering scenes. Stopped on the way to work by young men carrying rifles and jabbering about the dictatorship of the proletariat many muttered, 'Well it won't last long,' and went home. The rising lasted three days, at the end of which Valtin's assault group decided to split up.

I felt as if I should never be happy again . . . So much bloodshed.
It made a man want to turn his face to the clouds and roar, so great
was the pain. For what? . . . There was no chance to flee. The people

were hostile. Even the prostitutes mocked me. 'To the gallows with him,' one of them repeatedly chanted, swinging an empty beer glass.[54]

Larissa Reissner, a Russian communist journalist who witnessed the Hamburg fighting, described a socialist singers' festival two weeks later. Through her prose, dripping with irony, we can see how the old rituals of 1905 looked to the lost generation. 'A vast, half-empty, cavern-like hall. Several hundred unusually oppressed, taciturn and motionless workers . . . The round, jauntily upturned lid of a beer mug cannot be seen on a single table . . .' First there is a socialist speech; then a workers' choir singing 'exultations of pastoral bliss and pure love'.

> Not a stammer or a wrong note. Clearly the men have been prac-
> tising ensemble performance for at least two months despite hunger,
> unemployment, the howling of unfed children and the fascists'
> preparations for war. No, nothing can divert the SPD from peaceful
> cultural and educational exercises.[55]

This passage was written as a venomous attack on social democracy yet, unwittingly, it captures the essence of how the majority of German workers felt by October 1923. Surrounded by a world of chaos they would fall back on what they had themselves created: the world within a world of social democracy, no matter how bleak it looked to the revolutionary outsider.

'Hitler has no followers among the workers . . .': Jan Valtin would escape from police captivity after the Hamburg rising and live life on the edge: as Comintern courier in Shanghai, hit man for Soviet intelligence in San Francisco and prisoner in San Quentin jail. By the time he got back to Germany in 1929 the Nazis were about to become the second-biggest party in the Reichstag. The socialists and commu-nists were engaged in street fights with the brownshirts across the slum districts of Berlin. Because of the economic slump, 80 per cent of the communist party members were now unemployed.

Admitted once again to the inner circles of the KPD, Valtin was allowed an audience with Comintern chief Georgi Dimitrov, who was living incognito above a bookshop on Berlin's Wilhelmstrasse. Smelling of perfume and brandishing a cigar, Dimitrov told him,

> The Hitler movement has no followers among the workers . . . Don't let yourself be distracted. The biggest obstacle on the road to proletarian revolution is the Social Democratic Party. Our foremost task is to liquidate its influence. Afterwards we'll sweep Hitler and his lumpen-trash into the garbage can of history . . .'

In the general election of 1932, however, the Nazis won, with 13.75 million votes – 33 per cent of the total. The combined vote for the SPD and KPD was 37 per cent but the 'war between brothers' prevented the workers' movement from effective opposition. Hitler became Chancellor in January 1933, and suppressed the KPD on the pretext of the Reichstag fire. The SPD was banned later in the year. The largest communist party outside Russia and the largest socialist party in the world had been destroyed.

In February 1933 Toni Sender found a picture of her own face splashed across the front page of a Nazi publication entitled *The Jewish Mirror*. She fled to New York, where she died in 1964 after a career with the United Nations Commission on Human Rights.

Ernst Schneider, the revolutionary in the Baltic Fleet, was in exile in London by 1935 and active as an anarchist among London dockers after the war, producing a newspaper called the *Port Workers Clarion*.

Jan Valtin was 'turned' by the Gestapo in 1937 while under sentence of death in a Nazi concentration camp. He was released and ordered to infiltrate German communist networks operating from Scandinavia. Unknown to his controllers he was still working for the Soviet intelligence service, who had sent him a coded message while in jail. When he refused to obey further orders from Moscow he was kidnapped but escaped. He too fled to the USA. After serving in the US Army during the war, he was investigated by the House Committee on Un-American Activities. He died in 1951.

Oskar Hippe was, by 1933, a member of the Trotskyist opposition in the German communist party. He was involved in a street fight on the night of Hitler's torchlight victory parade. Imprisoned by the Nazis he was starved, whipped and beaten with an iron bar. He was released in 1936 and survived the war by moving to a remote island in the Baltic. In 1948 he was sentenced to 25 years by the Soviet authorities in East Germany for his activities as a Trotskyist. Released in 1956, he moved to West Germany, where he joined the SPD. He died in 1990. At his trial in 1934 he had told the judges,

> All the conditions had long been present to raise society to a higher, socialist, stage. If in the conflict between capital and labour, it had not been possible in 1933 to attain this new society in the interests of all mankind, then the blame lay with both the workers' parties.[56]

7. Totally ignorant labourers
The birth of the Chinese working class

If you strike it disturbs the peace and can bring no benefit.
We recognise that you are ignorant
So simply warn you against further blind recklessness
And urge you to return to work

Police anti-strike poem Shanghai, 1911[1]

New Delhi, India, 2005

They were not expecting the lathi charge; when it came the fero-
ciousness of the beating shocked the Honda strikers. Some 3,000 of
them were sitting in a lawned garden where the police had told them
to wait. They had taken their shoes off. Then, at 2.45 p.m. the riot
police surrounded them, closed the exits and let fly with their sticks.
'I have seen agitation but never this kind of violence,' said union official V.S. Yadav. 'If people covered their heads the police would pull
their arms out to get at them.'[2]

Eight hundred people were arrested, 60 of these forcibly removed
from the local hospital, which treated 400 casualties on that afternoon.
The next day, when they heard news of what had happened in the
park, the casual workers who had stayed at work inside the Honda
plant scaled the walls and ran away. 'We were scared that our fate
would be worse, as we were inside the factory,' said one. Three days
later Japanese managers at the plant agreed a settlement: full pay for
the time spent on strike, all sacked workers to be reinstated, a year's
freeze on all other demands and the union to be recognised. It was a
minor victory for the union, which had only just been formed. But
for the rest of India it was a shock.

Honda Motorcycles and Scooters India Ltd owns one of India's newest factories. Located in Gurgaon, one of two special economic zones on the edge of New Delhi, it employs 'lean' production methods and new technology. The workforce was a mixture of staff and casuals.

> In the Honda factory there were about 250 permanent workers who lived there. They were given air-conditioned rooms. Besides them there were 500–600 non-technical staff from outside and about 2,000 casual workers who slept in the same hall.[3]

By Indian standards take-home pay was good, though there were wide variations: most seem to have been on between £58 and £70 a month, higher than the minimum wage, and overtime was paid double. But as one worker explains, there was discontent.

> We were made to stay inside the factory under very tough conditions and were constantly under guard, with guards from the Group 4 Security Agency. About 2,000 workers had to sleep under one roof. There was no fresh air. I sometimes went in the lawn outside to sleep. We were given facilities like television and could call back home but we were not free to leave.[4]

The trouble started over a minor issue: one shift was given a pay rise, others not, and everyone was asked to sign a blank piece of paper, which they presumed was a way of getting them to agree to it. The workers went on hunger strike, working through their lunch break instead of eating. On 8 February 2005 they elected a seven-person committee to organise a union. On 25 June 1,500 workers from the A Shift held a rally well away from the plant. Two days later 2,700 workers were sacked. There had been no strike and no new pay claim. The registration of a union seems to have prompted the management's response.

The sacked workers took to sitting on a plot of land 100 metres from the factory gates. They took a register twice a day and remained there for a month. By 18 July protracted negotiations had led to an agreement to re-employ the workers 400 at a time but, angered by the raising of a union flag at the factory gate, the management reneged. That was what led to the mass demonstration on 25 July which ended with the lathi charge.

The Honda dispute was a wake-up call to India's trade unions. They had been formed under a different economic model, when India's economy was protected from global competition, when the state owned heavy industry and when labour laws guaranteed a range of benefits to workers in the 'organised sector'.

'Everything has changed – the general social pressure that used to be there from the government has totally vanished,' says Mohan Lal. He is general secretary of the Centre of Indian Trade Unions in Delhi. He meets me in the union's airless HQ where an electric fan is doing its best to cool the air between us. Behind him there is a bust of Lenin. There is a typewriter in the next room but neither in this nor in any of the three trade union headquarters I saw in Delhi was there a computer. They are up against companies whose bosses communicate by Blackberry, 24/7, across five continents, but they are barely in touch with the outside world. Mohan Lal's brand of trade unionism was not designed to deal with this.

> When I was a shop floor worker there were certain rules and regulations within the industry, now the employer can do anything, he can hire any worker, he can fire any worker – so a general change has taken place.

Though the challenge of globalisation has been obvious for at least a decade, Indian unions are only now beginning to try to organise the casual workforce summoned into existence by free trade. When I ask him if trade unions can survive in a world of globalisation he replies, 'The theoretical aspect of trade unionism is intact. It will not change; it will remain as it was in the past. The thing that has changed is that the workers don't understand the meaning of this philosophy, this theoretical aspect.'

Even the working class itself has been affected by globalisation, Lal tells me.

> They no longer think in terms of the old ideas – socialism, trade unionism – because they are more attracted by glitter now. It is very difficult to make an impact on them. Instead, small organisations are

coming up – local associations, NGOs – not trade unions in the old sense. They are working at grass-roots level but they don't have an overarching vision.

There are two special economic zones on Delhi's outskirts. Gurgaon in the west, Noida in the east. The archetypical landscape in these zones is a plate-glass office building next to a half-built road, surrounded by low brick huts, cattle, moto-rickshaw drivers and beggars. In Noida the kind of grass-roots unionism that Lal disdains is all they have got. The local office of the Hind Mazdoor Sabha (HMS) is a single room with two benches, a mobile phone, a water cooler and a fan. There is no bust of Lenin. It is in the middle of a working class housing complex, where children play on the streets, women squeeze washing dry from crumbling parapets and a herd of large brown cows sits passively in an excrement-filled paddock, their sounds and smells dominating the entire neighbourhood.

Mr Chouhan runs HMS in Noida. A generation younger than Mohan Lal, he has the job of trying to represent workers in the garment industry, where contracts of employment are rarely worth anything. On the benches sit young men who have been sacked or swindled by their backstreet garment bosses. One asked for his wages, another asked to see how much money he had accumulated in the insurance fund that was being deducted at source, another went to his village to see his family. All have been sacked at the factory gate and are deep in debt.

Sunil Chowhan (no relation) was working as a press operative. He is in his early twenties, with a wispy moustache and clothes that hang loosely from his seven-stone frame.

I consider myself one of the best press operators in the factory, and that's why I asked for a pay rise. The next morning when I got to the factory gate they told me I was redundant. I tried to pursue the owners for compensation, then I complained to the HMS. The problem is my income has totally gone. I am in debt. I am in a shattered position and I don't know what to do.

Inside Chowhan's factory, which makes velour cloth, the day is eight hours, but standard practice in Noida is to pressure workers to work a double shift if a big order is received.

> Some of them did it but I would only work a maximum of twelve . . . The factory looks very nice from the boundary wall but if you go inside you will find a lot of dust – it settles on our head and our hair gets white.

The Noida garment industry serves the booming export market and, as such, production units are subject to the 'codes' – which every union activist in the developing world has to know about. These are codes of conduct issued by name-brand companies under pressure from NGO campaigners in the developed world. But the system is not appreciated by the men in the HMS office. In the first place companies operate a scam whereby they set up a 'shop window' factory where it looks like they are doing all the processes to make the garment under one roof, says the union leader. That is what they show the visiting executives from the firm that owns the brand. A bigger problem is that the codes do not seem to match what the workers want. The codes insist on having toilet paper in the lavatories, one man tells me, 'yet Indian workers don't use toilet paper – we use water'. He says they would rather have a written contract than toilet paper.

Written contracts are in short supply here, though, and subcontracting to unregulated sweatshops is just the tip of the problem. In the factory itself foremen act as labour contractors, getting the workers' salaries paid directly to themselves. In turn, if individual workers have to take time off, they will subcontract their own job rather than risk losing the position. As a result you can have what looks like a factory system under one roof which is in fact a network of small contractors and agency workers, many of whom have no idea who they actually work for.

In 2003 the Uttar Pradesh government, which administers Noida, abolished the factory inspectorate. Now unions have to complain to a magistrate, who has to issue an order before the local labour department will investigate a complaint. In August 2005 Gurgaon's courts had a backlog of 6,000 labour cases outstanding. The office dealing with them has not had a secretary for over a year and does not have a typewriter.

The Indian labour movement was born under British rule and grew to maturity under the paternalistic gaze of the Congress Party. Its first mass strike, against the jailing of a Congress leader, was in 1908 and paralysed the Bombay textile mills. Its most recent was on 21 May 2003, when upwards of 40 million workers downed tools. Marxist parties govern in two states, but all the busts of Lenin have not stopped the unions' power in the workplace being relentlessly undercut. What is happening in Noida and Gurgaon is the creation of a brand new Indian working class.

Contract labour, casualisation, Japanese managers and baton charges; special economic areas where only the rules of foreign capitalism apply – there is a precedent for this in history, in a city that was once as glamorous as New Delhi is today . . .

Shanghai, China, 1919

It was nearing six o'clock, the hour of the night shift. In front of one of the great cotton mills a crowd of shivering humanity had gathered waiting for the Sikh policemen to throw open the gates. Faces were blue and pinched, shoulders bent, and hands drawn up for warmth inside the padded cotton sleeves.[5]

The city was Shanghai, China. The shift they were about to start would last 12 hours, with a half-hour break at midnight. The workforce was mainly migrant and mainly female.

One poor soul at last reaches the gate of the mill and drops all in a heap on the cold, wet ground to wait for the blowing of the whistle. 'Have you come far?' is asked of her pityingly. Half fearfully, half defiantly, as if braced for a reprimand, she struggles to her feet and answers, 'From Honkew,' a distance of nearly three miles. Let us hope she is one who works at a loom, for then she can have a seat at a narrow bench. The women and children who watch the spindles must stand the long night through.'[6]

There was cotton, child labour, strike action and at the end of it all a massacre. At one level the birth of the Chinese working class looked exactly like that of the British a century before. But in Shanghai in the 1920s there were also movie stars, communists, gangsters and religious cults. Over 80 per cent of the population were migrants, and there were more prostitutes per capita than anywhere else on earth. To the Western eye it was a gaudy paradise of sex, high finance and Hollywood glamour. 'So much life, so carefully canalised, so rapidly and strongly flowing – the spectacle of it inspires something like terror,' wrote the novelist Aldous Huxley, adding, 'It is life itself.'[7]

To Chen Du-xiu, the founder of Chinese communism, the city's inhabitants looked distinctly unreceptive to revolutionary propaganda.

A large portion are totally ignorant labourers who suffer privation and hardship. Another portion are traitorous businessmen who make a living directly or indirectly under foreign capitalism. Another portion are swindlers who sell fake Western medicines or lottery tickets. Another portion are prostitutes. Another portion are evil gangsters and police. Another portion are 'black curtain' writers and booksellers dealing in promiscuous romances, superstitious formulas and profitable new magazines. Another portion are gangster politicians . . .[8]

If that description sounds strangely prescient of the way Shanghai looks today it is not surprising. Then, as now, it was a booming, global city. It had started out as a trading port with 'concession' areas for foreign merchants, prototypes for today's special economic zones, but after losing a war with Japan the decrepit Manchu dynasty was forced to allow foreigners to build factories as well as to trade. In 1894 there were 36,000 factory workers in Shanghai; by 1919 the number was 260,000.[9]

How did the transition from farm to factory happen? Fan Lan-ying, a peasant girl from the Subei region, tells a story that would have been familiar to any factory worker at the time of Peterloo.

> We were very poor. When I was thirteen, a labour contractor from Shanghai came to our village to recruit children as contract workers. He said, 'Shanghai is a wonderful place. You can eat good rice as well as fish and meat. You can live in a Western-style house and make money.' So many parents in the countryside agreed to let their children go off as contract workers.[10]

Once inside the factory, the machines were the newest on earth, the management methods the oldest. In the silk-reeling factories children were employed to skin the raw cocoons in boiling water: 'The Chinese women overseers, passing constantly up and down the lines, occasionally punish a child's inefficiency, or supposed laziness, by thrusting the little hand into the bubbling cauldron.'[11]

But if the fines, the violence and obligatory silence were the same as in British factories of the early 1800s, Shanghai was different in one important way. The worker arriving there had to negotiate a maze of power networks that made it hard to discern a dividing line between workers and bosses but strangely easy to make out one between different groups of workers. The Shanghai factory was not at first a world of 'them versus us' more 'us versus us'.

In the first place there was the skills divide. Shanghai had a skilled labour aristocracy of 200,000 craftsmen: goldsmiths, carpenters, printers and foundry workers. Below that was the factory workforce, four fifths women and children, which endured the harsh mechanical drudgery of the spinning mill or the intense heat of the silk-reeling factory. Below them were the 'coolies': 80,000 men made their living pulling rickshaws, 50,000 were casuals on the docks, 20,000 women worked as prostitutes. Every job had a distinct subculture.

The skills divide was overlaid by ethnic rivalries. Craftsmen in Shanghai's engineering, shipbuilding and metalworking plants were mainly migrants from south China and spoke Cantonese. Each craft ran a guild system – with apprentices, initiation rites and deities – based in temples where masters and men mingled. In skilled workers' families only the man went to work. But factory workers inhabited a different world. Most were Mandarin-speaking migrants from the north and east of China and typically the whole family worked; the women and children in the factories, the men as rickshaw pullers, dockers or refuse collectors.

Each workplace was further divided by village loyalty. Factory foremen were allowed to recruit from their place of origin and as a result bonds between Chinese workers and foremen were persistently more durable than in the 'classic' factory system. Violent struggles over recruitment rights in a particular trade or factory were common. Even the city's 20,000 beggars were organised into five gangs by place of origin. Workers from each area would set up mutual societies, nurseries and 'same-place clubs' so the hierarchies and traditions of villages hundreds of miles away were preserved in the heart of the city. How you ate, how you wore your hair, the songs you sang – these were badges of identity that you clung on to in the hostile environment of Shanghai.

Xia Yan, the father of Chinese social reportage, captured these divisions when he described two queues of workers standing in the dark outside a cotton mill: on the one side local women, on the other migrant contract labourers who had just been beaten awake in their dormitories. 'These two groups seldom speak to each other on the road. Perhaps the workers from outside hold aloof because of the dirt, country ways and queer accents of the village girls, whom they despise.'[12]

Gangsters were a further complicating factor. Imperial China had been riddled with secret societies which the colonial powers recruited to run the opium trade. The result was the legendary gang culture that could be found whenever you scratched the surface of a Shanghai institution. Two major gangs, Red and Green, controlled drugs, prostitution, begging and the waterfront. Their political networks stretched from the gentlemen's club to the factory floor, where many foremen were gang members. Liu A-jiu, a cotton worker, recalled their powerful influence on working life:

The manager purposely encouraged all sorts of gangs among the workers so they would be divided. New workers were beaten up and prevented from working. There was no choice but to ask for help from the friend who had brought you to Shanghai. All the friend could do was introduce you to the gang leader . . . the new worker had to pay more than ten dollars to her new master and five or six dollars for [ceremonial] dinner. Adding this to the five dollars she paid the recruiter, she was already out more than twenty dollars. Having taken a gangmaster, you were stuck in the relationship for a lifetime.[13]

There was yet another factor that made loyalties in Shanghai complex: colonialism. Shanghai's two concessions were run respectively by France and an Anglo-US administration; they were much bigger than the old Chinese city and wrapped around it, dominating the riverfront. In the concessions the 'powers' ruled direct, with their own police force and their own courts. The majority of people who lived there were Chinese but even the richest knew they were second-class citizens. The concession system was what drew global capital into Shanghai, and it would survive even during the 1920s, as the rest of the city changed hands between competing Chinese warlords. Hostility to it would at times unite Chinese workers and their bosses.

Before 1919 strikes were not unknown – indeed as the value of wages fell during the First World War they increased. But they were sporadic and disorganised; sometimes factory foremen led them, sometimes the action was leaderless and moved swiftly from smashing machines to total surrender. Craftsmen as well as factory workers took strike action, reflecting growing polarisation within the guilds. But unions hardly existed.

To the rest of the world, China's working class seemed insignificant. When the International Labour Organisation was set up at the Versailles peace conference in 1919, no one blinked when a British civil servant reported, 'China was not present . . . for the simple reason that she has no labour problems.'[14] Within weeks that view would change.

* * *

4 May 1919: The Chinese urban middle class had been seething with anti-colonial feeling since the late 19th century. The nationalist leader Sun Yat-sen had overthrown the last Emperor in 1911, only to be replaced by a military junta in Beijing. By 1919 China was beginning to fall apart as rival military leaders built regional power bases, and for the next ten years these warlords would conduct a chaotic struggle for power.

On 4 May 1919 news broke that the Chinese government had agreed that Germany's colonial possessions in China would be handed over to Japan. Thousands of students demonstrated in Beijing, demanding the resignation of the ministers who had struck the deal. Across China committees of national salvation met, passed resolutions, sent telegrams; all the tactics of a modern velvet revolution were tried out by the May Fourth Movement. The men in power bided their time for a month and then cracked down, arresting hundreds of student activists.

The response in Shanghai was defiant. Shops were closed and students streamed out of the university, calling for the workers to join them. By 10 June 100,000 workers had responded to the call: the tactic of the 'triple stoppage' (merchants, students and workers) had been invented. Suddenly the Shanghai working class was in the thick of a national revolution and had become its decisive force. On 11 June the pro-Japanese ministers were sacked, the student leaders released and the Japan deal cancelled. In less than a week of strike action the workers of Shanghai had achieved what the students and the shopkeepers could not.

For the students, colonialism was an outrage against their national culture, for nationalist employers it was an attack on their profit margins; for the workers it was an abuse perpetrated against their bodies every day. In the foreign-owned factories they were treated 'like cattle and horses'. Body searches were obligatory, violence casual, verbal abuse routine. To visit the toilet a worker had to apply for a small bamboo permit: white to urinate, red to defecate.

There were no official unions in the 1919 general strike; in many cases it was the guilds, same-place clubs and foremen who organised the walkout. The gang leaders also backed it, ordering beggars and pickpockets to stop work. But at its root the action was spontaneous. It also posed an electrifying question for China's anti-colonial movement: what role would the workers play in national liberation and what would they get out of it? Would they have a walk-on part as extras in the drama – a role the Chinese peasantry had played for centuries – or would they do something new?

And it was a question they had started to answer themselves. On the first day of the strike, a group of 24 workers met to draw up the following declaration:

> The principles of universal justice will conquer tyranny. We, the hundreds of thousands of Shanghai workers, will sacrifice our lives and form the rearguard of the students' and merchants' struggle against barbaric tyranny. We propose that the workers act for themselves, that the workers in each trade organise various sorts of small workers' groups. Afterwards, they can come together to form big workers' groups. The first step is to launch a campaign of workers' demonstrations through the streets. The second step is to organise a big strike throughout industry. The third step is to sacrifice our red blood, the blood of hundreds of thousands of workers, in the struggle against this barbaric tyranny.[15]

Once the wording was agreed they cut their arms and signed it in blood. Within eight years the Shanghai workforce would move from the 'rearguard' of nationalism to its front line – and the offer of a blood sacrifice would be redeemed in full.

1919–23: The invisible underlings of the city were not slow to realise that if they could sink an international treaty, they could probably do something about their wages and conditions. Economic strikes and disputes intensified during the early 1920s, a period Chinese historians call the 'first strike high-tide'. Li Chung, a naval dockyard worker summed up the mood:

> The worst is not that they gain advantages from us, but that they grievously mistreat us, we the workers who provide for them . . .

In this way, we are forced to eat stinking food, wear stinking clothes, live in stinking houses – in all things our bitterness knows no limits. In such a situation, my face often turns ashen and I shed tears. Is it not true that we desire a great unity? First of all, we will settle the question of hours and pay, then we will settle the other questions . . .[16]

Workers' mutual societies were set up in partnership with sympathetic employers. Tram workers, electricians and mechanics formed independent unions each several hundred strong.

In 1921 the communist activist Li Qi-han began to agitate among tobacco and silk workers in the Pudong district, across the river from the main city. Li ran a workers' school and through it made contact with both the workers and the Green Gang foremen who kept them under control. During the first strike he organised at British American Tobacco, Li adopted the novel tactic of swearing allegiance to the local Green Gang boss and going through the initiation rights, including drinking cock's-blood wine. 'During the first period of the union's history, organisational activities were conducted secretly,' noted an observer, 'as the formation of workers' associations without the permission of the authorities made one liable to capital punishment.'[17] By September they were on strike for a second time, with Li bringing the mechanics and foremen out alongside them in a famous appeal to gang loyalty:

Most foremen are in the Green Gang, and they have taken the oath of brotherhood. But are not most workers also in the Green Gang? Bullying workers, who are brothers and nephews according to the same oath, is not something to boast about.[18]

Until this point the story of the Shanghai workers' organisations follows a pattern similar to that of the Lancashire workers before Peterloo: a political movement unlocks the door to action on the economic front. But the intervening century had destroyed the political space in which a fledgling workers' movement could experiment, indulge the naivety of its leaders and build do-it-yourself organisations. The world was now dominated by the competing ideologies of nationalism and communism. Both nationalists and communists had definite views about the role the working class should play. In fact the intellectuals in charge of both currents in China had been drumming their fingers in anticipation of its arrival on the stage for more than a decade.

Sun Yat-sen's nationalism was, from the beginning, imbued with commitments to social reform: sympathy for the workers was tempered by hostility to class conflict. Even the word used to describe the working class had connotations of harmony rather than conflict. The *gongren* – the 'working section of society' – was seen as a sacred part of the nation, as long as it knew its place. In 1919 Sun's party, the Kuomintang, had adopted demands for the eight-hour day, the legalisation of trade unions, social insurance and compulsory arbitration to settle strikes. By the early 1920s Sun had established a rebel government in the southern province of Guangdong (then known as Canton) and begun to reorganise the Kuomintang as a national political movement in the rest of the country. The communists meanwhile, mainly intellectuals who struggled to make their accents understood among the workers, made organising trade unions their main priority.

But the BAT strike alerted Shanghai's middle class nationalists to increasing communist influence. They formed an umbrella group to pull together 50 friendly societies and no-strike unions they had set up. The two strategies to liberate the nation – communism and nationalism – were now played out in the building of unions. At first they went side by side. In March 1922, after a mass meeting addressed by Li Qi-han, the cotton workers of Pudong formed a union. The same month silk-reelers formed an organisation called the Women's Industrial Progress Union, under the leadership of a female supervisor called Mu Zhi-ying; she was a Kuomintang supporter and a member of the Green Gang.

The communist-led union struck first, winning a 10 per cent pay increase after 3,800 women at the Nikko mills stopped work for nine days. They struck again in May, for 16 days, after management reneged on the deal. But the union leaders were sacked, and Green Gang bosses used their mob connections to get Li Qi-han arrested. By mid-June, with Li in prison, the mill workers' union had been completely taken over by the Green Gang.

Now, in the searing heat of August, Mu led 20,000 silk workers out on strike, stopping 40 silk-reeling factories across the city in the first mass strike of women in Chinese history. Their demand was simply for a day off due to the hot weather. They marched into the concession districts with banners saying 'Equality between the sexes' and 'Protect human rights' but were dispersed by the police, who arrested Mu and banned the union.

In November 1922 the Nikko mill workers struck again, after the company banned their union and closed down a school it had set up for workers' children. When the government tried to arrest the strike leaders, the workers at BAT, walking distance away, came out on strike in solidarity. Simultanously gold- and silversmiths in the area struck. Pudong, a small community on the 'wrong' side of Shanghai's big river, was now effectively on general strike. It was a hard-fought dispute. The employers set up rival unions and brought in strike-breakers; the workers staged a mass demonstration, beat up strike-breakers and smashed their houses. At the end of November the Pudong strikes collapsed, ending the first wave of union action among unskilled workers in Shanghai.

In a very short time two things had happened. First, workers in different industries, crowded together in the Pudong slums, had moved from individual strikes to coordinated solidarity action. This was something different from a general strike in support of shopkeepers, students and the 'nation', and it produced a violent reaction. No amount of cock's-blood wine and incense could keep the gangsters on board once they realised the unions were acting for the workers' wider interests, rather than just providing a bargaining tool for the gang's position in the enterprise. Second, the Kuomintang had shown that it too could organise workers, and it did not need communists to do so. This would produce a new tactic in the international communist movement which, as we will see later, backfired.

In any case, for now the lid was slammed shut on the strike movement when a warlord called Wu Pei-fu had 35 leaders of a railway strike in central China publicly beheaded. Across the country workers realised they were powerless in the face of the warlords' armies and the unions melted away. After the railway massacre, wrote one communist leader in Shanghai, 'nothing remained except a tiny group of printers and mechanics joined by a handful of shop clerks'.[19] It was a graphic reminder to both nationalists and communists, vying with each to build the new China, that the old China was still the main problem.

30 May 1925: On 30 May 1925 a British police inspector named Everson, finding his men surrounded by an angry crowd of Chinese students, drew his pistol and, at point blank range, gave the order to shoot. 'Blood and flesh flew in all directions, the scene was so appalling that people could not bear to look at it. The crowd scattered in confusion.'[20] Twelve were killed and seventeen injured. Everson's report on the incident noted that 'traffic became normal shortly afterwards' but he had set off a movement that within two years was to result in something highly abnormal: a workers' revolution in Shanghai.

The May Thirtieth Movement had its roots in the growing resentment of Chinese workers over their treatment by foreign managers, in particular the Japanese. The Nagai Wata Kaisha company operated 11 cotton mills in Shanghai. In February 1925 the workers struck and formed a union whose banner read 'Oppose Japanese Beating People'. This spread to nearby workplaces, including Japanese-owned silk factories and led to violence. The cotton spinners issued a leaflet: 'They often call us "worthless" and "slaves without a country".' The women silk workers' appeal said,

> Regardless of the fact that every day we work 12 hours, Japanese foremen still strike us with fists and sticks . . . The Japanese treat us as if we were cows and horses, our living quarters are worse than cattle stalls or stables . . . We ask you, where is China's national sovereignty now?[21]

What had in 1919 been an uprising against China's general weakness in the face of colonial power now became a concrete hatred of colonialism as personified by Japanese managers. Men threw away their factory headgear saying, 'We refuse to wear East Asian caps!' Japanese goods were boycotted.

Then Japanese foremen at one NWK plant shot dead a union picket. Strikes spread; nationalist sentiment ran high. News of the killing was suppressed in the Shanghai papers, prompting students to call a day of leafleting and public speeches inside the concession areas on 30 May. It was when they refused to disperse that Inspector Everson and his men opened fire.

In response to the massacre on 30 May both the nationalists and communists called for a triple stoppage in the city. The next day more than 200,000 workers downed tools, double the number in 1919. This time the strike was concentrated in foreign factories and on the docks, and was supported by the middle class and even Chinese factory owners. The 'working section of society' was no longer the rearguard in the anti-colonial struggle – it was leading it.

Now a new force emerged: the General Labour Union, hastily launched by the communists the day after the massacre. Within a month 117 unions had affiliated to the GLU, representing, it claimed with a precision born of exhilaration, 218,859 members.

The general strike against the colonial powers lasted for more than two months. Twenty-two gunboats, thousands of foreign troops and strike-breakers failed to make a dent in it; only by cutting the electricity supply did the British eventually force the Chinese factory owners to withdraw support. On 30 September the last of the cotton strikers marched back to work, flags flying, to the accompaniment of a brass band.

The GLU, though banned once the strike ended, had emerged as the first permanent independent workers' organisation. It had eclipsed the nationalist trade unions as the main organising body for Shanghai workers. The Communist Party, which had taken four years to grow from 57 members to 980, had 10,000 members by the end of 1925. Its anti-capitalist agenda had won it a small circle of working class adherents; the anti-colonial struggle was to quickly turn it into a mass force.

In June 1926 the GLU was ready to organise in the last bastion of nationalist trade unionism, the silk-reeling factories. Mu had ordered the women workers to stay at work during the general strike; now 25,000 went on strike against the extortionate dues she was levying. Mu's response to such insolence was swift, as the main communist women's organiser remembers:

> Mu Zhi-ying, wearing a white silk dress and clutching a leather pocketbook, rode by automobile with several factory forewomen to all the districts of women workers to admonish the women to return to work unconditionally. At first the workers were very surprised by this sight, mistaking her for a factory owner's wife. But when they heard Mu Zhi-ying harshly demand to see the strike leaders, they realised she was a scab. In unison they replied, 'We are all leaders! Down with the scab!'[22]

When it touched the world of the women silk workers, the labour movement had reached the lowest layer of the Shanghai workforce. It was now, in effect, in conflict with the old village culture that the first generation of workers had brought with them.

> Those brave and ardent young women workers who energetically supported the strike want to extricate themselves from the bonds of the family and march forward. But in the end they have to go home. I heard that some who returned after the strike were beaten and humiliated by their parents, brothers and sisters-in-law. They were refused food . . . The parents of another woman gave her a rope and a knife and told her to choose. Poor women workers. They don't sleep or eat well during a strike and then they have to go onto a tragic stage.[23]

The May Thirtieth Movement could have been the start of a strong labour movement across China focused on economic questions and independent of the Kuomintang. But for the Communist Party this was no longer mainly an economic struggle; it was a national struggle in which the Kuomintang was supposed to be an ally. In fact, on Moscow's insistence, the communists were supposed to be members of the Kuomintang.

★   ★   ★

'**The Soviet system cannot be adopted in China . . .**': While
the communists had been teaching Chinese workers to organise inde-
pendently of their Kuomintang foremen, a quite separate process of
collaboration at the international level was going on between the
Kuomintang and Moscow. The Soviet Union was the first state to
recognise Sun Yat-sen's rebel government in south China. In 1923
Adolf Joffe, a veteran of the Russian Revolution, signed a common
declaration with the nationalist leader:

> Dr Sun Yat-sen believes that the Communist organisation and the
> Soviet system cannot be adopted in China since China does not
> have the conditions to make this adoption a success. Mr Joffe
> completely agrees with this analysis.[24]

This was a complication the Lancashire cotton workers never had to
contend with – a disciplined international organisation with precise
views on what their unions could and could not do. Even the German
communists, who were getting the lion's share of instructions from
Moscow at the time, had traditions and leaders strong enough to argue
back. But the Chinese workers were about to become the first such
group in history to see their labour movement moulded under micro-
management from Moscow.

As part of the deal with Joffe, the Kuomintang was reorganised as a
political party modelled on the Bolsheviks, with commissars, uniforms
and tight discipline. The USSR brought the military leaders of the
Kuomintang to Moscow to be trained, and set up a military academy
in southern China. One of those trained was Chiang Kai-shek, the son
of a salt merchant and the Kuomintang's rising star. By 1924 the communists and the nationalists were ready not just for a formal alliance;
Moscow instructed party members to join the Kuomintang en masse.
China, it had been decided, must have its national revolution first. The
workers should concentrate on strengthening their own organisations
and support the Kuomintang against the warlords and the colonial powers.

To understand why this strategy looked sensible, you have to see it
in the context not of Shanghai but of the rest of China. The entire
urban working class of 4 million was at this point just 1 per cent of

the population. The rest were peasants. Moreover there was not much of a Chinese capitalist class outside the cities; in the countryside it was the anti-warlord struggle that animated the poor, not anti-capitalism.

Tsai Shu-fan was a miner in Wuhan 400 miles up the Yangtse river from Shanghai. He learned to read at a workers' club organised by a young communist agitator called Mao Tse-tung. By 1922, at the age of fourteen, he was a strike activist.

> Only the young boys joined in strike, the old men being more
> conservative. All the young men were radical and stood as pickets
> to keep the old men away from the mine . . . Luckily we persuaded
> the men in charge of pulling the whistle to go on strike, and as no
> siren ordered the men to work, nobody went![25]

Some 200 miles south, in Changsha, a teenage railway worker called Wang Cheng saw the May Thirtieth Movement spark the workers into action there: 'I had been a picket for the union during the [30 May] strike. When it was successful we were all surprised. Every worker felt happy to discover the new power of organised labour.'[26] But for both Tsai and Wang the world was about to get more complicated: the Kuomintang was about to advance against the warlords and they stood in the path of the advance.

In 1926 Chiang Kai-shek launched the so-called Northern Expedition, a military offensive into central China aimed at smashing the warlords, unifying China and then, from a strengthened position, resisting the colonialists. As far as the rest of the world was concerned, the Northern Expedition *was* the Chinese Revolution, a war of manoeuvre led by a Moscow-trained general aided by communist workers in the cities. And as far as the mass of Chinese people were concerned, the Kuomintang and the Communist Party were inter-changeable. 'I joined the Kuomintang in 1925, and when only sixteen was elected a member of the Changsha branch of the General Labour Union,' reports Wang Cheng.

> When the Northern Expedition began . . . all the workers eagerly
> supported the armies. Our economic conditions were much

improved, we had our union, and we felt that in working for the Kuomintang we were working for ourselves.[27]

All across China, in anticipation of the Kuomintang army's advance, unions sprung up 'like mushrooms after rain'. In Shanghai the workers began to prepare themselves to be liberated. But it was not to be so simple. Sun Yat-sen had died in 1925, provoking a split in the Kuomintang leadership into left and right wing factions. Chiang Kai-shek headed the right-wing faction, and in his home base of Guangdong threw the communist trade union leaders into jail.

A map of the Kuomintang military campaign would show three arrows pointing northward. The most inland axis of advance was led by the left-leaning generals of the Kuomintang. Chiang Kai-shek, meanwhile, led the march through the central and coastal provinces. Railwayman Wang and miner Tsai were lucky enough to be in the path of the left-wing arrow, where for now things went as planned. After Changsha was liberated, remembers Wang, 'We ourselves took charge of the railway and of all communications to support the army.' Where the Kuomintang's left-wing generals were in control, communist workers slotted in behind them as the rank and file. Wang found himself running a 'training class for labor leaders' in Changsha.

> . . . though I had only three years of primary school as a child and could barely read or write. This class was held for four months under the name of the Kuomintang but it was really directed by the Communist Party.[28]

By the end of 1926, Wang remembers, 'all the Changsha workers supported the Communists'. The Kuomintang government was transferred to Wuhan and in the area under nationalist control several new public holidays were announced, including May Day and 18 March, the anniversary of the Paris Commune.

But for the central and coastal prongs of the campaign, where Chiang Kai-shek was in control, things looked ominous. Everywhere his troops arrived they tried to suppress trade unions. And he was headed directly for Shanghai. At this point Jan Valtin re-enters the story. After escaping from the catastrophic rising in Hamburg in 1923 and spending two years in an American jail, this perpetual adventurer was ordered to Shanghai by his Moscow controllers. His mission was to help disrupt the foreign navies and prevent them from opposing the Kuomintang army when it arrived.

> We were blissfully unaware of our own grotesque audacity. Our combined force consisted of a score of assorted communists, including a handful of Japanese and two Scandinavians lusting for adventure. Equipped with a portable printing machine and a weekly allowance totalling a hundred Shanghai dollars we set out to 'pull the teeth' of the combined navies of Britain, France, Japan and America on the lower Yangtsekiang.[29]

Valtin's Chinese agitators worked as rickshaw pullers and 'plied every arriving bluejacket with tracts containing incitements to disobedience and mutiny'. They recruited some Chinese prostitutes to give the leaflets out, but these were sabotaged by émigré Russian prostitutes, who reported them to their pimps, and in the end Valtin had to go into the bars and engage the Western sailors direct. 'They resented our instructions unless we first invited them to a drink. For that, however, we lacked the money.' After three weeks of this his communist bosses shipped Valtin out of Shanghai. They had bigger guns to deploy . . .

At 4 a.m. one spring morning in Changsha, the communists called their supporters to the railway station to hear a delegation of foreign union leaders. Wang the railwayman does not mention it in his brief life story, but given his importance in the movement he must have been there in the crowd. One of the speakers remembered:

> Hundreds of peasant eyes peering through the night, in the dim reflection of a gaslight that was blown out occasionally by the strong gust of wind and rain, followed every word and gesture of the speaker. There were the bronze faces of men who still till the soil that is not theirs; there were the faces of railwaymen and others who had gone through and fought many a battle against butchers

like Wu Pei-fu. As I left the improvised tribune to return to the train, piercing cries filled the air. Long Live the International Workers Delegation. Long live the unity of the workers of the West with the oppressed peoples of the East! Long live the Chinese revolution![30]

The speaker was Tom Mann. At the age of 71 the veteran syndicalist, whose life as an agitator had taken him from the London docks to the Australian outback, had volunteered to go to China as part of a three-man delegation from the communist trade union international. Mann had become a communist in the early 1920s. Now this inveterate traveller was there to see first hand what was going on. Arriving in the city of Ganzhou, however, he sensed danger. A local trade union leader called Chen had been killed by Chiang Kai-shek's agents. Mann noted, 'Several more union officials were threatened with the fate of Chen and had been hiding since. The trade unions were holding their meetings secretly, all premises being occupied by troops.'[31] But Mann was by now either trapped in, or complicit with, a political machine that could see no evil in the Kuomintang. The delegation was able to send daily reports to left-wing papers in Europe and America. One official bulletin from late March 1927 read,

> Now that we are on the eve of taking Nanking and Shanghai, the imperialists are issuing reports about the so-called splitting tendencies within the Kuomintang . . . far from dividing, as the imperialists say, the Kuomintang has only tightened its ranks.[32]

April 1927: By the autumn of 1926 Shanghai had become once again a city of strikes and other industrial action. The communist-backed General Labour Union, though still banned, was able to conduct an effective campaign over wages and conditions. There were prolonged go-slows – a tactic that had been impossible when industrial action was organised through the gangs and foremen. But it was this very strength in the economic sphere that had begun to alter the balance of power within Chinese nationalism. The Chinese employers, who had shelled out hundreds of thousands of dollars in strike pay during the May Thirtieth Movement, now feared that the communist-led union was out of control. The British and French colonialists, tired of warlordism and not happy about their sailors being importuned by communist-minded prostitutes, saw Chiang as a man they could do business with. And the gangs decided that they too could do business with Chiang. The 'splitting tendencies' within the Kuomintang were all too real.

In October 1926 the communists in Shanghai launched an uprising timed to take advantage of infighting between local warlords and intended to open a new front for Chiang's army. It failed abysmally. A second uprising, in February 1927, was a more professional effort, but again the warlord armies moved decisively to put it down. At the main crossroads the heads of twenty strikers were placed on poles, while another 300 union organisers were arrested.

Undaunted, the GLU once more marshalled its forces. It printed leaflets outlining its highly moderate objectives – evict the warlords, an autonomous government for Shanghai, civil liberties and import controls. It recruited pickets and issued them with small white badges which they were ordered to keep at work and show to no one. On 20 March, with Chiang's forces advancing towards Shanghai, the GLU organised a secret meeting of 300 delegates from organisations loyal to the Kuomintang to appoint what was to become the Provisional Municipal Government.

The next day, with Chiang's reconnaissance troops on the outskirts of the city, the GLU announced a general strike and the third armed uprising began. By the afternoon 800,000 workers were on strike. At the British American Tobacco factory in Pudong, at precisely 1.35 p.m.

> . . . we shut off our machines. Shortly thereafter workers from the Rihua cotton mill, the Xiansheng ironworks and the Little Nanyang tobacco factory rushed into our workshop shouting, 'Comrades, those of you with badges please show them' . . . Now I pulled out my badge, pinned it on, and followed everyone out. Exiting by the gate for male workers we came to the third district police office.

Greatly frightened, the police handed over the guns to us . . . After arming ourselves we marched in rows – just like soldiers. We took shifts standing guard, replacing the police in maintaining public order.[33]

Five thousand pickets took over strategic points in the city and only in the northern industrial suburb of Zhabei did the warlord army manage to hold out, killing 200 workers. Chiang's strategy, like Stalin's at Warsaw in 1944, was to hold back and let the uprising be defeated, thereby ensuring total control for the invading army later. However, this misfired when the lead division of the Kuomintang army disobeyed orders and joined in the fighting at Zhabei. By nightfall on 22 March Shanghai was under the control of communist trade unions and Chiang's spearhead division was fraternising with the workers.

As planned, the union then ordered the strikers back to work and handed authority to the Provisional Government, which in its turn agreed to implement the limited economic programme the union had drawn up. The union busied itself mopping up the hundreds of new workplace groups that had been formed during the uprising. By the end of March the GLU claimed 821,282 members, roughly half the total population of Shanghai.[34]

A trade union is designed primarily to conduct relations between two sets of people, workers and employers. It can, at a pinch, stretch to organising an armed insurrection. What it is not designed to do is navigate the choppy and uncharted waters of a nationalist revolution, where war is raging across thousands of miles of countryside and the so-called liberating army is about to change sides. But a communist party *is* designed for just such a situation. It is the self-styled leadership of the working class and it comes, by 1927, armed with manuals about street fighting and a network of secret agents. Revolutionary war is supposed to be its element.

The story of how communist activists warned about Chiang and were overruled by Moscow has been told in detail by historians; the row was to be the catalyst for expulsions and crackdowns within communist parties across the globe.[35] On the eve of disaster, the official bulletin revealed that Moscow was in a state of denial:'A split in the Kuomintang and hostilities between the Shanghai proletariat and the revolutionary soldiers are absolutely precluded right now.'[36]

At 2 a.m. on 12 April 1927 groups of men wearing uniforms bearing the Chinese character 'labour' attacked the GLU's picket lines across the city. They were members of the Green Gang armed with 5,000 rifles supplied by the authorities in the French Concession, and they were acting on the orders of Chiang Kai-shek. The gangsters seized the GLU headquarters and handed the building over to a new union set up by Chiang, whose stance was outlined in an official statement: 'When labour leaders become a disturbing element, when they arrogate to themselves tasks that are detrimental to the movement and disruptive of law and order, labour must be disciplined.'[37] Everyone found in GLU headquarters that night was lined up and shot.

Immediately the communists called for a general strike against Chiang's coup, and 100,000 stopped work, paralysing the docks, the trams and about half the cotton mills. On 13 April a mass demonstration marched out of the mill district of Zhabei. Chiang's soldiers opened fire, pursuing the workers into their tenements with bayonets. Three hundred were killed and many more wounded. Despite the fierce repression, the general strike lasted until 13 May, with the *North China Herald* reporting 111,000 on strike even then. But it was not the rank and file Chiang was after, it was the communists. Over the next few weeks an estimated 5,000 Communist Party sympathisers were executed; by the year's end the death toll stood at 30,000 – a revolver in the mouth for the lucky ones, ceremonial beheading for the rest. This was what Chiang meant by 'labour must be disciplined'.

Among the victims was Li Qi-han; he was caught in a round-up in Canton on 15 April and executed. Tom Mann would report back to British trade union activists later that year, 'In some cases, as we have seen, the reactionaries gradually got their forces together and tried once more to set back the tide. In several places they succeeded, at least temporarily. We must not expect that revolution in China can be fought and won in a few months.'[38] In this speech, printed and circulated in thousands of copies, he made no mention of the Shanghai massacre. Jan Valtin, who was in a position to see the intelligence, was more frank: 'In the mass slaughter of communists which followed Chiang Kai-shek's break with Moscow in 1927, nearly all the Chinese comrades I worked with in Shanghai perished.'[39]

Spectators to a revolution: Chiang Kai-shek's coup was not the end of the Shanghai workers' movement; the Kuomintang-led unions, while effectively controlled by the gangsters, did organise strikes over bread-and-butter issues in the 1930s. But, more importantly, nor was it the end of the communists – though it might easily have been. In a series of kamikaze uprisings against the Kuomintang elsewhere they managed to destroy their presence in the cities. Amid the chaos Wang Cheng the railwayman fled Changsha and ended up in the army of a Kuomintang general in which 'communists were executed every day'. Eventually his squad deserted.

> We saw handbills and slogans of the secret party organisation, and thus knew there was one nearby. My men hid in the long reeds of the river bank while I went out to find a peasant to talk with. This peasant helped me find the Red Vanguards . . .[40]

He had stumbled on the communist guerrilla forces led by Mao Tse-tung. By the early 1930s, with Mao in command, the communists had discovered a route to power that bypassed not just Shanghai but the Chinese working class itself. In the legendary Long March they fought a peasant war against the warlords, the Japanese army and, in a final showdown, the Kuomintang itself. Both Wang and the miner Tsai took part in the Long March; laid-off miners formed the core of Mao's army in the early years. Both men were senior commanders by the time Mao took power in 1949. Tsai would recall: 'You ask what broke the labour movement in China? [The leaders] didn't believe in the power of the unions. The Chinese Communist Party was afraid of breaking the united front with the Kuomintang.'[41]

The workers of Shanghai played only an auxiliary role in the revolution that brought Mao to power in 1949. Lancashire cotton workers would remain actors in their own destiny for two centuries after Peterloo but the workers of Shanghai were to lose the freedom they enjoyed in the years 1919–27. They have not regained it yet.

8. Heaven and earth will hear us
Jewish workers fight for cultural freedom

> Heaven and earth will hear us,
> The light stars will bear witness.
> An oath of blood, an oath of tears,
> We swear, we swear, we swear!
>
> Semyon An-sky 'The Oath', 1902

El Alto, Bolivia, 2006

The crowd is silent; the eyes of the women tighten against the bright-
ness of the sky. Below, the capital city of La Paz looks unfeasibly small
and distant, like a swimming pool does from the edge of a diving
board. The Federation of Working Class Street Sellers unfurls its banner
across the road, with a picture of Che Guevara and the slogan 'Science,
Unity, Politics, Economics'. The women line up behind it in their
traditional Aymara finery – bowler hats worn at sharp angles, gold
earrings, bright tartan shawls. An old man shoots two fireworks in the
air and the demonstration moves off: three columns, single file. El Alto
is on the move.

El Alto is a city of just under a million, 80 per cent Aymara. Its
low brick buildings and tin roofs stretch as far as you can see across
the plain above La Paz. It is a do-it-yourself city built from nothing
over the last 20 years by peasants as they migrated off the land. When
the price of tin collapsed, tens of thousands of ex-miners joined
them. Although they are a majority of the Bolivian population the
indigenous peoples – Aymara, Quechua, Guarani – suffer levels of
poverty and exclusion that mirror those found under apartheid. The
government could not provide water, health or education in El Alto
so they did that themselves too. The typical El Alto shop sells bricks,

pipes, wire, steel rods, paint and plaster; the typical El Alto sound is somebody tapping a window frame into place in the cool evening sunlight.

El Alto's claim to fame is that it has overthrown two Bolivian governments. It surrounds the airport and hugs the main road that links La Paz with the rest of Bolivia, so when El Alto stages a roadblock, La Paz is paralysed. That's how it was in October 2003. The police had fired on a roadblock in an Aymara village, killing eight, so the unions called a general strike. Martial law was declared in El Alto bringing deep-seated grievances rushing to the surface. Eliodoro Iquiapaza says,

> First they privatised everything, saying it would attract new money and create new jobs. But instead there was more unemployment. They promised that Bolivia would have a very strong economic development, but all we got was a worse crisis than before, when the firms were in Bolivian hands.

Iquiapaza is the acting president of Fejuve, the Federation of Neighbourhood Committees in El Alto. These neighbourhood committees grew because local services were inadequate and chaotic; even now, he tells me, two of the nine districts here have no water. Fejuve acts as an alternative local government in the city but is also a highly effective campaigning network; it can grant you permission for a drain or summon you to an uprising. El Alto society is resilient because the Aymara have brought their social networks and customs here, and have not yet lost them. Traditionally they make decisions by consensus and, once taken, compliance is obligatory.

In October 2003, says Iquiapaza, they decided to paralyse Bolivia.

> If you don't give information to the people, they stay quiet. But once the truth is revealed, they revolt. In 2003 they were trying to defend their lives. More than 60 people died. And more than 400 are wounded, mutilated and can't work – adolescents, old people, men, women and children among them.

It was the shootings that turned revolt into revolution. After six days of running battles, house-to-house searches, fuel shortages and explosions, President Sanchez de Lozada left town in a helicopter and headed for the USA. After eighteen months of a technocratic government there was another uprising and, in January 2006, El Alto got its own man into power. Evo Morales nationalised Bolivia's gas industry on May Day 2006 but many in El Alto think that is just the start.

Abram Delgado leads the Movement of the Youth of October – as in the October of the 2003 revolt. I meet him at El Alto's Public University and he points out where they piled the bricks and stored the petrol bombs during the uprisings. 'The second time we were more coordinated because we used mobile phones,' he says. They had to fight to have their own university and for their degrees to be recognised. With its half-built roads and unpainted breeze block class-rooms, the whole university looks like it's been in a fight.

> At night we went to the oil and gas refineries in the south of the city. We organised blockades so that nothing could enter or leave La Paz. We had a confrontation with the police and almost got caught, but we managed to escape. Afterwards, we linked up with the peasants' movement, the indigenous and social movements. We coordinated with our people to use explosives . . .

Almost out of nowhere the people of El Alto introduced the world to a new version of working class republicanism, the fusion of 'social justice' demands with an intense desire for equality among Bolivia's indigenous community. The Che banners, which are everywhere, symbolise this. Ironically, this fusion of socialism and indigenism is what Che Guevara originally wanted to achieve – only he expected it to happen in the countryside, not amid dual carriageways teeming with ghetto-fabulous Aymara youth. Abram Delgado wants a deeper change – the '*ayllu* economy'.

*Ayllu*s are traditional social networks in the indigenous villages of Bolivia, horizontal economies based on kinship, communal property and the exchange of labour. They date from before the Incas and Delgado is deadly serious when he tells me he wants a 'return to the way it was before the Spanish came':

We don't mean by that that we want to go back to the situation that was lived at that moment. What we propose is that we should get back and rebuild the institutions that existed at that time. The *ayllu* is a social community system which functions in a rotational and circular way. It is not linear and hierarchical such as the capitalist or communist systems, where there is still a boss whether you like it or not.

Until Delgado and his comrades launched their uprising only anthropologists were interested in *ayllu*s; now all those interested in the politics of Latin America's most volatile city must learn about them. It is entirely possible that someone here will go beyond the traditional leftism of Morales's government and try to make an 'urban *ayllu*' a reality.

At the Public University, the first generation of Aymara women to reject the bowler hat and shawl is being educated but the Aymara language, in contrast, is going through a renaissance here. 'More people are speaking it since Evo came to power,' Delgado tells me. No one on the streets of El Alto believes that nationalising the oil and gas means the end of the revolution. Some, like Delgado, speak of the Pachakuti, the cosmic deluge of Inca mythology:

It is not over; the great Pachakuti is still to come. It started in 2000 with the social movements, blockades, marches, hunger strikes, social turmoil. To me, Evo Morales is a person who will open doors but who will also say, 'If I can't do it, there needs to be someone else to be able to make the transformation.' The Indian revolution is near but has not arrived yet.

It is this mixture of ethnic nationalism and radical socialism that the Bolivian elite – descended mainly from the Spanish colonialists – fears most. However, for all that it is lionised within the anti-globalisation movement, El Alto's resistance movement is also insular, localist and petty-bureaucratic. The Fejuve headquarters is a world of mobile phones alongside manual typewriters; the activists here can have instant verbal communication with their neighbours but, politically, it feels hugely distant from the outside world.

Ethnic oppression has combined with poverty and resistance to create a new identity for the people of El Alto. They have new dreams too – fantastic plans to build the world afresh as if capitalism and communism had never happened. For all its poverty and squalor, the city seems like the nearest place on earth to the 'world within a world' the workers' movement strived for in the early 20th century. There have been places like this before, and idealistic youth with not-dissimilar dreams of cultural freedom, but they did not survive.

Brzeziny, Poland

It is a small town in Europe between the wars. There are a handful of warehouses, a collection of workshops and grocery stores; from the railway station come newspapers and socialist lecturers. There have been strikes here, but they did not exactly shake the world. The cobbled streets clatter with the sound of horse-drawn carts and children skipping. The town was once famous locally for its garment industry but is now, on the surface, nondescript – typical of the towns people lived in during the decades when the workers' movement was at its height.

Yet Brzeziny is a town about which we know almost everything. We know not only how many tailor's shops there were but the names of the tailors. We know the names of the hooligans who had to be reined in so that the trade union movement could go about its business. We know what people argued about at work, what songs they sang, the names of the generous employers and of the mean ones. We know what street the first May Day procession went down, on 1 May 1928, the name of the man who carried the flag and that he remembered, 'The flag was so heavy – and the wind made it even heavier – that to this day, I feel its weight.'

We know so much about this ordinary town for an extraordinary reason: it was destroyed by the Nazis. First the Gestapo told the Jewish community leaders to choose ten hostages, then they hanged them. They rounded up every Jewish child and sent them to be gassed.

Neither crying, nor begging, nor asking for mercy helped . . . The lament and the wails of the unfortunate parents, while their children were torn from them and taken in trucks to the death camps to be annihilated, was something that words are too inadequate to describe.[1]

That was on 15 May 1942. The next day all the old people were rounded up. Before sending them to the gas chambers the Nazis ordered them to strip naked for a medical examination.

> They packed them all into a small room. Then the German doctors made jokes about our elderly. They pricked and tugged at the breasts of the women and the sexual organs of the men. The behaviour of the doctors was the behavior of loathsome, odious sex maniacs.[2]

Three days later the rest of the population was deported to the Jewish ghetto in the city of Lodz, 13 miles to the west. Most of those who did not die there were murdered in Auschwitz.

The Germans desecrated the cemetery in Brzeziny. They piled up the skulls of people who had once set up theatre groups, bickered about socialism and Zionism and played football on Saturday mornings. But because the Nazis destroyed Brzeziny so completely, the survivors decided to write its history down completely. Thanks to a memorial book compiled in 1961, we have a rare vantage point from which to study the history of the working class: a worm's-eye view of the action from a place that was never at the centre of the action, but typifies it completely.

The Bund arrives in Brzeziny: There was something going on among the apprentice boys in the autumn of 1904. They had started going into the woods together for secret meetings. As they trooped back, the warehouse owners, known as 'magaziners', would joke with them drily, 'How was your day at the office?' A rumour went round that the overthrow of the Russian Tsar was being discussed. 'It did not occur to our magazine owners,' remembers Aaron Fogel, an apprentice tailor, 'that there, at the meeting, they talked more about the magazine owners themselves than they spoke about Tsar Nicholas.'[3]

Brzeziny's garment industry was born in 1886 when a few Jewish craftsmen developed a system based on specialisation: one man sewed the arms of a suit, the next the collar, a third focused on buttonholes, and so on, all of them working at home. In the 1890s a wave of Russian Jews arrived and the town's population doubled to 16,000. The Russians brought with them a three-tier business model: the magaziners would send out batches of pre-cut cloth to a network of master tailors. They, in turn, employed apprentices, journeymen and seamstresses. The norm was to work 18 hours a day – 'the 108-hour week' they called it – beginning at 6 a.m. on Sunday or, for those really short of money, at sundown on Saturday night. David Lencicki remembers life in a typical tailor's shop:

> The apartments . . . consisted of two rooms, both of equal size, approximately four by four metres. The first room, where there was a walled-in stove, was a workshop that had kitchen fixtures. Two to three large machines stood there – to make the work easier and to iron – also a small table for the hand-stitchers and a half dozen stools . . . The second room consisted of: two beds, a wardrobe or two, a table and stools, a sofa, and packets of cut work.[4]

This was a traditional, observant Jewish community; memoirs describe the tailors singing 'cantorial melodies' to each other as they worked. But in the first years of the 20th century Aaron Fogel remembers that 'new winds began to blow'. Pamphlets appeared in the workshops which 'urged one toward a more humane life. In these booklets, it was written that the worker is exactly equal to the work giver.'[5] Another apprentice, Mojsze Frank, recalls that 'some light began to shine little by little':

> A man arrived from Lodz called Baruch Hoyker [literally, 'the hunchback']. He really was a hunchback. He was a very capable and intelligent person. He was sent by the Lodz worker movement, and he actually stayed in Brzezin long enough to organise all the workers. A strike committee with a secretary was appointed. Everyone had to pay twenty-five *kopeks* a week.[6]

One Sunday morning the precise subject of the apprentices' secret meetings became clear.

Everything was ready for work. The charcoal lay near the iron and only waited for the apprentice to come and set fire to it. The machines had been cleaned and oiled; the master had already evenly counted out the work and laid out the packets for the machine workers. The clock stood at six in the morning. The workers did not appear.[7]

The master tailors rushed to the town square, where it became clear that not a single apprentice had turned up for work. After letting off some steam the masters went home, considering the punishment they would inflict on their missing trainees. There they had a second shock:

As the clock stood at eight, all the apprentices and journeymen came to work. They came in a little embarrassed, but with a resolve that they would begin working from eight in the morning until eight at night and no longer. Such a 'revolution' our tailors had not anticipated.[8]

This was how the General Union of Jewish Workers arrived in Brzeziny. Known universally as the Bund, it had been formed by Westernised socialist intellectuals in 1897 to bring Yiddish-speaking Jews into the labour movement. By 1905 things had worked out differently. The intellectuals had embraced Yiddish culture and the Bund had become a movement for Jewish 'cultural national autonomy'. The theory was that the Jewish apprentices of Brzeziny were part of a 5 million-strong nation oppressed by Russian Tsarism and that only a social revolution could set them free. Joseph Shaibowicz witnessed the impact of the Bund on traditional life in the town.

At the beginning of the century, under pressure from the Bund, Jewish workers broke with the old leaders and antiquated traditional patterns and carried out a coup d'état in Jewish life. In 1905 the Bund organised strikes and street fights in Brzeziny.[9]

In response to the trouble, the master tailors formed their own union which, though banned under Tsarist law, was tolerated because of a bribe to local officials and because they hung the Tsar's portrait in their meeting room. The apprentices' movement, known as the United Youth, was also completely illegal. But it could not be stopped:

> A wave of strikes broke out in our town. Our proletarians made new demands. Now they asked for higher wages and also humane treatment of journeymen and even of apprentices. And if they still did not accede to their demands, the workers struck. The machines didn't operate; the cantorial melodies emanating from the workshops stopped. It became more lively outdoors.[10]

It had been lively throughout the Tsarist empire. In January 1905, when thousands of workers in St Petersburg marched to petition the Tsar for a shorter working day, hundreds were shot. The Bloody Sunday massacre set off a wave of strikes and political protest that was to culminate in a general strike and revolution before the year's end.

'An oath of life and death': In truth the young Jews of Brzeziny were up against more than just their local bosses. The defining problem in their lives was a crude system of anti-Semitism run from Moscow. For more than a hundred years Jews had been forced to live within the so-called Pale of Settlement, a band of territory from the Crimea to the Baltic. Forbidden to own land or to practise the professions, they were forced to live in small towns called *shtetls* or in the city slums. They spoke mainly Yiddish, worked in small workshops and developed an urban culture based on self-help and the *kehilla*, the elected religious council that ran every Jewish community.

Most educated people assumed that, as the Russian economy modernised, anti-Semitism – together with the Pale, the *kehilla* and Yiddish itself – would die out. But when industrialisation took off in the 1880s, anti-Semitism intensified. Tsarist police organised crowds of racists to rampage through Jewish areas, killing and maiming at random. Residency laws were tightened and in 1891 the Tsar expelled the Jews from Moscow and St Petersburg. It was this forced migration, of over a million people, that doubled the population of Brzeziny and towns like it. A factory system was growing rapidly in the cities

but Jewish workers were generally excluded. If they worked in factories at all they were the small ones, not the name-brand engineering
plants that became famous during the Russian Revolution.

In the year the Bund was founded, Jews made up 58 per cent of
the urban population in the area that is now Poland, Latvia, Lithuania
and Belarus. 'About 90 per cent of the whole Jewish population . . .
come near to being a proletariat,' wrote the Tsar's official sociologist.[11]

It was this increasing oppression plus growing urbanisation that gave
birth to a new national consciousness. In the same year as the Bund,
the World Zionist Organisation was founded. Its leader Theodore Herzl
argued that, given this upsurge of racist violence, Jews could not survive
within Gentile society and that emigration to a new Jewish state in
Palestine was the only future. Herzl boasted to Europe's rulers that
Zionism was 'taking the Jews away from the revolutionary parties'[12]
and he rejected socialism outright. But in *shtetls* like Brzeziny the spread
of Zionism, necessarily clandestine, contributed to the atmosphere of
subversion and cultural renaissance that the radical movements fed on.

For its part the Bund rejected Zionism as an ideology and emigration as a strategy. Its slogan was 'Our Home is Here'. It called for legal
equality, recognition of Yiddish as an official language in schools and
the legal system, and advocated cultural national autonomy – the right
to a separate Jewish parliament which could tax the Jewish population and provide education, culture and community services in Yiddish.
And while the Zionists remained uneasy about the secular lifestyle
spreading among young Jews, the Bund, as orthodox Marxists, revelled
in it.

In 1902 the writer Semyon An-sky wrote a poem in Yiddish called
'Di Shvue' ('The Oath'). Set to music, it became the Bund's anthem
and was once heard as widely on workers' demonstrations as the 'Red
Flag' or the 'Internationale'. Musically, it is a masterpiece of synthesis:
the verse follows the rhythm and melody of the classic Russian workers'
song, a dogged march in a gloomy minor key, but the chorus, which
begins 'Heaven and earth will hear us', takes the singer to a different
world – the Yiddish folk song, whose harmonies only resonate properly on the accordion – and into the high tenor range of the synagogue

cantor. The symbolism cannot have been lost on the young men and women who gathered in small meetings to sing it, secretly, in the run-up to 1905. 'The Oath' was, like the Bund itself, a fusion of socialism, internationalism and Jewish culture; it was poetry to slake their thirst for fanaticism, and its last verse held out a promise of martyrdom that would soon be fulfilled.

> We swear an endless loyalty to the Bund.
> Only it can free the slaves now.
> The red flag is high and wide.
> It waves in anger, it is red with blood!
> Swear an oath of life and death![13]

'The word of the Bund was law . . .': In the five days following the Bloody Sunday massacre in St Petersburg, hundreds of thousands of workers went on strike in the western cities of the Tsarist empire. The province around Lodz, which included Brzeziny, was the centre of the action: 650 workplaces were shut, and an estimated 100,000 struck. But as soon as the initial convulsion was over, with the Tsar announcing various minor concessions, anti-Jewish pogroms began in retaliation. The Bund ordered its members to commandeer weapons from police stations and set up armed self-defence groups. Battles raged on the streets of Warsaw and Lodz. Even in tiny Brzeziny, 'the socialists among us . . . began to promote fighting gangs, which had to be the protection brigade for Jews, to help when needed to repulse attacks by hooligans'.[14]

The figurehead for the Brzeziny Bund militia, which dressed in black with leather belts, was a master tailor called Blind Chone but its real leader was the hunchback Baruch Hoyker, who spent much of the time in hiding. Quickly the Bund became the civil power within the town, a phenomenon repeated across Poland according to one of its leaders:

> It was regarded as some kind of mystical being, with fear and hope.
> It could achieve everything, reach everyone . . . The word of the

Bund was law; its stamp worked like hypnosis. Wherever an injustice, whenever an insult, even when it had no relation to the workers' movement . . . one came to the Bund as the highest tribunal.[15]

For the apprentices of Brzeziny, this brief taste of control was an opportunity to change things not just in the workplace but in their daily lives as well.

For the time being, the power in the town was completely with the United Youth. People whispered to each other that not only did they not care about the rules of those in power, but also they started rebelling at Jewish customs. They did not pray any more . . . and smoked cigarettes even on Sabbath. This last act nobody had actually seen, but, how do we say it, 'Walls have ears'.[16]

In the summer of 1905, while the national situation teetered on the brink of revolution, Aaron Fogel remembers standing in a crowd of devout Jews praying at the Brzeziny cemetery when the United Youth arrived in their black shirts, led by Baruch Hoyker. The faithful were forced to listen to a stern revolutionary lecture.

'Comrades, you see here all the gravestones; they who lie there under the stones, they were once people like all of us. Now nothing of them remains but the stone. Be assured that in our time the same thing will happen to the Russian bureaucracy – with one difference – that from them not even a stone will remain.'[17]

With red flags flying, the militia would march through the streets belting out 'The Oath'. Even the local police chief stood to attention as they passed. But while Lodz was in the grip of bitter struggles between factory workers and their bosses, Brzeziny witnessed a realignment in industrial relations as the master tailors came over to the Bund.

A closer contact developed between workers and masters. The masters had learned a lot, and they themselves were well organised. The masters carefully thought over every worker demand in their small prayer house, and, if it was accepted, they turned to the magazine owners with new demands.[18]

In October 1905, faced with a general strike, it seemed for a moment that the edifice of Tsarism was indeed about to shatter. The Tsar promised to become a constitutional monarch, hold elections and even to legalise moderate political parties. But at the same time he moved to crush the workers' councils that had been formed in the major cities and the pogrom gangs were revved up to persecute Jews. Brzeziny did not escape.

> On the second day, about forty tailors were arrested. There were rumors that certain magaziners let the police authorities know who the revolutionaries were, so that those arrested would be exiled to Piotrków – where they indeed were banished. This provoked an absolute fury among the workers – the wives of those arrested broke almost all the windowpanes at the magaziners in retaliation.[19]

Baruch Hoyker was hunted down and 'mercilessly tormented'. The apprentice Mojsze Frank was warned by his master to go into hiding once the strike ended.

> When I was at home a week, a letter arrived at my parents saying that I should not dare to return to Brzezin, because they had arrested all the workers. Cossacks had gone through all the homes in which it was known just that someone who had helped carry out the strike was living there. One certainly could no longer talk about going back to Brzezin.[20]

A witness who brought news to apprentices hiding in an Orthodox Jewish school told them, 'I ran away from the town barely alive. It is darkness. Jews attack Jews. My eyes should never see again what I saw, what they did to the United Youth.'[21]

The story was the same across Russia, for the Bund and the rest of the labour movement. At this point the Bund had a membership of more than 25,000 and influence over millions. If you flick through the pages of the photographic history published in the 1950s by Bund veterans in New York you can see how things suddenly changed. Before 1905 the book is mainly group shots of middle class people in collars; straw boaters and crinolines dominate; there is even the classic Edwardian device of posing two men horizontally, on their elbows, at the front. In 1905 there are still group shots, but they are of large groups and of gruffer individuals. Usually they are standing in the snow, holding revolvers across their chests, and are sometimes in uniform – and instead of dreamily posed young fellows at the front, there are often the bodies of those killed in that day's pogrom, draped with flags.

By 1905 the Bund had become the mass party of the Jewish working class in Poland and the rest of the Russian empire. By 1910, under severe repression, it had shrunk to just 609 members. Many of its activists, including some of the Brzeziny writers quoted here, emigrated to the Americas. But the Bund was already a legend in the *shtetl*s and slums of Eastern Europe.

1918–39: As the First World War ended, the geopolitics of Europe were changing dramatically, shrinking the world in which the Bund would operate and altering its political dynamics: Russia had become a workers' republic; Poland had won its national independence; the retreating German army was about to stage a revolution of its own. Added to this, Britain had promised the Jews a homeland in Palestine. The Bund's strategy of cultural autonomy within the Tsarist empire was now a dead letter while winning any kind of cultural freedom in the new Poland would be a challenging task, as proved by the three days of pogroms that accompanied its creation. Meanwhile the way to Palestine was opening up, strengthening the arguments of Zionist leaders and giving fresh impetus to a 'labour Zionist' movement which would grow to rival the Bund. Plus, the Bund itself had been diminished: its members to the east had disappeared into the political chaos of Soviet Russia. Having styled itself an international movement the Bund was now effectively just a party in Poland and the Baltic states.

In November 1918, on the day the war ended, a left-wing provisional government was set up in Warsaw and workers' councils formed in Lodz, Warsaw and Lublin to support it. Abraham Abramowicz, a union activist in Brzeziny, remembers that this 'reverberated like a flash' in the town.

On the day when workers took over the management of the town, the workers' council had before it a very serious question about providing food for the hard-suffering, hungry inhabitants. The workers' committee issued orders to a number of magaziners the first day, to others the next day, and so on, continuously, to prepare meals for groups of fifteen, twenty, or more workers. So it continued for the short time of the life of the workers' council.[22]

But the councils were talking shops and by mid-1919 were disbanded. The new government was powerless to stop a wave of anti-Semitic riots, with the new Polish armed forces and police repeatedly involved in murders, beatings and economic boycotts of the Jews.

For the next two decades, the Jewish workers' movement found itself trapped within a state being fought over by two political factions: the right-wing anti-Semites of the 'Endeks' party and the right-wing militarists led by socialist-turned-nationalist Josef Pilsudski. 'Brzeziny, between the world wars, was like a two-sided coin,' remembers Abe Rosenberg. 'On one side, the blooming of a community, secular life, elementary education for children, libraries, lectures, cinema, and theater-performances – on the other side, economic decline and hopelessness.'[23] The First World War had ruined Brzeziny's tailoring business. The magazine owners had gone east with the retreating Russians while many tailors sold their sewing machines to avoid starvation. Work remained scarce until 1923.

The Bund was not the only Jewish workers' party in the town. Some of its members had split off to form a branch of the Polish Communist Party's Jewish Section. In addition there was a strong branch of the labour Zionist movement, Poale Zion (PZ). Its ideology was a mixture of Marxism and Zionism: it advocated the creation of a Jewish state in Palestine as a means to the higher goal of unleashing a 'normal' class struggle within the Jewish nation. It organised migration to Palestine and set up the first kibbutz there. In 1920 PZ split into left and right wings. The Left PZ wanted a Yiddish-speaking Soviet Palestine with Arabs and Jews as equals, in which Jews could become train drivers and steelworkers instead of tailors and cobblers.

This vision, which with hindsight seems to some historians simply crazed fanaticism, was at the time for many young Jews a cause worth dying for. The Left PZ went head to head with the Bund for the franchise to provide an authentic 'Marxism of the Yiddish street' in Brzeziny and many other places like it.

For most socialist parties in history the main aim has been to gain political power, how and when being the main sources of division. For the Bund and the Left PZ, it was different: they recognised there was no chance of the labour movement coming to power in Poland. The main workers' grouping, the Polish Socialist Party, was in its own way a mirror image of the Bund – a socialist party tinged by nationalism. Since Polish nationalism was heavily tainted by Catholic anti-Semitism the PSP would lose Polish votes to right-wing nationalists if it formed an alliance with Jewish parties, even if it was inclined to (which it was usually not).

The response of the Jewish labour movement to this political paralysis was to embark upon a cultural and social revolution within the working class community as a kind of palliative for being unable to change the wider world. The scale of their achievement has rarely been seen in the history of the working class. The impact on Brzeziny, Abramowicz remembers, was profound:

> Drama groups sprang up, sports clubs, libraries, and also other activities ... The thing that really was unusual in the town was the rapidity of the tempo spurring on the radical process, the very extreme attitude to issues, the general, boundless fanaticism that helped no one.[24]

The Bund had never supported the communist vision of revolution; its strategy was a slow, cumulative 'social revolution' which would set aside the need for a Russian-style seizure of power. It was precisely this that the Bund set out to achieve in the early 1920s, by organising a broad network of workplace, community and cultural organisations.

At the centre of this was the Yiddish language. The Bund's founders had been intellectuals and had to learn it, swear words first, from the workers they were trying to recruit. Now the organisation was rooted firmly in the post-war generation of Yiddish speakers. From all sides they could feel Yiddish culture maturing, becoming modern, even as it was vilified by racist politicians. The father of modern Yiddish literature, Isaac Peretz, had been a Bund fellow-traveller. In his poem 'Monish' (1888) the hero ridicules the decrepit state of the language, which Jews called the 'old jargon':

> Differently my song would ring
> If for gentiles I would sing,
> Not in Yiddish, in 'Jargon'
> That has no proper sound or tone.
> It has no words for sex appeal,
> And such things as lovers feel.[25]

Peretz set out to rectify this, along with a circle of populist and socialist writers who poured out a stream of Yiddish plays, novels and poetry after the 1890s. As they got their mouths around old sounds, moulded into tantalisingly new words and phrases, Yiddish speakers noticed with surprise that it sounded 'just like French'.[26]

By the early 1920s the workers' movement had built a network of institutions based on Yiddish. In 1920 there were 58 Yiddish schools in Poland, including 23 run by Poale Zion and 14 by the Bund. By 1929 there were 114 primary schools, 52 night schools and even a teacher training college, in total covering more than 100 towns and with a school roll of 24,000. In Brzeziny it was the Left PZ which had the bigger franchise.

> The leftist Poale Zion, which had been able to attract a young and energetic membership, created evening courses for adults. Many of the working youth got their only education there. The Poale Zion also had a well-run library.[27]

The Bund even had a children's movement, so it was possible to live your whole life in the workers' movement: at school, in the playground, at the youth club and on into apprenticeship, and it didn't stop there.

In 1926 the Bund launched a sports organisation called Morgenshtern (Morning Star). The idea was that 'mass sport' was better at fostering a spirit of comradeship among workers than individual competition. So the official literature promoted cycling, gymnastics and swimming, while boxing was banned and football frowned upon. 'Sports business, commerce in football . . . our sportsmen leave . . . for the Left Poale Zion with its stars, of whom some think so highly,' sneered the Bund's youth paper.[28] But the allure of the beautiful game was to prove overpowering.

Abe Rosenberg recalls that organised sports were unheard of in the town before the war, but in the early 1920s football took off dramatically:

> In a short time, hitting the ball took on epidemic proportions. At dawn on Saturday summer days, instead of going with one's father to pray, the young people, through roundabout detours in order to avoid the 'evil eye', were drawn to the playing field. There, they threw off their Sabbath clothing, put on short pants, shirts, and special shoes and with great zeal took to training.[29]

Rosenberg has left an ecstatic description of a match day, in which 'the superb youth of my generation', taller and fitter than their parents, take on a rival local side watched by the whole town, including the Hassidic Jews in their long coats and black hats. The goalkeeper is fouled, the crowd runs onto the pitch, a brawl ensues. At the final whistle Brzeziny have lost, but while the elders go to the bars to drink beer and analyse tactics, the youth head for the forests to sing socialist songs and talk politics.

> The forests shone in the pale-golden light of the full moon swimming in the dark blue sky. The night lay still, heavy and fragrant. We had finally sung all the songs. We did not want to go home. The pleasure of the past day slowly evaporated. The morning ahead lay gray and cheerless.[30]

How could the Bund resist football? By 1929 it had several football teams of its own and by the mid-1930s it had given the OK to boxing too, on the grounds that it was useful for self-defence. In 1931 Morgenshtern sent a team of 100 athletes to the Workers' Olympics in Vienna – their group portrait, preserved in the Bund archive in New York, shows them lined up in modish uniforms, the women's hair stylishly bobbed, the men's slicked back in the style of matinee idols, their lives a world away from those of the apprentice boys of 1905.

Beyond sport there was a strong demand for Yiddish theatre, which the workers' movement took the lead in supplying. In Brzeziny the Bund and Left PZ formed rival theatre groups and, says one participant, the Bund lost 'after a violent fight'. At national level the Bund and the Left PZ engaged in the same bitter rivalry across sport, theatre, literature and even film, even as the economic hardship and bitter racism that might have coaxed them together closed in on the *shtetl*s.

To conquer the world: It was not all football and culture; Brzeziny provided a ready audience for the agitators and lecturers sent by the Bund and Left PZ. Jacob Pat, who later became a Bund leader in the USA, relives the experience of arriving to give a speech in the town:

> Soon people will empty into the street, in a group. Jews will come out of their doors, remain standing on the cobblestone pavement. Youngsters will run closer, 'Greetings, comrade. Greetings comrade'. The town sees, the town knows that 'the speaker has come'. He is already here; there he goes with his friends. Hasidim were displeased with this; older Jews were upset. The speaker will lead the children astray from the straight path . . . But one can do nothing; no one can help. It is such a time, a new time.

Pat recalls being welcomed with the same atmosphere of 'joy and holy dread' that would have greeted a famous rabbi decades earlier. He would speak to crowds of more than a thousand in the town's biggest hall.

> We were all together then in a higher world, a brightly lit one . . .
> The exclamation 'Comrades – male and female' floats down, and

they marshal themselves with a passionate dream of a new world, of new people, new Jews for a greater freedom that will come. Whoever was worthy of having the honor of seeing the way the poor young tailors from Brzezin dreamed, they would at that time have been able to conquer the world.[31]

The political world the Bund was building did indeed have a dream-like quality if we remember that these idyllic descriptions of mass meetings, football and theatre groups date from years in which Jews were being driven out of the civil service and regularly attacked by gangs on the streets of Warsaw and Lodz. You can sense the frustration in this passage from an editorial by one of the Bund's leaders:

The Jewish worker worries too little about himself and too much about others . . . At Jewish labor rallies called for specific purposes, discussion veers to all sorts of foreign issues and away from the point at issue. Jewish workers live much more each day with the problems of Germany, Russia, England and America than with the immediate issues, which we must solve.[32]

There had been a relaxation of official anti-Semitism after Josef Pilsudski's military regime came to power in 1926 (he was more anti-Russian than anti-Jewish) but it was still virulent in society. Now the Bund's tactics slowly changed. It had previously boycotted elections to the Polish parliament but in 1928 formed a modestly successful electoral alliance with the Polish Socialist Party. That year saw the first ever May Day demonstration in Brzeziny and active collaboration between Jewish workers and non-Jewish socialists. Abramowicz remembers:

On the day of the first of May, the various factions marched with their slogans and flags up to the marketplace. There the great demonstration was formed. It was still early, and the marketplace was already full of people. With red flags and banners, the march moved noisily in the direction of Rogow Street. Chants and slogans in Polish and Yiddish deafened the streets through which the demonstration moved . . . We gave the Poale Zion Left Party (I was then the party secretary) the honor of bearing the flag. The flag was so heavy – and the wind made it even heavier – that to this day, I feel its weight.[33]

In 1929 an alliance of workers' candidates led by Poale Zion won seats on the town council, replacing the mainstream Zionists who had until then represented the Jews. But gerrymandering meant the council was controlled by Christians. When the leader of the Jewish workers' group made his first speech, asking the council to provide welfare to the unemployed, he was shouted down.

The session exploded, and this was the beginning of subsequent conflicts between Jews and Polaks in the town council. That is how the situation continually deteriorated until the Jewish population realized that future cooperation in the town council was not possible.[34]

The hollow triumph: For most of the inter-war period the Bund lost ground to the Left Poale Zion. The Left PZ-aligned youth movement, Hashomer Hatzair, had an even more attractive policy than self-defence plus socialism, namely self-defence plus Palestine. In addition, because the Left PZ was strongly pro-Soviet (the Bund was strongly anti), they garnered the valuable kudos of association with Stalin's Russia. As a result the Bund would play second fiddle in small-town communities like Brzeziny to the organisations of Labour Zionism.

But the death of Pilsudski in 1935 and the resurgence of official anti-Semitism that followed propelled the Bund back into a leading position among Polish Jews. 'Jews are too numerous,' announced one of the ruling colonels in a radio broadcast. 'The answer is mass emigration . . . We can however not wait for the problem to solve itself with the disappearance of the Jews. We must without delay find work for the Polish population in trade, industry and the handicrafts.'[35] It was an unmistakeable call for Jews to be thrown out of skilled workplaces, and at street level the racist attacks became more organised.

The new situation hit the Bund's leadership like a bucket of cold water. Its leaders, Victor Alter and Henryk Erlich, had struggled to achieve engagement with the wider political crisis, but now they steered the Bund towards a formal alliance with the Polish Socialist Party and turned seriously to election work. Until 1936 the Bund had never properly participated in the elections to Jewish *kehillas* – the religious councils – but now it did, and immediately won hundreds of seats across the country. In Warsaw, Lodz, Lublin, Vilnius and Grodno it became the majority party. In Warsaw the Bund took control, but the Polish government effectively dissolved the council, choosing a group of mainstream Zionists to govern in its place. In Lodz a coalition of the Bund, the PSP and German-speaking socialists actually controlled the main city council, but it too was dissolved. In any case, electoral success would come too late.

In March 1936 there was a police-backed pogrom in the town of Przytyk. The Bund and the Left PZ ensured the Jewish districts across Poland stopped work completely in response. Mainstream Zionist politicians, who refused to support the strike, lost face. So as catastrophe loomed, Jewish workers turned to the Bund in large numbers.

The municipal elections of December 1938 were to be the last test of political strength before the war, and in them the Bund won a majority of the Jewish vote and a landslide in the cities. The Bund's political trademarks had always been active self-defence against racist violence, the rejection of Zionism, scorn for emigration and hope for an alliance with the Polish workers. Now, as Europe and America closed their borders to refugees, Jewish workers turned to the organisation which had always told them, 'Our home is here'. The shift in allegiance was as much a gesture of national solidarity as it was of socialist radicalism, but the Bund's leaders were determined to press home the advantage they now had over the Zionists.

At the moment of its electoral triumph Henryk Erlich defiantly set the tone of the movement's relationship with Zionism during the tragedy that would follow:

> [Jewish unity] cannot involve cooperation with reactionaries . . . Zionism has become an ally of anti-Semitism. The worsening situation of Jews throughout the world is exploited by the

Zionists. The Zionists regard themselves as second-class citizens in Poland. Their aim is to be first-class citizens in Palestine and make the Arabs second-class citizens. The Bund therefore cannot see the Zionists as partners in the struggle against the reactionary forces in Poland.[36]

Instead, the Bund saw itself as the only conduit for an alliance between Jewish and Polish workers. For the Bund leaders, the experience of the 1938 election taught them that they could at last speak for the majority of Polish Jews and that the long-delayed alliance with the Polish workers' movement was about to happen. And for all the hardship, solidarity made life feel good in the *shtetl*s.

Icchok Janasowicz, a Brzeziner who became famous as a writer after emigrating to Argentina, sums up what the Jewish workers' movement in the town had achieved on the eve of its destruction:

> Even in the years between the two world wars . . . a definite patriarchal quality was still preserved in the way of life and left a certain stamp on the battle between wage earners and the master and between the master and the magaziner. True, in Brzezin they carried out the same social battles as in Lodz, and strikes there were not infrequent, but all the battles lacked the sharp bitterness of the large cities, and they almost never led to the outbreak of serious hatred . . . Even though I would not want to exaggerate the idyllic quality in their attitudes in comparison to other towns, there certainly was an idyllic quality.[37]

In September 1939 Germany invaded Poland and the idyll was destroyed. The Nazis occupied Brzeziny within days of the outbreak of war, burned the synagogue and in 1940 instituted a ghetto, cramming 6,000 Jews into a few tiny streets of their own town. The *kehilla* postponed deportation by negotiating a contract with the Wehrmacht to sew army uniforms, an arrangement which kept the ghetto alive for the next two years. But after Hitler decreed the 'final solution' in January 1942, its fate was sealed.

The town had a society for workers' evening courses, a seven-grade

Jewish secular school, six libraries, four drama groups, two cooperatives, a professional workers' union, two artisans' unions and active branches of the Bund, Left and Right Poale Zion and in addition 'revolutionists and communists'. That is the final inventory of the Brzeziny workers' movement as described by a survivor. By May 1942 Brzeziny was destroyed. There were fifteen members of the Brzeziny branch of the Bund among the deportees who arrived in the Lodz ghetto.

The ghetto fights: The last action of the Bund in Poland is known to history as its most heroic. On 17 April 1943 its youth movement in the Warsaw ghetto joined with youth from the Left PZ and mainstream Zionists in a doomed uprising against the Nazis. But the decision to fight came at the end of three years in which the Bund had struggled against the odds to maintain a workers' movement behind barbed wire, and had resisted an alliance with Zionist fighters until most of Warsaw's Jews had been slaughtered.

With the German invasion the Bund's national leaders, Erlich and Alter, were ordered to leave Warsaw and escape to the east. But the Soviet Union had agreed a division of Poland with the Nazis and the two were arrested by Stalin's secret police as part of a widespread crackdown against the Bund in the Soviet sector. In Warsaw the veteran Bund leader Shmuel Ziegelboim took charge and was nominated to serve on the Judenrat, the Jewish Council set up by the Nazis to replace the *kehilla*. But after Ziegelboim made a speech urging resistance to any attempt to set up a ghetto, he had to be spirited out of Poland and became the Bund's representative on the Polish government in exile in London.

In November 1940 the Warsaw ghetto was set up behind a ring of barbed wire and bayonets. After a chaotic fortnight of two-way migration the Bund found itself operating amid a population of just under half a million Jews, living seven to a room. Escape was punishable by death, education for Jewish children banned and a regime of random killings, beatings and extortion began immediately. Bernard Goldstein, the leader of the Bund's self-defence group in pre-ghetto Warsaw, managed to reconstruct it through a system of cells – 'fives and tens' – who knew only their immediate commander.

In mid-1941 the Nazis relaxed the ban on education and the Bund's youth network sprang to life with night schools and kindergartens wedged into the corners of housing blocks and offices. Goldstein remembers:

> Educational and cultural activity took on new importance . . . Indeed to defend ourselves against the feeling of helplessness that engulfed us, we tried to rebuild and strengthen all the prewar institutions, to create at least the illusion of the life that used to be.[38]

During the first 18 months in the ghetto there was an explicit understanding that resistance would be passive, but the Bund still published an illegal paper called *The Bulletin* (later named *The Call*). On 17 April 1942 the Gestapo carried out the first wave of mass executions, on the pretext of stamping out illegal newspapers. A large number of printers and intellectuals were rounded up and shot. That night began the first phase of the destruction of the Warsaw ghetto, during which Gestapo groups would beat, shoot and loot randomly, collecting individuals for deportation. But at this point the concentration camp at Treblinka was not ready. It was on 22 July 1942 that extermination began on a mass scale. The Gestapo ordered the Judenrat to organise the deportation of 60,000 'unproductive' Jews at the rate of 10,000 a day to what they said were work camps, and took hostages to secure compliance. The president of the Judenrat, Adam Czerniakow, swallowed cyanide rather than sign the order.

Now the Bund's leadership in Warsaw began to pass to members of its youth movement, Zukunft (The Future). The Left PZ had symbolically dissolved itself at the start of the war, but the left–zionist youth movement, Hashomer Hatzair, had remained active. The same pattern emerged among the mainstream Zionists, with the Hechalutz youth group emerging as the leading force. Under circumstances of extreme danger, the 'superb youth' of the inter-war generation were faced with the hardest question: when and how to fight.

Led by Zukunft, the Bund had already decided that it would organise armed resistance but at this point was still trying to acquire weapons.

At any hour we expected to hear that the long-awaited shipment of arms had arrived. But we knew that armed resistance would doom the whole ghetto instead of only sixty thousand. And who, no matter how convinced that the whole ghetto was doomed in any case, could take upon himself the responsibility for precipitating such a catastrophe?[39]

The problem was that most people in the ghetto did not believe the rumours that the Germans had begun mass extermination. So mass support for armed resistance did not exist. Instead, there was a scramble for work permits and for jobs. Rich Jews gave their entire fortunes to become floor-sweepers in workshops exempt from deportation. It was in this context that the Bund refused the first approach from the Zionist youth groups to form a united military force. In addition to the traditional mutual hostility, the Bund clung to the belief that that there would be a united Polish uprising – that building links with the Polish socialists leading the resistance on the other side of the wire was more important.

Faced with inertia among the population, the Bund set out to do two things: puncture the atmosphere of denial among the Warsaw Jews and persuade the Allies to act to stop the Holocaust, if necessary with punitive measures against the German population. Individual acts of bravery would be required if the world was to see evidence of the Holocaust.

The Bund sent youth organiser Zalman Friedrich on a desperate mission to Treblinka. Friedrich had grown up in the Bund's schools, edited its sports paper and studied politics and literature in its youth group. He accepted his task unflinchingly. Friedrich was tall and blond, 'a Nazi propagandist's dream' according to Goldstein, and his mission was to get over the wire, out of the ghetto and follow a shipment of deportees to its destination. And then come back. In July 1942 he followed a train to Treblinka where, in a nearby forest, he found and interviewed two escapees, one a Bund member. They described the mechanised extermination methods in use in graphic detail. Friedrich then returned to the ghetto, to certain death, to file the first eyewitness account of Treblinka, which was published in the Bund's newspaper on 20 September.

All of the trains carrying Warsaw Jews went to Treblinka, where the Jews were murdered in a horrifying fashion . . . The camp at Treblinka is 1–2 kilometers in area . . . The newly arrived people . . . were undressed, [gathered] in groups of 200 and sent to a 'shower' . . . from which they never emerged.[40]

Meanwhile the Bund activist Leon Feiner smuggled the Allied secret agent Jan Karski first into the ghetto and then, disguised as a guard, into a death camp. After making his way back across occupied Europe with evidence of the Holocaust, Karski linked up with Ziegelboim, the Bund's London representative, to confront senior British and American politicians with what was happening, though he was met with initial disbelief on both sides of the Atlantic.

September–October 1942 saw 300,000 Jews deported from the ghetto, driven by the whips and boots of the Gestapo and the Jewish police to the Umschlagplatz – the transit point. From there they were put in cattle trucks and taken to Treblinka. The Bund did its best to rescue people from the transit point using a mixture of bravery and bribery, but in the process some of those sent do deals with guards were instead deported. Marek Edelman, a youth organiser with the Bund, recalls that 'during this time we lost almost all of our comrades. Just a few dozen of our members remained from our original group numbering more than 500 people.'[41]

The Bund, through the unions, had good connections with the managers of the factories where a pass meant exemption from deportation, and it had also used its printing press to produce thousands of fakes. Bernard Goldstein survived because workers in a clothing factory hid him; his close friend Sonia Novgorodsky, also a Bund activist, was seized during a raid on the factory and deported. Edelman remembers a conversation with Sonia the day before she was taken which explored the central dilemma for a movement that had always lived in close connection with the workers. She told him,

My place is not here. Look who remains in the Ghetto, only the scum. The working masses march in formation to the Umschlag. I have to go with them. If I shall be with them then, perhaps, maybe they will not forget that they are human beings, even during their last moments, in the cars and afterwards . . .[42]

By October the 'liquidation' of the ghetto was almost complete. Only about 60,000 Jews remained – 33,000 in the factories, 3,000 council workers and the rest hiding in bunkers, the so-called 'wild people'. Goldstein, who had been rounded up for deportation but escaped, described his return:

> Everything looked strange. There was no trace of the tumultuous pushing, spirited multitude, which only six or seven weeks ago had been the Ghetto. Stores gaped open and empty. Houses were abandoned . . . gloomy desolation hung over everything.[43]

At this point the Bund decided to join the Jewish Fighting Organisation, known as ZOB. There was no risk of embroiling the wider civilian population in the fighting now since they were largely dead. Goldstein was ordered to escape to the 'Aryan' side of the wall, to help link up with the Polish resistance and to procure arms. ZOB's commander was Mordechai Anielewicz, a 24-year-old youth organiser from Hashomer; Marek Edelman was the Bund representative on its command group. From then on, he says, 'Our comrades lived with the others just as members of a close family. A mutual aim united us. During this period of over half a year there were no quarrels or struggles, which are common among adherents of different ideologies . . . all fought equally in this heroic life and death struggle.'[44]

At the end of December, ZOB received its first delivery of weapons from the Polish resistance: ten pistols. The first major skirmish took place on 18 January and resulted in most of the Jewish fighters involved being killed, after a surprise attack by the Germans forced them into open street fighting. Its impact was dramatic. At the Oppel arms factory, outside the ghetto, Jewish forced labourers clamoured to get back inside to join the fight. Inside the ghetto, at the Toebbens factory, its German owner made a speech denouncing ZOB, which Jan Mawult, a Jewish policeman who was later to join the final uprising, was present to hear.

Whatever the reason the idea of resistance is growing . . . The Fighting Organisation is on everybody's lips; people talk about it and think about it. By mentioning it in his polemic, Toebbens actually wins more adherents to the combatants' cause than weeks of their own propaganda.[45]

Now ZOB began hit-and-run attacks and sabotage, and built up its arsenal. By the time of the decisive uprising, according to Edelman, each partisan had a pistol, ten to fifteen rounds, five hand grenades and five Molotov cocktails. Each sector had three rifles. There was just one machine gun.

There were two types of detachments, 'special garrisons', who positioned themselves around the ghetto in strategic locations, and the factory-based groups. The Bund, orthodox Marxists to the very end, insisted on basing most of its fighters within factories. Goldstein wrote,

The Bund, under which almost all the factory fighting groups were organised, contributed only four groups to these special garrisons. We were fearful of unduly weakening our factory strongholds . . . Our goal was to broaden the resistance and give it mass character . . . Our reliance on the people proved to be justified, for when the final battle was joined our factory groups were able to draw into them all the factory workers. Even the so-called 'wild' people, the illegals without any credentials who lived wherever they could hide, joined the struggle.[46]

In February 1943 news came over the radio that Victor Alter and Henryk Erlich had been executed for 'subversive work against the Soviet Union'. Erlich was the man who had moved the resolution for Polish independence in the St Petersburg Soviet. Alter had attended the founding of the Comintern. Together they had been the public face of the Bund between the wars. Goldstein wrote,

I can still see before my eyes the faces of our people during the first days after we learned that our two most beloved comrades and leaders had been shot to death in Stalin's GPU dungeons. Heads were bowed in deep sorrow and bitter anger.[47]

The SS attacked the ghetto at 6 a.m. on Sunday 19 April 1943, signalling the start of their attempt to liquidate the remaining Jews and the month-long battle known to history as the Warsaw Ghetto Uprising. Though armed with tanks and machine guns and in full battle gear the 850-strong German force advanced in a road column, totally unprepared for fighting. ZOB units opened fire and hurled Molotov cocktails against the tanks. A second German attack was hit by a huge bomb, which inflicted many casualties. By 2 p.m., Edelman writes, 'not a single live German remained in the Ghetto area'.

The first phase of fighting lasted five days, at the end of which Anielewicz, in his final communiqué, summed up the results:

> What happened exceeded our boldest dreams. The Germans ran twice from the ghetto. One of our companies held out for 40 minutes and another for more than six hours. I feel that great things are happening and what we dared do is of great, enormous importance . . . Beginning from today we shall shift over to the partisan tactic.[48]

ZOB knew the uprising was part of a much bigger change in the direction of the war. The Germans had surrendered at Stalingrad in January – now the fighters talked of 'Ghettograd'. Meanwhile the mood among the Polish working class began to lift. On 23 April ZOB issued its manifesto to the Polish workers: 'We the prisoners of the ghetto send you our heartfelt brotherly greeting . . . This is a fight for your freedom and ours, for your and our human, social and national pride!'[49]

After the first week, the Germans, having lost two tanks and 93 soldiers, stood off from the assault. Instead, they methodically set fire to areas, forcing ZOB to retreat to its bunkers: 'On May Day the ghetto fighters undertook a one-day "offensive". In the evening they held a roll-call of their decimated ranks and sang the "Internationale".'[50]

On 8 May the Germans discovered ZOB's headquarters and attacked with poison gas. Around 80 fighters were caught inside. Many, including Anielewicz, committed suicide rather than surrender. On the night of

12 May, with sporadic fighting still under way, a radio bulletin brought news that Ziegelboim, the Bund's representative with the Polish government in exile, had killed himself in protest at Allied inaction over the Holocaust. His suicide note said:

> My comrades in the Warsaw ghetto fell with arms in their hands in the last heroic battle. I was not permitted to fall like them, together with them, but I belong with them, to their mass grave. By my death, I wish to give expression to my most profound protest against the inaction in which the world watches and permits the destruction of the Jewish people.[51]

'The meaning of Artur's suicide was bitterly clear to all of us,' wrote Goldstein. 'He was tendering us the balance sheet of all his efforts on our behalf.'[52]

When ammunition ran out, the Polish resistance arranged for ZOB to escape through the sewers. Edelman's group, by then 'human skeletons', escaped the ghetto after 48 hours in the tunnels. Zalman Friedrich made it out but was caught and shot. Goldstein remained in Warsaw and would take part in the wider Polish uprising there a year later. The Bund maintained contact with two battle groups in the ghetto until June, by which time some seventy ZOB fighters had regrouped as partisans in the forest. On 16 May the SS commander in charge summed up the operation:

> Of the total of 56,065 Jews caught, about 7,000 were exterminated within the former Ghetto in the course of the large-scale action, and 6,929 by transporting them [to Treblinka], which means 14,000 Jews were exterminated altogether. Beyond the number of 56,065 Jews an estimated number of 5,000 to 6,000 were killed by explosions or in fires.[53]

'How much poorer the world became': Most workers' movements exist to change the world but the Bund faced a unique problem – the world that had formed it proved impossible to change. Its response was to create a world within a world, a world which was at its most idyllic when sealed within *shtetl* communities like Brzeziny.

Through the Warsaw Ghetto Uprising the Bund sent a final message from that world to the one we live in now.

Those who had seen it rise, and could compare it with workers' movements outside Poland, knew the Bund was unique. It did not have to separate itself from the national culture it worked within; it had helped create that culture. As a result, the Bund has left probably the most successful example of concentrated community organisation in the history of the working class. Isaac Deutscher, a Jewish communist who opposed the Bund and rejected its ideology, nevertheless eulogized its achievement:

> A quarter of a century has passed since I had the good fortune to work in their surroundings . . . nowhere have I again found this broad political horizon, this devotion to ideals, this sacrifice, this courage, which animated the Jewish worker of past generations in East Europe. I know just how much poorer the world became when the heart of that worker ceased to beat.[54]

But it did not cease to beat entirely. Marek Edelman survived to spell out for history the philosophy of the Bund and the lessons of the uprising. He said,

> My idea of socialism is no state monopoly. There should be stress on the subjectivity of the human being. You need good material conditions, a high level of culture, much freedom and friendship. And it won't come today or tomorrow. It's a long and winding road . . .[55]

In the year he made those comments Edelman was a busy man: he had recently been released from jail and he was still trying to help a semi-legal workers' organisation fight a crumbling dictatorship. The organisation's name was Solidarnosc. The year was 1989.

9. Joy brought on by hope
When workers controlled the factories

> Sometimes song and laughter are heard and there is also a
> sense of fascination with the novelty of the moment. Red
> banners are flying, guards at the doors, bivouac in the court-
> yards, meals eaten almost communally, a sense of waiting for
> the unknown and of joy brought on by hope.
>
> *Corriere della Sera*, Milan, 2 September 1920

Neuquén, Argentina, 2006

For Raul Godoy it was a last resort after months of stalemate; with
Bob Travis it was a hastily improvised tactic to prevent the machine
tools being removed; for Maurizio Garino and Simone Weil it was
nothing less than liberation in the workplace. The act in question is
a sit-down strike. Garino was the leader of the Turin metalworkers'
union in 1920, Weil a lowly operative at Renault in Paris in 1936;
Travis was head of the auto workers in Flint, Michigan in 1937. Godoy
leads the union at Zanon Ceramica, a tile factory in Argentina, and
at the time of writing he and 460 fellow workers still control the plant
they seized in 2001. He says,

> At the beginning it was not clear if the entire workforce would be
> sacked, so we occupied only partially. That is, we continued to work
> our normal shifts as a way of guaranteeing that the machinery and
> stock was not removed. The mood was one of uncertainty – we
> didn't know what to do.

The Zanon factory is one of the biggest in Neuquén, and a high-
tech installation, so when the owners tried to close it, sack the workers
and remove the ovens in October 2001 there was dismay throughout

this industrial town. But the economic crisis skidded out of control, provoking a currency devaluation and a run on the banks. With unemployment spiralling to 20 per cent, unemployed pickets blocked the highways. Hundreds of workplaces were taken over by their employees in December 2001. 'It was an uprising,' says Godoy. 'Everybody felt the sky was the limit; radical demands were on the agenda because the situation was about to explode. We were part of that process.'

They took over the plant and voted to continue producing tiles, spurred on by a court ruling which outlawed the management's attempt to lock them out.

> Without bosses and without foremen we organised production from the bottom up, just as we did in our trade union. We voted on production plans – for example, type of tiles, quantity, designs, suppliers. Each department elected a coordinator who takes the everyday problems to the daily Coordinators' Meeting, which operates like a workers' council.

On top of that there is a regular, day-long assembly of the whole workforce, which takes the medium-term decisions. One of the first they took was to work less hard.

> We have three, eight-hour shifts and the same hours and salary for everybody. We also work at half the rate that we used to work under the bosses. We used to operate the tile press – which sets the pace for the whole process – at 14 to 15 beats per minutes, which was terrible because it made you lose all feeling in your arms. Now we work at half that rate and we are keeping a good level of productivity.

Sorting out the production process was only the start of their problems. At first regular suppliers refused to deliver and their output was impounded for lack of a tax code number. But connections with the wider social revolt kicked in: the Mothers of the Plaza De Mayo, an organisation of those whose children had been murdered by the military dictatorship, donated their invoice number, and indigenous people in dispute with Zanon's former owners gave the workers access to their clay.

243

Of the factories occupied during the 2001 upheaval, about 160 remain under workers' control. Some are demanding to be nationalised permanently; others want to remain cooperatives, or want government grants to become solvent again under new managers. Long after the mass movement they were part of has ebbed away, they have remained in a parallel universe to the rest of Argentine business. At Zanon they have boosted the workforce by nearly 50 per cent since taking over, hiring people from the unemployed movement, and have built a steady market for their goods. Before the occupation, says Godoy, there were an average 300 reportable accidents a year, half of them severe, and on average one fatality. Since the occupation there have been 33 accidents, none severe, and no fatalities.

It is rare for factory occupations to last so long. In history they have usually appeared at violent turning points, provoking strong reactions. But the Argentine workers' occupations have survived because it suits the left-nationalist government that came to power during the 2001 crisis to allow them to. Men and women used to the daily grind of work have found themselves stars of the show in the anti-globalisation movement. There have been three films made about Zanon, and it relishes the label 'the biggest factory in the world under workers' control'.

Are they aware of the history of factory occupations? Godoy, a Marxist, says he is. 'Many workers saw this as a leftist fantasy, but when all the other options were closed, they started to realise that this was the only real alternative to fight for,' he says. But what were the precedents? He lists an Argentine occupation in the 1970s, the Chilean occupations in the years before Pinochet, some factories in Bolivia and Peru. As for the sit-down strike tsunamis that washed over Italy, France and the USA in the decades between the two world wars, these seem like legend, not history. Yet the fundamental similarities are there, right down to the basic emotional response of those involved: there is a sense of joy and freedom. Says Godoy,

> We feel more free, especially because of our struggle. You start to feel free when you start fighting, when you can see the problems

and identify the enemy, understand what the bosses do, and the union bureaucracy. We can show the world what we have done; although we are only a grain of sand on a huge beach, our experience shows what workers can do . . .'

Italy, 1920

In September 1920, managers all across northern Italy were taking instructions from their workers. A correspondent for a Milan newspaper wrote,

> We have visited the various plants and have noted that in several . . . the foremen, white collar workers and even the directors are taking orders from the factory councils. In other plants, Marelli, Breda, Spadaccini, etc., from which the foremen, directors and office workers have stayed away, fearing the reprisals of the industrialists, labour goes on . . . under the direction of workers . . . selected by the factory councils.[1]

Half a million metalworkers were in control of their factories and the managers had only the choice of staying or leaving. The sit-in strike had come after two years of riots, wildcat walk-outs and popular revolts but it was not the product of chaos or social breakdown; it was a meticulously planned attempt by skilled workers to capture control of their lives at work.

Italian heavy industry was modern and highly concentrated. The cities of Genoa, Turin and Milan formed an 'industrial triangle' whose workforce had grown quickly during the First World War. The Italian labour movement was unusual because it had both a strong syndicalist union and a strong socialist one. The socialist union federation, CGL, had 1,930,000 members and was led as in Germany by moderates. The liberal government that had ruled Italy before 1914 gave the union leaders a recognised consultative role over wages and conditions. But many of the factory militants were not in the CGL. The syndicalist federation USI had 800,000 members, and its whole outlook was modelled on direct action. In the crucial city, Turin, there was a complication: the metalworkers' union FIOM contained both syndicalists and socialists.

There was rivalry between the two groups but the 'war between brothers' that was destroying the German workers' movement had not yet begun in Italy. Maurizio Garino, a syndicalist metalworker, remembers the political culture in the Turin metalworkers' meeting halls:

Everybody was free to join the USI or the FIOM and was immersed, naturally, in the spirit of direct action. Yes, even the reformists could have their say – they had maximum freedom of speech – but they were few . . . We were friends, we collaborated in a real sense – without hatred, and without fighting.[2]

In this atmosphere groups pursuing similar strategies emerged within both syndicalist and socialist unions. The replacement of traditional trade union leaders with a shop stewards' movement was their common aim.

Antonio Gramsci, a Marxist intellectual fired up by the idea of direct action, moved into the industrial district of Turin in 1918 and set up a newspaper specifically aimed at organising a stewards' movement, *L'Ordine Nuovo* (The New Order). Its first issue appeared on May Day 1919. Meanwhile Garino and his syndicalist group were on the point of taking control of the metalworkers' union. It was not long before the two men realised they were treading the same path.

In August 1919 workers at the Fiat-Centro plant scrapped their official union committee and formed Italy's first 'factory council'. It was essentially a committee of shop stewards – though they labelled themselves commissars – each elected by a group of about 20 workers to which they had to report back. Garino remembers:

The key characteristic of the councils was the ability of the rank and file to recall any delegate immediately. Every workshop chose a commissar, in the person of a worker who had to study the whole production process and communicate that knowledge to the comrades in his own unit, in order to eliminate completely the managerial hierarchy inside the factory . . . Now these councils had to be preparatory organisations in two ways: technical and organisational preparation for the eventual replacement of capitalism with socialised production; secondly to prepare the elements of a revolutionary culture, in order to proceed towards the foundation of a socialist society.[3]

In other words, the Fiat workers thought they were learning both to control their own production line and Italian society.

Gramsci developed this into a nationwide strategy in his report of the vote at Fiat-Centro:

The workers' organisation which will exercise communist social power . . . can be nothing but a system of councils elected at the workplace . . . coordinated in a local and national hierarchy to realise the unity of the labouring class above and beyond the determined categories of the division of labour.[4]

Other factories rapidly adopted the idea and Gramsci was invited to speak at meeting after meeting. By 31 October 1919 the movement was able to call a conference of delegates from 30 factories representing 50,000 workers.

At that meeting a 'Programme of the Workshop Commissars', penned by Gramsci, was adopted. It called for the fusion of all non-religious unions into a single organisation. The shop steward, it said, must exercise control over conditions in the workplace. But these workers, who were used to rapid innovation and if truth be known worshipped it, had no intention of holding up technological progress:

The commissar must study and urge comrades to study bourgeois systems of production and labour processes and call for criticisms and suggestions of improvements to ease labour and speed up production . . . Wellbeing will be achieved not by disorder in production or a weakening of labour discipline . . . For similar reasons, the commissars must study the internal technical innovations proposed by management and not decide about them until they have discussed them with the comrades . . .[5]

The problem with the factory council theory was this: in Gramsci's mind it was a single idea that solved two problems – the problem of power and the problem of control. As well as being the means of running a communist state it was a means of educating the workers for the future. But when the decisive moment came, the Italian workers would be faced with a choice. Did they want the factory councils to rule Italy, or merely to run the factories from below in consultation with the management? It is a nice choice to have if you are radically minded, but they were to face it unprepared.

The leaders of the socialist union federation had scorned the factory council movement but they could not ignore it. On 1 November 1919 the factory councils took over the leadership of FIOM in Turin. The man they put in charge was Maurizio Garino. With a syndicalist in charge of a nominally socialist union, it would not be long before some direct action followed. He spelled out the plan: 'First, immediate action; second, to guarantee the continuity of production in the insurrectionary period; third, to be perhaps the basis for communist management.'[6]

On 8 November the issue of Gramsci's *L'Ordine Nuovo* carrying the shop stewards' manifesto sold out by lunchtime. Fiat, Lancia, Alfa Romeo . . . the roll-call of firms with factory councils reads like a hall of fame of Italian motoring. By February 1920 around 150,000 workers were part of the Turin factory councils. By April the movement was prepared for battle.

The national contract that FIOM had negotiated with the engineering employers stipulated that union committees should not have access to the shop floor and could only meet outside working hours. The factory councils were in breach of this and a struggle over recognition ensued. When some shop stewards were sacked, a general strike began in the Turin metal factories and spread to the region beyond.

During this strike the Italian Socialist Party's national committee was in session. High on the agenda was the issue of how to bring about soviets in Italy – that is, how to establish the Russian revolutionary model on Italian soil. The plan was to form local councils, organised by the party itself, which would claim a permanent role in the governance of post-war Italy. It did not occur to the socialists at this stage that the shop stewards in the factories would have a part to play; indeed they saw the shop stewards as a troublesome distraction from the revolution. So they refused to support the strike. Isolated, the Turin strike ended in defeat.

But the socialist trade union leaders were now confronted with a fresh problem. Inflation, driven by the devaluation of the lire, was eating into wages. Weekly living costs for an average family rose from 120 lire in June 1919 to 190 lire in December 1920. The minimum daily wage for a metalworker was 13 lire. The unions demanded a 40 per cent wage rise, but the claim was stonewalled by the employers, who now decided to form a national federation of their own, Confindustria. In August 1920 the wage claim was finally thrown out, with the employers' leader famously telling the union men, 'All discussion is useless. The industrialists will not grant any increase at all. Since the war they've done nothing but drop their pants. We've had enough. Now we're going to start on you.'[7]

Bruno Buozzi, the national leader of FIOM, was steeped in the pre-war traditions of socialist trade unionism. He was a long-time opponent of syndicalism, declaring himself 'against the theory that the organisation, and the organiser, must follow the masses even if they are disorganised. Such a theory – to put it bluntly – renders the organisation useless. It creates rebels but not a revolutionary consciousness'.[8] But the employers' attitude meant Buozzi had to organise a fightback. To preside over a rapid erosion of wages would lead to all the things he feared – desertions from the union, the growth of factory councils and his own replacement by syndicalists. So he called for a go-slow in the engineering factories. With hindsight this was clearly a way of resisting a national strike and at the same time putting pressure on the employers. He ordered:

> Reduce production to a minimum; no one to move from his workplace; no one to use tools unsuitable to the work in hand; take as long as possible over the repair of every machine; do not work at

jobs you are not trained for; clean and lubricate no machinery until it is stopped; if the company sacks anyone for this behaviour, make him come to work notwithstanding . . .[9]

Finally, as a concession to the militants, Buozzi ordered: 'If the company claims a lockout, occupy the factory and work there on your own account.'[10] This was to be done 'by all available means' – union code for physical force. Under pressure from the rank and file on one side and intransigent bosses on the other, Bruno Buozzi was about to start an epic battle, though his whole intention was to avoid one.

On the morning of 31 August 1920 managers at the Alfa Romeo car plant in Milan declared a lockout. FIOM promptly ordered its members to occupy 300 factories in the city. The city's newspaper reported,

> From outside, the factories yesterday evening presented a singular spectacle. One reached them through crowds of women and children, coming and going with dinners for the strikers, voluntary prisoners of the factories. Nearer to them, here and there, on the pavement or the grass, were the debris of the day's bivouac. Entrances were strictly guarded by the groups of workers. Not the ghost of an official or police officer in sight. The strikers were complete masters of the field. Whoever passed, in car or cab, was subjected to control as if he were crossing the frontier.[11]

In response the employers decided to make the lockout national. As news reached production lines all over Italy on 1 September, the workers calmly prepared to stay overnight. There was no big mobilisation of the police, nor did the employers obstruct the seizure of the gates and offices. They wanted the showdown and they wanted it to be decisive – not just in order to take on and defeat the unions but to rein in the government of liberal politician Giovanni Giolitti, who they saw as soft on the unions.

By Saturday 4 September, 400,000 metalworkers had occupied factories throughout Italy. In many smaller cities this was a minor if dramatic local event involving one or two factories, but in the industrial triangle of Genoa, Milan and Turin the whole of society was gripped by the action.

> The spectacle could not fail to be impressive, especially towards evening, when the red guards, straddling the walls, weapon in hand, were silhouetted against the night sky and the wail of the sirens rang the whole length of the Adda to echo in the Resegnon.[12]

Crucially, this was not a sit-down strike but a mass work-in – the first in history. The factories were ordered to keep production going but only at the pace of the existing go-slow, with an average shift of 12 hours: eight at work, four at rest or on guard duty. The clear intention was that, by maintaining production, the union leaders would signal that this movement – though massive – was neither a challenge to the civil authorities nor a prelude to revolution. But that was not the intention of the factory council leaders in Turin. For them it was the opportunity to stage a giant experiment in workers' control.

At Fiat-Centro in Turin, the factory council took over the management of production, pausing only to pose for a group photo around the desk of their famous boss Giovanni Agnelli. Here, as in many factories during the first days, the technicians and office workers stayed on to help. The first communiqué from Fiat-Centro's factory council read,

> The workers' internal commission, in agreement with the technicians' internal commission, calls upon all workers to remain at their workplaces and carry on work as in the past (the go-slow) in reciprocal respect. Workers! Show that you can run this factory without employers. Your internal commission will watch over your interests and will summon you at the opportune moment.[13]

Production at Fiat-Centro had been 67 cars a day before the dispute. Under the go-slow it had fallen to 27 a day. Under workers' control it managed 37. It was here in Turin, where the doctrine of workers' control had been spread by Gramsci and Garino, that the experiment was in full swing. The contrast with Milan, where the occupation was led by the traditional union leaders, was obvious.

The first thing which strikes you in Milan are the red flags flying from every stack and chimney. In Turin, even today on the fourth day of our occupation, around the workshops of the periphery, external symbols of the achievement are rare. An occasional red flag, the odd sentry on the parapet, but energies are concentrated inside. What the workers prefer to concentrate on is the technical organisation of labour, both in the individual plant and in the industrial complex of the city.[14]

The occupations sparked a social crisis across Italy, with the action spreading beyond metalworking, notably to the chemical and textiles industries, the shipyards and the docks. But there was a problem with money. In many factories the occupying workforce was demanding to be paid, and with the FIOM leadership offering no solution other than solidarity donations, the less committed began trying to back out of the confrontation, while the more militant wanted to escalate it. With branches all over Italy calling on the unions to launch a general strike, all minds became focused on 10–11 September, the date of a prearranged national council of the CGL.

This meeting goes down as one of the most extraordinary events in the history of the workers' movement. Here the idea of revolution, once the preserve of small outlawed groups, was openly debated and voted on by the trade union congress of a developed country. When the meeting began, there were an estimated 500,000 workers in occupation. What the CGL leaders wanted to know from their local agents was whether the factories were in a condition to launch an insurrection – to sally out from behind their barbed-wire barricades and take on the armed forces. The answer was no. The best-armed factory had only 5,000 rounds of machine-gun ammunition. So they resolved to negotiate, and to forget the seizure of power.

But they had reckoned without the addiction to rhetoric of the socialist party leaders. The Italian Socialist Party was a mass party like the German SPD or the British Labour Party, but unlike its counterparts it had, early in 1919, gone over en masse to membership of the Communist International. Its leaders were moderate men, no more revolutionary in practice than their counterparts elsewhere, but to them Marxism was like an old religion they could not renounce. To the chagrin of the real communists within the party, they refused to let the 'war between brothers' break out on their own soil.

Now, on the first day of the union council, the socialist leaders declared that, since this was a 'political' strike, it was their job to direct it; they would take over control and organise the seizure of power by the working class. Stung by this, the union leaders proposed a different way forward: to broaden the objective of the work-in. Instead of a 40 per cent wage rise, the aim would be nothing less than 'the recognition by employers of the principle of union control over industry'. They would boost financial aid to the metalworkers but not call out the rest of the union movement.

What happened next was later seen as farcical: they decided to put it to a vote. The block vote mechanism designed to determine issues like a pay claim or a union election was used to decide whether the Italian workforce would now rise up and seize power. The proposal was defeated by 591,245 votes to 409,569. The revolution was in effect called off, and in a matter of days a national vote was under way within FIOM for the ending of the occupations.

The relief of the employers was audible. But while they wanted now to move in for the kill, Giovanni Giolliti, the liberal premier, had his own ideas. Seeing the chance to engineer permanent peace in the factories, he brought forward his own proposal on workers' control. The unions should be incorporated into the joint management of the factories, on the management's terms but with a permanent role in decision-making:

A final solution lies in the integration of the workers, if necessary as shareholders, into the structure of industry in full practical participation . . . so that they learn the real conditions of industry and the state of profits.

It was not such an outlandish idea. Giovanni Agnelli, the boss of Fiat, made a grudging public offer to turn the company into a cooperative, uttering the famous complaint, 'How can one build anything with the help of 25,000 enemies?' And read this conversation between Albertini, the editor of *Corriere della Serra,* and liberal politician Giovanni Amendola, four days *after* the crucial conference vote against revolution.

> Albertini: The only way to avoid the revolution is to give power to the CGL.
>
> Amendola: To do what?
>
> Albertini: The factory council, anything they want ... but at least there'd then be some order ... The only thing left is to resign and to give power to the CGL. They must be told: you are the masters now, so take power legally.[15]

Giolitti's offer of industrial participation turned what could have been a humiliating climbdown into a victory for the moderate leadership of both the unions and the socialist party. The party summed up how most workers saw the ending of the factory occupations:

> As in all battles, won or lost, there are those who find things to criticise, as they even criticise today's magnificent trade union victory. We thus find some who lament the fact that the historical and pro-letarian moment was not seized upon to abolish industrial privilege completely ... Let us have no illusions. The recent events are the preface to others which the psychic evolution of the masses will carry to completion ...[16]

It did not turn out that way. The morale of the trade union movement collapsed and Gramsci set about organising the split that would create the communist party. Meanwhile the employers – frustrated with Giolitti – poured money into the fascist movement. Two years later the unions would be forcibly dissolved by gangs of strike-breakers loyal to a man called Mussolini. Bruno Buozzi would write, in exile,

> To raise the question of whether the occupation of the factories could have resulted in political action which could have prevented the rise of fascism and led Italy towards socialism is perhaps a waste of time. One thing however we must say if we want the experi-ence of the past to serve as a lesson for the future: what the Italian

socialist movement really lacked was decision . . . The party could make up its mind neither on revolution nor on participation in government.[17]

'Speeding up the slow men . . .': Sit-down strikes on this scale were a new phenomenon but so were the scientific management techniques that had begun to transform the workplace. The first two decades of the 20th century saw the introduction of methods invented by Henry Ford and Frederick Winslow Taylor: mass production of standardised goods, the moving production line and precise measurement of the 'time and motion' involved in manual labour. These, in turn, created a new kind of worker, the semi-skilled operative, thereby breaking the stranglehold of the skilled craftsmen over the pace and quality of work.

Taylor was the theorist, Ford the practitioner. Ford's first production line, opened at Highland Park, Michigan in 1913, aimed to iron out all unevenness within the workforce, 'slowing down the fast men and speeding up the slow men'. Taylor's theory of scientific management had shot to national prominence in 1911 as a result of a Congressional row over the trouble it was stirring up in factories. Taylor's aim was to break down skilled labour into measurable smaller tasks, in the process destroying the autonomy of the skilled worker.

In both systems the trade-off for the robotisation of work was higher wages. Before rationalisation, the workforce at Highland Park was 13,000 but Ford was hiring and firing 50,000 workers a year. When Ford raised wages from $3 to $5 a day and cut the working day from nine hours to eight, turnover fell to 5 per cent. Indeed, for Ford higher wages were there not just to reward higher productivity but to create a market for the cars they were churning out.

> All other considerations aside, our own sales depend in a measure upon the wages we pay. If we can distribute high wages then that money is going to be spent and it will serve to make storekeepers and distributors and manufacturers and workers in other lines more prosperous and their prosperity will be reflected in our sales.[18]

Fordism and Taylorism were to shape the industrial landscape of the 20th century, but, initially the new techniques met resistance. In 1913 the French union federation, the CGT, warned its members,

> The worker is reduced to the position of a brute, in which he is forbidden to think or reflect; he is reduced to a machine without a soul, producing intensely and excessively until his premature exhaustion turns him into a non-value . . . Taylorism is pitiless; it eliminates the non-values and those who have surpassed the age of full muscular strength.[19]

During the First World War, with strikes banned in belligerent countries, with an influx in unskilled labour to 'dilute' the skilled engineering shops, conditions for the new techniques were ideal. Yet, outside America they were only applied thoroughly in a few show plants, in part because of opposition by the unions. However, after the war, a major change took place in the thinking of union leaders about the new techniques, known popularly as 'rationalisation'. In Italy, Bruno Buozzi wrote,

> Those American technocrats who call themselves anti-socialists, but who propose a rational organisation of production and distribution, albeit subordinate to the profit motive, are, without knowing it, potential Marxists . . . Prejudice against rationalisation is childish.[20]

In France the leaders of the CGT were converted to the same idea. By 1920 the union's guru of workplace sociology, Hyacinthe Dubreuil, was advocating a kind of 'workers' Taylorism' modelled on conditions in the Bata shoe factory in Czechoslovakia. Workers should embrace the rationalisation of production and the new technology involved, but struggle to impose their own control on the speed of work and participate in the innovation process. In the USA it was the death of veteran craft union leader Samuel Gompers in 1924 that opened the way for the unions to accept Taylorism as progressive.

The conversion to Taylorism was not just the result of moderation; the union leaders could see both advantages and necessities. Higher productivity could shorten the working day; team work eradicated the last vestiges of craft mentality and, as Buozzi observed, 'narrowed the collaboration between workers and managers'. Above all, by weakening the autonomy of the individual worker over the pace of work, scientific management had shifted the question of control to the level of the whole factory. Albert Guigui, a French metalworker, summed up the deal the unions were trying to make with Taylorism: 'Expertise has passed from the man to the team, certainly in the workshop and sometimes even in the factory. To the worker who has lost his skill the union can offer, in exchange, the mastery of industry.'[21] Only after 1926 did anything like Taylorism get implemented widely in French factories, and again the emphasis was on new machinery and paternalistic schemes rather than measured and disciplined work.

It is no accident, however, that all three of the big sit-down strike waves of the inter-war period centred on automobile factories. Car workers were always the laboratory rats of the Taylor theory because this was a brand new industry where to be as efficient as Henry Ford was a life and death issue. Walter Moore, a communist party organiser in the US auto industry, did his best to describe the inside of a Taylor-designed workshop to the uninitiated:

> Did you ever see a house in the country on fire? They tear up the carpets, rip out the furniture, throw everything out of the windows and doors, work at white heat while great, red flames shoot up to the sky. Well, that's a shop, only in a shop it goes on and on; the fire never goes out.[22]

So in the major industrial battles of the 1920s and 30s, employers faced a workforce which was more robotised, more alienated from work, but whose material standard of living was higher. Among them there was acceptance that the production process had to be rationalised, but no agreement that it should be to the detriment of the workers.

France, 1936

To be a communist in France in the early 1930s was depressing; to be a socialist probably even more depressing. French Communist

Party (PCF) numbers had fallen to just 29,000. The Socialist Party with 191,000 members seemed doomed to remain in parliamentary opposition forever. Even if you added together the pro-communist and pro-socialist sections of the CGT they had less than half the members they had registered in 1918. In 1931 came the Depression. Then, in January 1933, Hitler rose to power in Germany.

It was the sudden danger of fascism in France that changed things, most dramatically when fascist demonstrators tried to storm parliament on 6 February 1934, resulting in 15 deaths. The CGT called a one-day general strike which brought millions out of their factories and forced the socialist and communist leaders to forget the 'war between brothers' and unite. In October 1934 the PCF issued the call for a Popular Front against fascism, discarding its previous theory that the socialists were worse than fascists. In September 1935 the two trade union federations voted to merge, with their membership now rising on the back of a wave of economic disputes.

Simone Weil, a 25-year-old socialist schoolteacher, knew instinctively that the coming crisis would be decided in the factories; she had, in any case, been shunted around the school system after going on too many anti-fascist marches and factory work was all she could get. She took a job at the Renault factory at Billancourt, where her diaries and notes comprise an unparalleled record of life inside a typical Fordist workplace in the years when it was about to become a battleground.

She describes the process of working up to the required speed of the metal press: 400 pieces of metal pressed an hour is a lot, but the target is 800 – more than 13 repetitions of the same task every minute. She manages it by the second day. 'What did I gain from this experience?' she asks, after being harangued by her foreman.

> . . . the feeling that I had no right, whatever, to do anything at all (and be careful not to lose it). The capacity to make do, mentally, on my own; to live in this latent state of perpetual humiliation without seeming humiliated in my own eyes; to savour intensely each moment of freedom or comradeship, as if it should be eternal.[23]

It was feelings like this, multiplied across hundreds of factories, that fed the workers' enthusiasm for the Popular Front. In the factories they felt worthless; on the streets they knew they were the only force that could save France from fascism. In its manifesto the Popular Front called for the defence of civil liberties, the disbanding of fascist squads, the defence of secular education and union rights. It also promised a reduction in the working week without loss of pay, and a new system of social security with pensions and unemployment benefits for workers. Half a million people demonstrated in Paris on 14 July 1935 in support of the Popular Front, the economic grievances spilling over into the political space.

In the French elections on 3 May 1936 the Popular Front won an outright majority and there was dancing in the streets. Fascism had been sidelined, in part because the socialist and communist parties had swallowed their differences, in part because they had moderated their demands. But it was just the start. Simone Weil described the normal atmosphere of the factory as one where 'nobody raises their head, never; nobody smiles; nobody says a word; how alone one feels'.[24] But the election victory let them raise their heads. A wave of sit-down strikes would soon begin that would dwarf those seen in Italy.

In France there was no background of revolutionary agitation, no factory council movement, no newspaper like *L'Ordine Nuovo* to encourage the takeover of the factories. All French workers knew was that ordinary strikes usually failed; that the police would be used if things got nasty on the picket line. And they knew that workers had used the occupation tactic and won – there'd been sporadic sit-down strikes in Poland, Romania and the British coal mines in the early 1930s.[25]

Now, a week after the election victory but before the Popular Front took office, two almost identical strikes took place in the cities of Le Havre and Toulouse. Both were caused by the sacking of union members who had taken the day off to attend May Day marches. Following the euphoria of the election result this seemed like a slap in the face to the workers concerned. In each case they called a strike but stayed in the plant overnight; in each case the dispute was swiftly resolved through arbitration by local mayors. On 14 May a third factory, an aircraft plant, decided to adopt the sit-down tactic too. Only on 24 May did the communist daily *L'Humanité* comment on the strikes and point out the rare, complete victories they had won.

By then, however, momentum was growing and the issue was not sackings but the programme of the Popular Front itself. Workers at three major engineering factories set down a list of demands along the lines of what the new government had promised and at Hotchkiss, in the Paris suburb of Levallois, workers seized the plant. They asked for union recognition, a significant wage rise, paid holidays and the abolition of overtime, plus no recriminations and full pay for the time spent occupying the factory. They won everything.

Now most of the engineering workers in Paris decided they would like the same thing. Since they could get what they'd voted for just by sitting down, the workers decided not to wait for the socialist premier Leon Blum to take office. When Renault-Billancourt, the heartland of French trade unionism, was occupied it signalled a national crisis. By 28 May 100,000 workers were sleeping inside their factories. As social commentators chewed their pens over the cause of the strikes, Simone Weil went straight to the point – it was the Popular Front.

> As soon as one felt the oppression weaken, immediately the suffering, the humiliation, the bitterness silently accumulated over the years became a force strong enough to loosen the bonds. That's the whole story of the strike: there is no other.[26]

By the day of Blum's inauguration the sit-ins had spread from engineering to the chemical, food, textiles, furniture, transport and oil industries. All newspapers except the three belonging to Popular Front parties had been stopped by their print workers.

The French president ordered Blum to broadcast immediately to the nation on the radio, promising to enact his social programme as soon as the parliamentary session began. But the strike movement did not stop. It spread across the French provinces and into industries where unions barely existed. Three Paris department stores were occupied, the builders working on the site of the Paris Expo took it over, and the entire cinema industry from studios to usherettes went on strike, mounting 'proletarian' programmes for the strikers. This in turn transformed the movement's character and took it beyond what the Italian metalworkers had achieved: every main street, every housing district was transformed.

In the early hours of 8 June 1936 Blum brokered the first Matignon Accord, so called for the name of the building where he, the union leaders and the employers met. Faced with social upheaval the employers caved in completely. Blum, who gave an unvarnished account of the events at his trial by the Vichy regime in 1942, described the scene:

> The CGT representative said to the representatives of big business: 'We will undertake to do everything in our power, but we cannot guarantee success. With a tidal wave like this, the best thing is to give it time to run its course. Maybe now you will start to regret using the years of deflation and unemployment to weed out systematically all our union militants. There are hardly any left to exercise the necessary influence on their workmates for our orders to be carried out.' And I can still see Mr Richemond, who was sitting on my left, bow his head, saying: 'It's true, we were wrong.'[27]

The Matignon Accord guaranteed collective bargaining, union recognition and a 12 per cent pay rise, graded so that the lowest paid received the most. A minimum wage, no victimisations, paid holidays and the 40-hour week were to follow, backed by legislation. Effectively the strike movement had circumvented the parliamentary process and implemented Blum's entire manifesto within four days of his taking office, and from below. A second Matignon Accord was signed three days later to stop workers bringing forward wage rises in advance of the new national deal.

Leon Jouhaux, the veteran leader of the CGT, broadcast to the nation on the significance of the victory. For him it was proof that old-style syndicalism worked better than revolutionary Bolshevism.

> For the first time in the history of the world a whole class has won an improvement in its conditions at the same time. These events

prove beyond doubt there is no need of a dictatorial and authoritarian state to achieve the elevation of the working class to its rightful role of collaborator in the national economy.[28]

By this time there were a quarter of a million workers in occupation in the Nord region alone. French prefectures put the official figure for the June strike wave at 1.8 million workers in 12,000 workplaces, three quarters of which were occupied.[29]

But the Matignon Accords were not enough. Workers found their bewildered managers still trying to bully and belittle them. While many of the strike resolutions had spoken about wages and hours there was also the persistent theme of dignity – and the lack of it – in the relationship between manager and employee. This, plus the sheer euphoria of the strike, goes a long way to explaining what happened next: the movement refused to demobilise.

In defiance of the wishes of the union, the government and the Communist Party, the occupations continued. It was at this moment that, having pushed hard within the unions to get the strikes called off, communist leader Maurice Thorez issued his famous statement: 'One must know how to end a strike.'

It was at this relatively late stage that the occupation movement began to take on some of the proto-soviet forms that had been seen in Turin. Mass meetings of delegates from across the engineering industry were called under the auspices of the CGT. On 10 June Weil reflected the growing fear that the strikes could simply lead to nationalisation of the factories and 'a return to drudgery':

> I myself see another possibility. It is, to tell the truth, delicate to speak about it publicly at present . . . Tough! Each has to shoulder his responsibilities. I think, myself, that the moment could be favourable, if you knew how to use it, to create the first embryo of workers' control.

Hers was not a lone voice. So Thorez called together a mass meeting of 700 communist organisers and instructed them that there was 'no question' of letting the wage issue slip into the background and going all out for workers' control of production. The message was spelled out on the front page of *L'Humanité* and became the theme of the speeches of communist organisers in the workplaces: no workers' control. By 13 June the strike movement started to unwind.

What turned two sit-ins to defend sacked militants into the biggest wave of factory occupations the world has ever seen? It was not agitation; neither the unions nor the communists agitated for the sit-in tactic, though they went with it at the time. Nor was it a 'revolutionary situation'; the governmental crisis had been resolved and the danger of fascism was receding. If anything it was a mass act of opportunism, with workers seeing the chance of a one-off change in the power balance in the workplace.

However, there was also something else at work, a visceral desire for liberation within the factory. The labour historian Lefranc called it 'a great collective feverish escapism'. Danos and Gibelin, historians who were activists at the time, remember:

> Contagion, imitation, certainly played a decisive role in a large number of cases. The very novelty of the undertaking was a source of attraction – with its creation of a whole set of new situations – the feeling of escape from the routine of everyday life, the breaking down of the barrier between private lives and the world of work, the transformation of the workplace into a place of residence, fulfilment of the desire for action, of the need to 'do something' at a time when everyone felt that important changes were coming. All these elements played a part in the spread of the occupations and helped to account for participants' universal enthusiasm and cheerfulness.[30]

The movement of May–June 1936 was bracketed by two mass demonstrations. The first, on 14 May, to commemorate victims of the Paris Commune, attracted 600,000. The second, on Bastille Day, brought over a million onto the streets of Paris. For about a month workers found themselves living in a wonderland where strikes could win, where the factory was transformed from a place of robotic drudgery, where the streets were alive with red flags and comradeship. The movement achieved major social reforms and a shift in the balance of power within the workplace, but it had also produced something intangible, something which made it taste sweet, whereas a normal strike tastes like necessarily bitter medicine. Weil wrote,

> The very act of striking is a joy. A pure and unalloyed joy . . . I have been to see my pals in the factory where I worked a few months ago . . . what joy to enter the plant with the smiling authorisation of a worker guarding the gate. Joy to roam freely through the shop where we were chained to our machines . . . joy to hear laughter instead of the pitiless din of machinery . . . joy to walk near the foreman with our heads held high . . . to live the rhythm of human life amongst the silent machines . . . of course the hard existence will begin again in a few days but no one is thinking of that now . . . at last for the first time different memories will haunt these heavy machines, souvenirs of something other than silence, constraint, submission.[31]

The 1936 sit-ins mark the point when factory workers in a major industrial country collectively lost their illusions about 'scientific management'. A far-fetched judgment? Well, hear it from the horse's mouth. It was Citroen's owners who pioneered Taylorism in France. Today the official corporate history of Peugeot-Citroen concedes:

> Although Taylorism enhanced productivity and promoted the employment of unskilled labor, it soon became apparent that the only way to increase production was to push workers to the limit. Reduced to the rank of automatons, workers saw their intellectual and social prospects decline. The monotonous tasks and lack of intellectual stimulation were discouraging.[32]

The gains of Matignon were short-lived; they were rolled back at gunpoint in the Renault factory in 1938 once the Popular Front had been replaced by politicians who would later surrender France to the Nazis. But the strikes had killed stone dead French managers' ability to impose the harsh form of Taylorism they had been reading about in American textbooks. And, within months, the American texts would have to be rewritten anyway.

★　★　★

Flint, Michigan, 1937

There was something new happening to politics in America. Franklin Delano Roosevelt had come to power in 1933 promising a 'New Deal', essentially the application of state intervention and corporatist policies to get the economy out of depression. The 1935 Wagner Act had given unions new legal rights to organise and ballot for recognition and prompted resistance from employers. In November 1936 Roosevelt was re-elected with a landslide, with active support from the union movement.

Something new was happening in the unions too. Membership of the American Federation of Labor was limited to skilled workers; its leaders actually opposed the organisation of unskilled workers. What they opposed in particular was unskilled workers being organised across their grades and specialisms into so-called 'industrial unions'. The ultra-moderates who led the AFL were haunted by the ghastly memory of the Wobblies, and had no intention of letting the phenomenon of 'one big union' return.

However, there was a growing reform movement within the AFL. In 1935 it formed the Committee for Industrial Organisation (CIO) with the explicit aim of organising industrial unions. In September 1936 the AFL leadership expelled the CIO unions, creating in effect a rival union federation one million strong. A small taste of the bitterness with which the inter-union battle was fought out can be gained from the comments of AFL leader Arthur Wharton.

> Many employers now realise that [the Wagner Act] is the law of our country and they are prepared to deal with labor organisations. These employers have expressed a preference to deal with the AFL organisations rather than [the CIO leaders] and their gang of sluggers, bums, expelled members of labor unions, outright scabs and the Jewish organisations with all their red affiliates.[33]

The Flint dispute at General Motors (GM) was what put the CIO on the map. GM at this time employed 60 per cent of the automobile industry workforce. Though built on Taylorism and Fordism, GM was run by a third great mind in the pantheon of scientific management, Alfred P. Sloan. Sloan's achievements included bringing financial management to bear on the shop floor and designing a range of cars at different price brackets that did not compete with one another. Today one of the top management schools in the world is named after Alfred Sloan. Leo Connelly, a drill presser in 1936, recalls what Sloan's management style meant at the level of the workplace:

> They treated you like a dog, you know. If you wanted to go to the restroom or the toilet, you had to ask them, and they pulled a watch on you to see how long you were gone, and they pulled a watch on you come back to see how long you'd gone, you know. Stuff like that, that's what brought on this whole thing.[34]

Fred Ahearn, an assembly line worker at GM remembers:

> I've gone home so completely exhausted and my hands so swollen that I couldn't get my fingers between each other. And rather than eat my dinner in an evening, I would lie down and go to sleep and get up the next morning and go back at it again, not knowing if I was going to work that day or whether I was going to be laid off.[35]

GM was making $173 million a year in profits. It was also spending the best part of a million dollars a year on detectives who would root out union-minded workers by posing as activists and trying to recruit them. GM was paying its workers an average $900 a year at a time when the poverty threshold for wages was set at $1,600.

When markets were depressed speeding up the line was the most simple, brutal and effective way for manufacturers to defend their profit margins. The workers would have to work harder and, with the flick of a switch, could be forced to – so the advocates of Taylorism believed. Today exchanging gossip next to a tank of cooled mineral water is considered part of workplace life, but there was no such thing as the 'water-cooler moment' at Sloan's GM.

> It was a fast pace is right. I had a water fountain back behind me – you probably heard some say that and I can tell you that's God's truth,

that water fountain wasn't over ten feet from me – I worked for an hour and I wanted a drink of water and I didn't have time to get it.[36]

Hiring and firing was relentless. Men who could not work fast enough would be sacked. The newly initiated quickly found out they could not keep down food, such was the pace of work. Others worked voluntarily through meal breaks to catch up with the line. Ray Holland, who worked in the Chevrolet assembly plant, explains what recruitment and retention meant for GM in 1936: 'I have absolutely, and tell the truth, seen them hire a hundred men and fire a hundred all the same day. That's what the thing's all about. If you never knew whether you had a job or not.'[37]

It was the back-room struggle between the AFL and CIO that inadvertently chose the GM plant at Flint, Michigan as the place where these employment practices would be challenged. The United Auto Workers had been founded in 1935 by CIO supporters, but by the summer of 1936 it was led by an AFL supporter, Homer Martin, a moderate. He ordered the left wing of the union to run a recruitment drive in Flint, which he assumed would be a disaster and would discredit it. Instead the union began to grow rapidly. Roy Knotts remembers:

You were asked to join on the QT, 'cause you didn't know who in the heck was gonna squeal on you if you did join, you know. If they got to know you, you were asked to join. And you knew that the guys around you was workin' or already belonged, you know, but you didn't say anything. But you knew that they belonged. And you more or less figured if you didn't join at that time, you ain't gonna have anybody talk to you . . . [38]

In mid-November, the election landslide for Roosevelt signalled that the time was ripe to take on Alfred Sloan. Isolated strikes had broken out in parts of the GM empire but no national strike for recognition would be called until three strategic plants were ready to act: the Fisher Body plants in Flint and Cleveland, and the Chevrolet 4 plant in Flint, which together produced the dies and chassis that all the other factories needed. Bob Travis, a CIO supporter, was put in charge of preparations. On 17 December the union submitted a claim for recognition. On 18 December the plant in Cleveland struck and was occupied. With a strike planned to begin on 1 January at the Fisher Body plant in Flint, the management made preparations to move the crucial stamping dies out of the factory. It was this that sparked the sit-in.

When the railway trucks arrived to remove the dies, workers rushed from shed to shed shouting, 'Strike on!' At this time big strikes in America meant big trouble. The workers knew they would be hit by a combination of armed police, the National Guard and private detectives, so they prepared accordingly.

> The workers inside immediately began to secure the plant against any attacker. They moved scores of unfinished Buick bodies in front of all entrances to form a gigantic barricade. With acetylene torches they welded a steel frame around every door. Bullet-proof metal sheets were put in position to cover every window, while holes were carved in them and threaded to allow the nozzles of fire hoses to be screwed into them. Wet clothes were kept in readiness to be placed on the face as protection against tear-gas attacks. Large supplies of metal parts were placed in strategic spots. Paint guns for spraying would-be invaders were located throughout the plant.[39]

On 3 January, the UAW called a national conference. Three hundred delegates representing ten cities met in Flint and formulated their demands: recognition for the union, no victimisations, a last-in-first-out principle for any layoffs, an increased minimum wage, a 30-hour 5-day week, time and a half for overtime, abolition of piecework and a slowdown of the assembly line. By the end of the first week of January, 100,000 GM workers were on strike.

> Inside, every worker had a specific duty for six hours a day. They were on duty for three hours, off for nine, on three and off nine,

in each 24-hour period. Every day at 3 p.m. there was a general cleanup. No matter how cold the weather, all windows were opened wide and teams of workers moved in waves on, and in between, the assembly lines for the entire length of the plant, leaving it spick-and-span.

GM's initial response was to seek a court injunction and the union was ordered to pull the workers out of the plant within 24 hours. However, when newspapers revealed that the judge involved owned GM stock worth $219,000, the company decided not to press the injunction. Instead, on 11 January it tried to seize the plant by force, beginning with the smaller and more vulnerable Fisher 2 plant.

In what became known as the Battle of Bulls Run, the police – having failed to storm the gates – fired tear gas through the windows. Genora Dollinger, a woman UAW member inside the plant, remembered how they fought back:

> We didn't have any body contact. This was all shooting, you know. We had the water hoses from the plant and the hinges and the stones, that's all. Those hinges were kind of heavy hinges, you know; the old car door hinges was a different thing . . . the blackjacks would do no good; there was no hand-to-hand combat. Those cops had rifle shot and buckshot; there were fire bombs; and there were tear gas containers. We would run out and grab – the men were faster at that, they were better pitchers, I didn't try anything like that – the tear gas canisters and hurl them back. And the fire bombs, they usually got those things – I mean they attempted to; the timing on those were very important.[40]

The police retreated when a large crowd of women, who had assembled to watch the battle, broke through the police lines to join the strikers.

The next day 8,000 flying pickets arrived, not only from other GM plants but from across the auto industry. The National Guard was mobilised and the stand-off continued. There was an extensive support network for the strike within the city of Flint, with meals being centrally produced and brought in to the strikers. By this time most of GM was shut down: production had fallen from 50,000 units a day to 1,500. Flint had become not only a national symbol for the rise of industrial unionism but a practical rallying point for trade unionists across the state of Michigan. At one mass demonstration in support of the plant, 150,000 assembled in Detroit.

Inside the plant the occupiers were organised into 'social groups' of 15 involved mainly in patrolling and cleaning rotas. There were two meetings a day of the 1,200 workers inside Fisher Body 1, with a central organising committee and subcommittees for 'food, police, information, sanitation and health, safety, "kangaroo court", entertainment, education and athletics.'[41]

The company announced it would begin negotiations on 18 January and some plants began to evacuate, with one banner promising, 'Today GM. Tomorrow Ford!' But it became clear that GM was preparing to recognise not the UAW but its own pro-company union. Negotiations ended and the entire industrial union movement now watched to see whether the workers in Flint could win the showdown.

The union organisers made their last throw of the dice. Walter Reuther, the legendary union organiser from Detroit, arrived in Flint with a team of union enforcers. One strike activist remembers:

> You probably remember seeing some of these old movies, where these fellows carried violins, and they weren't musicians . . . they claimed that Reuther had his own, you know, 'musicians', see, because they carried these violin cases.[42]

Reuther's 'violinists' would soon be serenading the Chevrolet 4 plant, whose 7,000 workers made the engines for a million cars a year, and had remained at work.

The union staged a diversion. They started a pitched battle at the Fisher Body plant, exchanging gas canisters and iron hinges with the police and creating general mayhem. Meanwhile union activists crept into the Chevrolet plant, pulled the switches and ordered everyone to stop work. There was sporadic fighting between pro- and anti-strike workers but it was soon over. At an impromptu meeting about half the workforce agreed to stay overnight and occupy the plant; meanwhile a large women's demonstration surrounded it. Industrial cranes were used to build three-storey barricades. Joe Sayen, one of the organisers inside the plant addressed the crowd,

> We want the whole world to understand what we are fighting for. We are fighting for freedom and life and liberty. This is our one great opportunity. What if we should be defeated? What if we should be killed? We have only one life. That's all we can lose and we might as well die like heroes than like slaves.[43]

Eleven days later GM signed an agreement recognising the UAW at Flint and twenty other plants. It also opened negotiations on increased pay and unilaterally raised piece rates by five cents an hour. In the two weeks that followed, 87 factories were occupied throughout Detroit. Chrysler, General Electric and United States Steel – at that time the biggest steel company in the world – each subsequently signed recognition deals with the CIO. John Thrasher, a worker at one of the GM feeder plants recorded the moment his team packed up to leave the sit-in:

> As the exhilaration of our first union victory wore off the gang was occupied with thoughts of leaving the silent factory . . . One found himself wondering what home life would be like again. Nothing that happened before the strike began seemed to register in the mind any more. It is as if time itself started with this strike. What will it be like to go home and to come back tomorrow with motors running and the long-silenced machines roaring again? But that is for the future . . . Now the door is opening.[44]

'We were happy . . .': Each strike has its own peculiar features but there are too many similarities between the sit-down strikes of the interwar period for there not to be a pattern. Each was part of a battle between radicals and moderates in the union movement; each happened during a political situation which tied the hands of the employers; each won a tactical victory. Each of the big sit-down strike movements had, at its heart, a major automobile plant: Fiat-Centro in Turin,

Renault-Billancourt in Paris, Fisher Body in Flint. Each plant was seen at the time as a showcase for scientific management. Agnelli, Renault and Sloan had created these factories as dedicated spaces for auto-mated production, skill-free and interchangeable workforces, moving production lines, meticulous time and motion. And in each case the robots rebelled.

The intensity of work inside the modern factory had turned the workplace into a symbolic space, and the experience of occupying it, rather than simply striking, seems to have presented the workers with a direct route to personal liberation within the factory. And they took it. In each case the sit-down was designed to get round the main pitfalls of mass strikes in the interwar years: violence and the seizure of union funds. Henry Kraus, a Flint strike activist, explains how the French sit-downs inspired the Americans:

> The whole idea of the sit-down was the fact that you were exposed over the usual strike, the strikes were illegal, you couldn't strike in Michigan . . . besides that, there is the question of violence. You strike, you have a picket line, they'll break it up for sure, one way or another, and arrest people . . . So, when we saw them having the very successful 1936 just around the same time, we saw this was brilliant, it was just the answer and we had something we had to do.[45]

Significantly, each strike ended with a change in the relationships between workers and foremen, as one of the Flint strikers remembers:

> We were treated more like human beings, and, if you wanted to talk to your supervisor . . . you could stop and talk to 'em and tell 'em your problems, where before, you could not. They ignored you, or they threatened you that if you didn't behave, you was just a troublemaker, you'd lose your job. So things improved in that way.[46]

The most lasting memory for those involved was the most intangible: the feeling of personal liberation in the place where they were normally treated like cogs in a machine. Simone Weil captured that moment of elation as she toured the Renault plant in July 1936:

Relaxation is complete. There is none of that fierce nervous energy, that determination mixed with pent-up anxiety so often associated with strikes in the past. We are determined certainly, but no longer anxious. We are happy.[47]

Afterword: Louise Michel with fairy wings

> There is no heroism: people are simply entranced by events.
>
> *Louise Michel*

Jack was a miner, he'd been working down Astley Green Colliery since the age of thirteen. A devout Christian, he once threw a novel into the fire because it had the word bastard in it. But he was also a devout Guinness drinker and in his wilder days was reputed to have thrown a fascist through a chip shop window, put a man's eye out in a pub fight and regularly gambled away his wages at the local race-track.

Jack married Ellen, a mill girl. She'd been thrown out of her family home when Jack got her pregnant. How did they survive during the long miners' strikes of 1921 and 1926? In preparation, coal bargemen they knew would kick some of their cargo into the canal at the end of their street. During the strike Jack would dive to the bottom of the canal, retrieve the coal, sell it and buy food.

Their daughter Irene always remembered the 1930s with a scowl and a head shake; Jack and Ellen never spoke of the decades before the Second World War – the tiniest detail had to be prised out of them: the rent man, the means-test man who would come into their house and order them to sell their furniture, the terrifying power of the doorstep loan shark. When, in the 1970s, they stripped back the wallpaper in their house there were crude white polka dots all over the plaster. 'Irene did that with whitewash and a sponge,' Ellen remembered. 'We hadn't enough money for paper.'

Ellen's first surviving son was John; she'd had two who had not lived. By the time John got his first job, just after the war, the world

274

this family had fought for was a reality. The coal mine he started in was freshly nationalised; no one had to pay for medical care any more. Then he got a job on the railway, also nationalised. And soon they were not poverty-stricken anymore. Real wages rose. Sometime during the 1950s somebody bought a camera and, for the first time, a generation of this family would be remembered by more than just names written into the back of a Bible.

The earliest photographs of John show him in a sharp suit with Brylcreemed hair. He has two jobs, driving a truck by day, playing in a dance band by night. Both jobs are unionised – even as swing gives way to rock and roll no musician can play without a union card. At the electrical engineering factory he drives for, the union is an institution. Or rather the unions – plural. The engineers and electricians who supervise the machinery have their own, separate unions; they're paid almost double what a driver gets and, John suspects, vote Conservative. By 1960 John is the first member of his family to own a house, albeit one with flagstones on the kitchen floor and an outside toilet. That is the house I was born in.

I lived for the next eighteen years in this tightly knit working class town where people had jobs for life, where everybody was in a union, where the only party that ever won elections was Labour. They manufactured cotton, cranes, electrical system boards, asbestos and giant wire cables; they dug coal – you could tell the time by the shunt of the winding gear in the distance. During those eighteen years, despite two miners' strikes and numerous walkouts at my father's factory, I never once saw a red flag or a demonstration. The first miners' banner I ever saw was embroidered with a scene showing an evening cricket match, with players wearing white and the sun setting behind colliery winding gear. That seemed to be the extent of their dreams. Nobody mentioned the word capitalism; people who used it were seen as radical, and only middle class people were radical . . . and who wanted to be middle class?

What the miners had fought for were pit-head baths, a pension scheme, free health care, sports fields and the leisure time to play on them – and above all jobs. The visceral shudder that older people gave if someone mentioned the Depression told you, as no textbook or documentary could, what it had meant for them to be unemployed and in debt. Now they had got what they had fought for. And in case anybody failed to understand the distinctly non-radical principles they adhered to, another miners' banner carried the slogan 'Socialism through Evolution'.

That is what the labour movement looked like across the developed world during the four decades after 1945: ubiquitous, passive, barely political, static. It was a different world to the one I've described in this book. To understand how it all collapsed you first need to know how it came about.

In 1945 fascism was beaten but the labour movements of the world had paid a massive price. The independence, radicalism and gut anarchism that had driven them for decades were expunged. In America, Britain, Italy and France the unions allied themselves with employers and conservative politicians to defeat fascism. What they won in return was the welfare state, the European 'social model', or in America's case, a cut-down version involving healthcare and pensions for the core workforce. Germany and Japan had strong trade unions and welfare models imposed on them by their Allied occupiers; in Italy the workers' movement was so strong that a parallel state based on secrecy and corruption had to be built to run the country.

In the democracies the period 1945–89 saw unions take an unprecedented central role in economic life: they were seen as guardians not just of contracts in the workplace, but of a social contract involving pensions, healthcare and a strategic settlement between the classes. The Second World War had given another major push to scientific management in the workplace. During and after the war, life on a production line looked a lot like the workers' Taylorism dreamed about by trade union thinkers in the 1920s; likewise the 'industrial democracy' offered by liberal governments in Italy and Germany in the early 1920s now came into being. The 'union way of life' did not die immediately but it became a parallel lifestyle, separate from but not opposed to that of the upper classes. And eventually it withered away in all but the mountain strongholds of leftism: the Welsh valleys and Tuscan hill towns, the Buenos Aires docks.

In Russia, China and eastern Europe a different deal was imposed: in return for subservience and the absence of democratic rights, the worker – above all the heavy industrial worker – was guaranteed a social wage and a job for life and was vaunted in the public ideology of the Stalinist states. In sporadic revolutions the workers of east Europe tried to fight for more – democracy and national independence – but were crushed with tanks. Elsewhere they lived the deal summed up in the famous Russian workers' saying: 'We pretend to work, they pretend to pay us.' After 1947, for the first time in history, the world's working class was strategically divided; workers in the communist countries lived utterly different lives to those in the west.

As for revolution and class struggle, they became the playthings of the forces ranged against each other in the cold war, in eastern Europe and the developing world. For forty years, working class rebels would be either assassinated by the CIA or trained by the CIA, depending on geography. Meanwhile the war between brothers that had opened up within the labour movement in the 1920s began to heal, partly because in the Western democracies communism had no ambition to overthrow the status quo. The Comintern itself had been dissolved on Stalin's orders in 1943, as a gesture of goodwill to the Allies.

Then, in the 1980s, these post-war compromises fell apart. Economic crisis had summoned up the dormant militant soul of the unions during the 1970s: from Bologna to Detroit, the swiftness of shop-floor radicalisation shocked the employers. In response, governments in the West tore up tacit agreements with the unions and adopted the neo-liberal policies which led to mass unemployment. They passed anti-union laws and freed capital to move across borders. The iconic photograph of the 1980s was of the leaders of the American air traffic controllers' union chained hand and foot. By the time he dies in 1986, John – my father – knows once again all about the dole queue. And he has seen the old miners' banners, full of soft-soap imagery about progress and evolution, carried into battle for the last time by a doomed workforce, which suffers shattering defeat.

History moves swiftly now: after 1989 communist regimes collapse everywhere except in China, Vietnam and North Korea, and even here, except in the unreal kingdom of Kim Jong Il, communist governments are pursuing neo-liberal policies. This, in turn, ushers in the era of globalisation.

Industrialisation in the global south together with marketisation in the East has doubled the size of the global working class. A billion waged workers in the less-developed countries, together with 1.47 billion in India, China and the former Comecon states now dwarf the 460 million workers of the developed world.[1] And their lives are articulated together as never before. Globalisation has stretched the manufacturing process across continents and time zones. Digital communications allow the lives of workers in different countries to be massively more transparent to each other – and more similar.

Before looking at what these changes mean for the modern labour movement, it is worth considering what they mean for labour history. During the long post-war boom working class history was reshaped in order to justify the status quo. While Stalinism was all-powerful in the East, and influential in the West, it was the Moscow version of history that came to be accepted as definitive. In that version everything workers do before 1848 is seen as something of a preamble to the arrival of Karl Marx. In the Paris Commune, Eugene Varlin is in the wrong while middle class supporters of revolutionary terror are in the right. The story of the great upsurge of the unskilled worker, 1889–1914, is seen through the lens of the Second International. Bill Hayward, Jim Larkin, Tom Mann and Elizabeth Gurley Flynn all became communists in the 1920s, renouncing the anti-political stance of syndicalism – so what's the big deal? The story of the split in German socialism is told as triumph not tragedy; the story of the Shanghai workers in 1927 is remoulded by Maoism to become a one-dimensional struggle against foreign ownership. The Bund's memory is kept alive in a crumbling New York brownstone by old men tending newspaper archives written in a language their grandchildren cannot read.

On the social democratic side there is amnesia. Kier Hardie is remembered as the man who built the Labour Party, his speech denouncing the war, thrown into the teeth of a heckling mob in August 1914, forgotten. Bruno Buozzi, the Italian union leader who fought against revolutionary shop floor activism, is remembered – but more for his heroic death at the hands of the German occupiers in 1944 than for his union legacy. The reunification of the communist, socialist and Christian trade unions he had overseen did not survive the outbreak of the Cold War.

Even Walter Reuther is canonised. The man who arrived at the Flint strike flanked by hard men carrying violin cases is eulogised by *Time* magazine as one of the top 100 'founders and titans' of America.

> In 1940, a year before Pearl Harbor, he proposed converting available capacity in auto plants to military production . . . His plan was harshly criticized by the corporations, which were unwilling to give up any part of their profitable business. When the Japanese attacked Pearl Harbor, the rapid conversion to military production validated Reuther's vision.[2]

In short, during the post-war period 'official' labour history was devoted to rationalising the deal made in 1945 between employers and workers on both sides of the Iron Curtain.

Only at the edges did academics begin chipping away at the monolith. Edward Thompson's *Making of the English Working Class* initiated a school of labour history based on the micro-story, not the macro-narrative. Much of the insight we now have into the Bund, French syndicalism and Chinese workers in the 1920s comes from work by scholars following Thompson's approach. But in this 'new' labour history what gets lost is often story and significance. In reaction to the narratives superimposed on facts by Moscow, modern academics tend to avoid 'big truths' within the life stories of those they have rescued from oblivion.

I think there are two big truths contained in the stories I've unearthed. The first is that workers, faced with the thrills and hardships of rapid industrialisation, organise unions because of the very same economic forces that make rival companies compete and managers cut costs. As they organise, they hear from socialists and anarchists that they can only be free by abolishing capitalism; that something in their miserable way of life makes them the 'bearer' of a new kind of society. But what they actually try to do, at first, is create the new society *within* the old, building co-ops, fighting for autonomy in the workplace, creating a union way of life. Only when this world within a world is made impossible do they directly confront corporate power. And when history hands full employment, affluence and an element of control to them on a plate – as it did in Europe after 1945 – the red flags are relegated to the museum.

The second big truth is that when there is a globalised economy, a global labour movement begins to take shape. It has only happened twice – once in the run-up to the First World War, and the second time right now. But here is the difference: during the first great era of globalisation, the primary economic unit was the nation state. Major corporations were sometimes more powerful than nation states but, when war came, they aligned with the governments they saw as representing their vital interests. As a result, the first period of globalisation was also a period of rampant popular nationalism – a gut nationalism that eventually swamped the resolution-based internationalism of the syndicalists and socialists.

It is very different now. Today the transnational corporation is the primary form of economic life. In addition, global consumer culture is breaking down all that was local, insular and closed in working class communities. There is, for the first time, a truly global working class. But it has not yet had its 1889 moment and most of those who would like to make it happen are pretty realistic about what stands in the way.

In the first place the workforce is more stratified. What was added during the 1920s – a white-collar stratum within the unions, scientific management and mass consumer culture – has been strengthened by neo-liberalism and globalisation. Not only is the workforce of the developed world highly 'incorporated' into civil society, but the new workforce created by globalisation is born with more rights, more access to the media and to justice, than the workforce of 100 years ago. Self-organisation, in the form of unions, cooperatives and political parties, does not seem as urgent to them, yet. And even where it does, it is overlaid by the remnants of village and religious loyalty and plagued by organised crime – the same factors that made it so hard for Shanghai's workforce to create stable organisations and survive repression.

Second, there is the culture of individualism born of technological progress. The communications revolution has created a young generation that thinks more individualistically, cares more about its individual rights than its collective ones, and is – to the frustration of union organisers – less inclined to join organisations. If the union way of life was in the 1890s the only positive identity on offer to young workers, today they are adept at playing with multiple identities: Shenzhen shoe worker by day, World of Warcraft dwarf by night, retro-punk rocker at the weekend. And the phenomenon is growing in the global south as mobile phones and Internet cafes arrive there.

Third, the cotton spinners at Peterloo had Shelley and Sir Robert Peel to plead their case; the London dockers of 1889 had Beatrice Webb. But during globalisation, as official socialist parties have adopted neo-liberalism as the consensus, a new kind of social reformism has emerged, and from an unlikely quarter.

The anti-globalisation movement that hit the streets of Seattle in 1999 did not spring from nowhere; it was an alliance of eco-activists, anarchists and those inspired by the surrealism of the Zapatista guerrillas in Mexico. On its own it would have remained as separate from the workers' movement as the Saint-Simonians were from the *canuts* of Lyon, but it found itself in alliance with multi-million-dollar global aid agencies pushed into a more radical stance by the seeming indifference of those in power. There was an ideological crisis too in the headquarters of those bodies supposed to oversee the economic order: they could see that existing 'anti-poverty' strategies had actually worsened poverty. But what ensured the Seattle demonstration would shape history was the presence of organised labour. Whatever else you can say about a steelworker from Pittsburgh, you cannot truthfully describe him as a hand-wringing liberal, especially not when he is steaming into a line of Seattle riot cops.

Suddenly here was a coherent opposition to economic globalisation not simply based on anarchist radicalism or Marxist nostalgia.

Even then, had the world's boardrooms been shining models of corporate probity it might have been ignored. But first came Enron, Worldcom and Parmalat; then came acceptance by mainstream scientists and politicians that catastrophic climate change is a major danger. Basically, those in power have had to listen, and the proliferation of 'corporate social responsibility' executives and 'carbon neutrality' monitors within large companies testifies to that.

The new social reformism is strong. For a trade union activist in the developing world fighting poor conditions or anti-union violence, exposure in the Western media by a major NGO is often a far more powerful weapon than striking. Of course Tom Mann and Beatrice Webb had influence with the Lord Mayor of London and the Catholic hierarchy after the 1889 strike, but not such systematic and public influence as their modern counterparts in ActionAid and Oxfam wield.

Organised labour is a part of this movement, but a junior part; the leaders of major unions do not get their calls answered as readily by investment bankers as the leaders of major NGOs. It is in that sense that things are at a pre-1889 stage, though it is clear that battles in any post-1889 stage would be very different to those fought by Haywood, Griffuelhes and Mann. It is also clear that China is the big unknown in this equation. In China human rights are severely curtailed, NGOs have little sway, the huge urban workforce is the only part of the global working class not involved in the debate about globalisation. If that changes, many other variables will change as well.

As a result of what has happened since the 1980s, the lives of my family in the post-war boom seem to belong to another epoch, while the lives of people like Bill Haywood, Li Qi-han and Louise Michel seem modern. They are being re-lived in the sweatshops of India and China, in the slums that house a sixth of all humanity, and on the demonstrations that have harassed the world's decision-makers since Seattle.

And these were great lives. If the people I have chosen to write about had one thing in common it was their refusal to be doctrinaire, their embarrassment at the crazy non-sequiturs sometimes demanded by socialist or anarchist theory, their deep engagement with the lives of the people they were fighting for. They fought, as was said of Jim Larkin, 'for the flower in the vase as well as the loaf of bread on the table'. I don't believe they were born heroic; they were simply – as Louise Michel once wrote – entranced by extraordinary events.

Bill Haywood would always have been remembered as a leader of tough white men; it was the arrival of several million dirt-poor migrants on America's doorstep that gave him the chance to bestride the continents. Well, that is a chance every hard-talking union organiser in the world has today, with migration altering the demographics of the workforce beyond recognition.

Li Qi-han would have been executed as a communist in 1927 in any event; the fact that he refused to believe Chinese workers were ignorant, organised them into unions and drank cock's-blood wine with them in gangster temples to win their trust marks him out as an inspirational union leader. Today there are half a billion Chinese workers still waiting to take the first steps along the path Li set out on in the 1920s.

As for Louise Michel, she was always destined to be just another radical bohemian dreamer, writing poetry for the entertainment of slum children. Only when the workers decided to take control of Paris – and their lives – did the world become big enough for her dreams and poetry. I have seen the young Louise Michel dancing to a samba band in a field outside the Gleneagles summit; her face was painted and she was wearing pink fairy wings. She still has a lot to learn.

Notes

Some of the following references cite only web sources, undated pamphlets or leaflets and transcripts of speeches and oral testimony; they are as complete as possible.

Introduction

1   Larkin, E. *James Larkin, Irish Labour Leader, 1876–1947*, London 1965, p.11
2   Michel, L. *Red Virgin: Memoirs of Louise Michel*, Alabama 1982, p.52

1. Rise like lions

1   Lee, A. 'Breaching the Great Wall', *Chinascope*, April 2005
2   Chow Chun-yan, 'Shenzhen workers protest at beatings', *South China Morning Post*, 3 November 2005
3   Bamford, S. *Passages in the Life of a Radical*, London 1967 p.146
4   Ibid.
5   Ibid. p.147
6   Ibid. p.151
7   *Manchester Observer* 10 August 1822. Quoted in Read, D. *Peterloo: The 'massacre' and its background*, Manchester 1958
8   Sir William Joliffe in Bruton, F.A. *Three Accounts of Peterloo by Eyewitnesses*, Manchester 1921 p.53
9   Bamford, S. op. cit. p.152
10 Ibid. p.153
11 Prentice, A. *Historical Sketches and Personal Recollections of Manchester intended to illustrate the progress of public opinion from 1792 to 1832*, Manchester 1831
12 Holmes, R, *Shelley: The Pursuit*, London 1974
13 Shelley, P. *Shelley's Revolutionary Year: The Peterloo Writings of the Poet Shelley*, London 1990
14 Jolliffe, op. cit. p.56
15 Bamford, S. op. cit. p.157
16 Read, D. op. cit. p.142
17 Bamford, S. op. cit. p.158
18 *Ashton Chronicle*, 23 June 1849
19 Brown, J. *A memoir of Robert Blincoe, an orphan boy sent . . . to endure the horrors of a cotton-mill*, Firle 1977 p.28

20　Ibid. p.57
21　Gaskell, P. *Artisans and Machinery*, London 1968, p. 81
22　Bamford, S. op. cit.
23　Home Office Papers 42. 178, July 29 1818. Quoted in Hammond, J.L. and Hammond, B. *The Skilled Worker 1760–1832*, London 1919, p.99
24　Ibid.
25　Ibid.
26　Quoted in Hammond, J.L. and Hammond, B. *The Town Labourer 1760–1832*, London 1978, p. 308
27　*Manchester Observer*, 8 May 1819. Quoted in Read, D. op. cit. p.48
28　*Black Dwarf*, 2 June 1819. Ibid. p.50
29　*Sherwin's Political Register*, 5 June 1819. Ibid. p.51
30　Bamford, S. op. cit. p.123
31　*Manchester Observer*, 26 June 1819. Quoted in Read, D. op. cit. p.53
32　Bamford. S. op. cit. p.132
33　Norris, J. 12 August 1819. Quoted in Bamford, S. op. cit. p.138
34　Norris, J, 10 August 1819. Ibid. p.139
35　H.O. 42/188. Quoted in Read, D. op. cit.
36　Ibid. p.222

2. Everything connected with beauty

1　Benoît, J. *Confessions d'un prolétaire*, Paris 1968, p.41
2　Ibid. p.45
3　Sala, A. *Les ouvrieres Lyonnais en 1834, equisses historiques*, Paris 1834, p.10
4　Ibid.
5　Rude, F. *Les Révoltes des Canuts: 1831–1834*, Paris 2001, p.14
6　Villermé, L-R. *Tableau de l'état physique et moral des ouvriers employés dans les manufactures de coton, de laine et de soie*, 2 vols, Paris 1840, I p.377
7　Quoted in Cottereau, A. 'The Fate of Collective Manufactures in the Industrial World: the silk industries of Lyons and London 1800–1850' in Sabel, C.F. and Zeitlin, J. *World of Possibilities: Flexibility and mass production in western industrialisation*, Cambridge 1997, p.75
8　Rude, F. op. cit. p.15
9　Romand, J.-C. *Confession d'un Malhereux, Forcat Liberée*, Paris 1846, p.61
10　Ibid. p.61
11　'*L'Echo de la Fabrique*'. Quoted in Rude, F. op. cit. p.8
12　Benoît, J. op. cit. p.33
13　Ibid. p.44
14　Ibid. p.46
15　Bernard, M. and Charnier, P. 'Rapport fait à M. le Président du Conseil des ministres, sur les causes générales qui ont amené les évènements de Lyon', Lyon 1833
16　Blanc, L. *L'Histoire de Dix Ans: 1830–1840*, Paris 1840, p.56
17　Quoted in Rude, F. op. cit.
18　*L'Echo de la Fabrique*. Issue 1, 25 October 1831
19　Romand, J.-C. op. cit. p.76
20　*L'Echo de la Fabrique*. Issue 2, 6 November 1831

21 Romand, J.-C. op. cit. p.80
22 Romand, J.-C. op. cit. p.88
23 Montfalcon, J.-B. *Histoire des insurrections de Lyon*, Lyon 1834, p.82. Quoted in Popkin, J. *Press, Revolution and Social Identities in France 1830–1835*, Pennsylvania 2002 p.303
24 Romand, J.-C. op. cit. p.101
25 Romand, J.-C. op. cit. p.103
26 Montfalcon, J.-B. *Le Temps* 13 April 1834. Quoted in Rude, F. op. cit.
27 Girardin, S.-M. *Journal des debats*, Paris, 8 December 1831. Quoted in Popkin, J. op. cit. p.2
28 Chevalier, M. *A Lyon*, Menilmontant 23 November 1832
29 Quoted in Rude, F. op. cit. p.82
30 Benoît, J. op. cit. p.51
31 Anon. 'Curieux journal d'un ouvrier de la Croix-Rousse, president d'une societé patriotique, sur les événements auxquels il a pris part' in Sala, A. op. cit. p.150
32 *L'Echo de la Fabrique*, 1832

3. This is the dawn . . .

1   Valles, J. *L'Insurge*, Paris 1970
2   The interviewee asked for his name to be changed and the identity of his company to be withheld.
3   Foulon, M. *Eugène Varlin: Relieur et Membre de la Commune*, Clermont-Ferrand 1934, p.72
4   Foulon, M. op. cit. p.31
5   Quoted in Ranciere, J. and Vauday, P. 'Going to the Expo: the worker, his wife and machines' in Rifkin, A. and Thomas, R. *Voices of the People: The Social Life of 'La Sociale' at the End of the Second Empire*, London 1988, p.28
6   Ibid. p.31
7   Ibid. p.28
8   Ibid. p.31
9   Ibid. p.33
10 Foner, P.S. *History of the Labor Movement in the United States*, New York 1947, Vol. I, p.374
11 Marx, K. Letter to Engels 4 November 1864, in Marx, K. and Engels, F. *Collected Works*, Vol. 42, London 1987, p.11
12 Varlin, E. *Practique Militante & Ecrits d'un Ouvrier Communard* (ed. Lejune, P.) Paris 2002, p.21
13 Quoted in Ranciere, J. and Vauday, P. op. cit. p.41
14 Brocher, V. *Souvenirs d'une morte vivante*, Paris 1976, pp. 61–2
15 Varlin, E. op. cit. p.34
16 Charles Keller, quoted in Varlin, E. op. cit. p.37
17 It was on Rupert Street, just north of Leicester Square.
18 Villetard, E. *Histoire de l'Internationale*, Paris 1872, p.149
19 Michel, L. *Red Virgin: Memoirs of Louise Michel* (ed. Lowry, B. and Ellington Gunter, E.), Alabama 1981, p.81
20 Michel, L. op. cit. p.83

21 Michel, L. op. cit. p.52
22 Quoted in Thomas, E. *The Women Incendiaries*, New York 1966, p.31
23 Dalotel, A. and Feiermuth, J.-C. 'Socialism and Revolution' in Rifkin, A. and Thomas, R. op. cit. p.264
24 Ibid. p.260
25 Ibid. p.281
26 Michel, L. op. cit. p.54
27 Varlin, E. op. cit. p.66
28 Michel, L. 'La Commune', Paris 1999, p.29
29 Bouvier, A. 'La Canaille'
    (http://fr.wikisource.org/wiki/La_Canaille
30 Brocher, V. op. cit. p.102
31 Ibid. p.146
32 Ibid. p.151
33 Michel, L. 1999 op. cit. pp.139–140
34 Varlin, E. op. cit. p.153
35 Ibid. p.154
36 Quoted in Jellinek, F. *The Paris Commune of 1871*, London 1937 p.111
37 Brocher, V. op. cit. p.157
38 Guillaume, J. *L'Internationale* Vol. 2 pp.133–4. Quoted in Cordillot, M. *Eugène Varlin: Chronique d'un espoir assassiné*, Paris 1991, p.220
39 Jellinek, F. op. cit. p.406
40 Valles, J. op. cit. p.286
41 Foulon, M. op. cit. p.237. Based on an interview with the Commune member Camelinat, who was one of those who tried to intervene.
42 Lissagary, *History of the Paris Commune*, London 1976, p.302
43 Brocher, V. op. cit. p.159
44 Ibid. p.178
45 Ibid. p.190
46 Ibid. p.206
47 Michel, L. 1981 op. cit. p.59
48 Michel, L. ibid. p.83
49 Vallès, J. op. cit. p.288
50 Michel, L. 1981 op. cit. p.68
51 Brocher, V. op. cit. p.210
52 Lissagaray, op. cit. p.309

4. Every race worth saving

1 Quoted in Foner, P.S. op. cit. Vol. 1 p.437
2 Federation of Workers Councils and Unions in Iraq leaflet, 26 April 2006
3 Foner, P. S. op. cit. Vol. 1, p.433
4 Irons, M. 'My Experiences in the Labor Movement', *Lipincott's Monthly Magazine* Vol. 37 June 1886, p. 618
5 Ibid.
6 Ibid.
7 *Iron Moulders Journal*, June 1875. Quoted in Foner, P.S. Vol. 1 op. cit. p.475
8 Irons, M. op. cit.

9   *John Swinton's Paper*, 17 October 1886. Quoted in Powderly, T. *The Path I Trod*, New York 1968
10 Ibid.
11 Proceedings of the General Assembly, 1882. Quoted in Foner, P.S. Vol. 1 op. cit. p.508
12 *Journal of United Labor*, 15 August 1880
13 Joe B. Kewley letter to Powderly, 14 May 1883. Quoted in Foner, P.S. op. cit. p.68
14 Powderly, T. *The Path I Trod*, New York 1968, p.59
15 Northrop, Life and Achievements of Jay Gould, 1892, p.480. Quoted in Allen R., *The Great Southwest Strike* (University of Texas Publication 4214) Austin 1942, p.13
16 'Investigation of Labor Troubles in Missouri, Arkansas, Kansas, Texas and Illinois', 49th Congress Report No. 4174, Washington 1887
17 Quoted in Bimba, A. *The History of the American Working Class*, London 1927, p.179
18 Foner, P.S. Vol. 2 op. cit.
19 Quoted in Foner, P.S. Vol. 2 op. cit. p.106
20 'Investigation of Labor Troubles . . .' op. cit. (I) p.131
21 Ibid.
22 Ibid. p.133
23 Ibid. p.117
24 Ibid. p.469
25 *Fort Worth Gazetter*, 11 April 1886, p.4. Quoted in Allen, R. op. cit.
26 Quoted in Allen, R. op. cit.
27 Ibid. (I) p.375
28 Spies, A. *An Autobiographical Sketch by A. Spies*, Manuscript August Vincent Theodore Spies papers, Chicago Historical Society, Chicago Illinois
29 Ibid.
30 *Alarm*, quoted in Foner, P.S. Vol. 2 op. cit. p.102
31 People's Exhibit 91, Arbeiter–Zeitung (newspaper) article, editorial notice, 1886 Apr. 22, Chicago Historical Society
32 Bisno, A. *Abraham Bisno Union Pioneer*, Milwaukee 1967, p.66
33 *Chicago Tribune*, 26 April 1886. Quoted in Hirsch, E.L. *Urban Revolt, Ethnic politics in the late 19th century Chicago labor movement*, Berkeley, 1990
34 *Chicago Tribune*, 2 May 1886. Quoted ibid.
35 Bisno, A. op. cit. p.79
36 Ibid. p.81
37 Knights of Labor, 8 May 1886. Quoted in Hirsch, E.L. op. cit. p.75
38 Investigation of Labor Troubles (II) p.462
39 Debs, E.V, *His Life, Writings and Speeches*, p.274. Quoted in Allen, R. op. cit. p.148
40 *Chicago Tribune*, 10 October 1886
41 Powderly, T. op. cit. p.115

5. A great big union grand

1   Quoted in Kornbluh, J. *Rebel Voices: An IWW Anthology*, Chicago 1987, p.138
2   Roberts, R. *The Classic Slum*, London 1971, p.28
3   Tillett, B. *Dock Wharf and Riverside Union: A Brief History of the Dockers' Union*, London 1910

4   Webb, B. *My Apprenticeship*, Harmondsworth 1938, p.345
5   Ibid. p.368
6   Mann, T. *What a Compulsory Eight-Hour Working Day Means to the Workers*, 1886
7   Calculated using a pure GDP deflator scale. Source: *http://eh.net/hmit/ukcompare/*. Using average earnings (what £30,000 meant as wages to 30,000 dockers) it comes out nearer to £13 million.
8   *London Evening News & Post,* 26 August 1889
9   Burns, J. 'The Great Strike', *New Review,* Vol. 1 No. 5, October, London 1889
10 Mann, T. op. cit. p.18
11 Quoted in Pelling, H. *A History of British Trade Unionism*, London 1976, p.104
12 Griffuelhes, V. *L'action syndicaliste*, Paris 1908
13 *Qu' est-ce que la grève générale?*, Girard, H. and Pelloutier, F., Paris 1895
14 Steele, H. *The Working Classes in France, A Social Study*, London 1904, pp.16–17
15 Griffuelhes, V. op. cit.
16 Body, M. *Un Ouvrier Limousin au Coeur de la Révolution Russe*, Paris 1981, p.16
17 Ibid.
18 Louis M.-V., *Le droit de cuissage: France 1860–1930*, Paris 1994
19 *Le Siècle*, 22 April 1905. Quoted ibid.
20 *Le Réveil du Centre*, 23 avril 1905. Cited in ibid. p.295
21 Ibid.
22 Ibid.
23 Stearns, P. *Revolutionary Syndicalism and French Labor: A cause without rebels*, New Jersey 1971, pp.121–35
24 *L'Action*, 24 April 1906. Quoted in Vandervort, B., *Victor Griffuelhes and French Syndicalism 1895–1922*, Baton Rouge 1996
25 Confederation General du Travail, 1906
26 Quoted in A. Rosmer, *Le mouvement ouvrier pendant la Première Guerre mondiale*, vol.1, p.27
27 Archbishop Croke, *Freeman's Journal*, Dublin 1889. Quoted in Geraghty, M.J. 'Argentina: Land of Broken Promises', *Buenos Aires Herald* 17 March 1999 (http://www.irishargentine.org/dresden.htm)
28 Gaughran, Father M. *Southern Cross*. Quoted ibid.
29 *La Protesta Humana*, 3 September 1899. Quoted in Abad de Santillan, D. *La F.O.R.A:, ideologia y trayectoria*, Ch. 3, Buenos Aires 1933
30 Gilimón, E. *Un Anarquista en Buenos Aires: 1890–1910*, Buenos Aires 1971, p.28
31 Quoted in Oved, Y. 'The Uniqueness of Anarchism in Argentina', in *Pensamiento Político en América Latina*, Estudios Interdisciplinarios de America Latina y el Caribe, Vol. 8 No 1, Tel Aviv 1997
32 Gilimón, E. op. cit. p.84
33 Wilde, E. *Obras Completas*, Buenos Aires, 1895, Tomo II, pp. 29–30. Quoted in Suriano, J. *La huelga de inquilinos de 1907*, Buenos Aires, 1983
34 Gilimón, E. op. cit.
35 *Caras y Caretas* No. 468, 21 September 1907. Quoted in Suriano, J. op. cit.
36 Jones, M.H. *Autobiography of Mother Jones*, Chicago 1925
37 University of Missouri-Kansas City Law School, Haywood Trial, Defense Summation
    (http://www.law.umkc.edu/faculty/projects/ftrials/haywood/
    HAYWOOD.HTM)

38 http://www.law.umkc.edu/faculty/projects/ftrials/haywood/
    HAY_SUMD.HTM
39 Haywood B. *Big Bill Haywood's Book*, New York, 1929 p.219
40 Haywood, B. ibid. p.181
41 Gurley Flynn, E. *Memories of the Industrial Workers of the World*, 1977
    (http://www.geocities.com/CapitolHill/5202/rebelgirl.html)
42 American Institute of Electrical Engineers, Schenectady Electrical Handbook,
    Schenectady, 1904
    (http://www.schenectadyhistory.org/resources/seh/ge.html)
43 St John, V. *The I.W.W.—Its History, Structure and Methods*, Chicago 1912
    (http://digital.library.arizona.edu/bisbee/docs/019.php)
44 Miller, J. in Bird, S., Georgakas, D. and Shaffer, D. *Solidarity Forever: The IWW; an
    Oral History of the Wobblies*, London 1985, p.40
45 http://www.peoplesvoice.gov.au/stories/nsw/brokenhill/
    brokenhill_c.htm
46 Mann, T. op. cit. p.186
47 Ibid. p.188
48 Ibid. p.193
49 Connolly, J. *Socialism Made Easy,* Chicago, 1909
50 Mann, T. 'Prepare for Action' in Brown, G. (ed) *The Industrial Syndicalist,* Nottingham
    1974, p.53
51 Boyle, J. *The Minimum Wage and Syndicalism*, Cincinnati 1913, p.87
52 Quoted in Bookchin, M. *The Spanish Anarchists: The Heroic Years 1868–1936*, New
    York 1977
53 Quoted in Kornbluh, J. op. cit. p.45
54 Henry, A. *The Trade Union Woman*, New York 1915, p.93
55 Beal, F. *Proletarian Journey*, New York 1937. Quoted in Kornbluh, J. op. cit.
56 Ibid. p.178
57 Ibid.
58 Quoted in Kornbluh op. cit. p.159
59 Gurley Flynn, E. op. cit. p.128
60 Stannard Baker, R. 'The Revolutionary Strike', the *American Magazine*, May 1912,
    p.24. Quoted in Kornbluh, J. op. cit. p.157
61 Ibid.

6. Wars between brothers

1 Scheidemann, P. *Memoirs of a Social Democrat*, London 1929, Vol.1, p.281
2 Locksmith, age not given, in Levenstein, A. *Die Arbeiterfrage: Mit besonderer
   Berücksichtigung der sozialpsychologischen Seite des modernen Grossbetriebes und der
   psycho-physischen Einwirkungen auf die Arbeiter*, Munich 1912, p.285. This and other
   quotes were taken anonymously from social democratic workers in the first major
   study of social attitudes among the German working class.
3 Carpetweaver aged 42, ibid. p.321
4 Wilhelm König 'Turnen und Kniepe'. *ATZ*, 15 May 1902, pp.109–10. Quoted in
   Lidtke, V. L. *The Alternative Culture: Socialist Labor in Imperial Germany*, Oxford 1985, p.52
5 Audorf 1878. Quoted ibid.
6 Listed ibid. App. IV

Notes

7   *Hamburg Echo*, 8 August 1905. Quoted ibid. p.94
8   Bebel, A. *Woman and Socialism*, New York 1910, Ch. XXVIII
9   'Touristverein Naturfreunden' Arbeitersportfest, p.22. Quoted in Lidtke, V.L. op. cit. p.64
10 Hippe, O. (trans. Drummond, A.) *And Red Is the Colour of our Flag*, London 1991 p.12
11 Sender, T. *The Autobiography of a German Rebel*, London 1940, p.19
12 Ibid. p.21
13 *Vorwärts*, 25 July 1914
    (http://www.zlb.de/projekte/millennium/original_html/vorwaerts_1914_2507.GIF.html)
14 Hippe, O. op. cit. p.12
15 Ibid. p.13
16 Mendel, H. (trans. Michaels, R.) *Memoirs of a Jewish Revolutionary*, London 1989, p.142
17 Sender, T. op. cit. p.52
18 Scheidemann, P. *New York Volkszeitung*, 14 September 1914. Quoted in Schachtman, M. 'Old Wine in New Pails', *New International* Vol. 5 No 6, June 1939, pp. 179–182
19 Sender, T. op. cit. p.65
20 Hippe, O. op. cit. p.15
21 Ibid.
22 'Liebknecht's May Day, 1916, Speech' in Liebknecht, K. *The Future Belongs to the People*, New York 1918
23 Hippe, O. op. cit. pp.16–17
24 Quoted in Scheidemann, P. op. cit. Vol. II p.55
25 Valtin, J. *Out of the Night*, London 1941, p.8
26 Ibid. p.7
27 Schneider, E. *The Wilhelmshaven Revolt, 1918–1919,* London, 1944
28 Valtin, J. op. cit. p.10
29 Hippe, O. op. cit. p.29
30 Ibid. p.30
31 Sender, T. op. cit. p.87
32 Sender, T. op. cit. p.92
33 Müller, R. *Die Novemberrevolution*, Berlin 1976, p.11
34 Scheidemann, P. op. cit. Vol. 2 p.580
35 Ibid. p.565
36 Ibid. Vol. 1 p.281
37 Sender, T. op. cit. p.114
38 Schneider, E. op. cit.
39 Scheidemann, P. op. cit. p.565
40 Hippe, O. op. cit. p.35
41 Unfortunately this is one episode from workers' history where acronyms are unavoidable.
42 Paul Levi, *Rote Fahn*, 5 September 1920. Quoted in Harman, C. *The Lost Revolution*, London 1982, p.70
43 Schnieder, E. op. cit.
44 Remarqe, E. M. *All Quiet on the Western Front*, London 1929
45 Jünger, E. 'Fire' in Kaes, A. Jay, M. and Dimendberg, E. *The Weimar Republic Sourcebook*, London 1994, p.19

46 Zuckmayer C. 'Erich Maria Remarque's *All Quiet on the Western Front*' in Kaes, Jay and Dimendberg op. cit. p.23
47 Hippe, O. op. cit. p.54
48 Hippe, O. op. cit. p.55
49 Valtin, J. op. cit. p.36
50 Sender, T. op. cit. p.209
51 Ibid.
52 Ibid. p.213
53 Valtin, J. op. cit. p.68
54 Valtin, J. op. cit. p.77
55 Reissner, L. (trans. Chappell, R.) *Hamburg at the Barricades*, London 1977, p.37
56 Hippe, O. op. cit. p.159

7. Totally ignorant labourers

1 Shibao, 10 August 1911. Quoted in Smith. S.A. *Like Cattle and Horses: Nationalism and Labor in Shanghai 1895–1927*, Durham 2002, p.73
2 'Lathi charge on the HMSO Workers on July 25 2005 in Gurgaon: A Citizens Committee Enquiry Report', New Delhi 2005, p.22
3 Ibid. All worker evidence other than from union officials was anonymised in the report of the enquiry, which was carried out by a team of academics, union leaders and NGO researchers.
4 Ibid. p.15
5 Gamewell, M. N. *The Gateway to China: Pictures of Shanghai,* New York 1916, p.217
6 Ibid. p.224
7 Huxley, A. *Diary,* 1926
8 Chen Du-xiu 'Shanghai shehui' (Shanghai Society). Quoted in Perry, E. J. *Shanghai on Strike; The politics of Chinese labor*, Stanford 1993, p.85
9 Smith, S. A. *Like Cattle and Horses: Nationalism and Labor in Shanghai, 1895–1927*, Durham 2002
10 Transcript of interview, Labor Movement Archives of Shanghai Academy of Social Sciences Institute of History. Quoted in Perry, E.J. op. cit. p.56
11 Gamewell, M.N. op. cit. p.232
12 Xia Yan, 'Contract Labor' in *Chinese Literature* 8 1960, pp.47–63
13 Quoted in Perry, E.J. op. cit.
14 'Report on the Commercial, Industrial and Economic Situation in China', UK Department of Overseas Trade, London, 1919. Quoted in Chesneaux, J. *The Chinese Labor Movement 1919–1927*, Stanford, 1968
15 'Proclamation of the Shanghai workers' (trans. Benton, G.) Quoted in *Militant*, London 17 March 1972
16 Li Chung, 'Letter of a Shanghai Dockyard Worker' (trans. Benton, G.) Ibid.
17 Lowe, C. H. 'Facing Labor Issues in China' in *Shanghai Chinese Papers*, Banff Conference 1933, Vol. 11, p.661
18 5 November 1921. Quoted in Smith, S.A., op. cit. p.137
19 Deng Zhong-xia quoted in Perry, E.J. op. cit. p.76
20 Teng Chung-hsia 'Chung-kuo Chi-kung Yun-tung Chien-shih', Beijing 1949, p.183. Quoted in Rigby, R.W. *The May 30 Movement: Events and themes*, Canberra, 1980

21 Quoted in Rigby, R.W. op. cit. p.28
22 Zhihua,Y. 'Thoughts during the strike movement of Shanghai women silk workers in 1926'. Quoted in Perry, E.J. op. cit.
23 Yang Zhi-hua op. cit. pp.3–7. Quoted in Gilmartin. C.K. *Engendering the Chinese Revolution: Radical Women, Communist Politics and Mass Movements in the 1920s,* Berkeley 1995, p.144
24 http://www.stetson.edu/departments/russian/sunjoffe.html
25 Tsai Shu-fan, interview in Wales, N. *Red Dust: Autobiographies of Chinese Communists,* Stanford 1952, p.84
26 Ibid. p.90
27 Ibid. p.93
28 Ibid. p.92
29 Valtin, J. op. cit. p.138
30 Mann, T. *What I Saw in China,* London 1927, pp.22–3
31 Ibid. p.11
32 *La Correspondence Internationale,* 23 March 1927. Quoted in Isaacs, H. *The Tragedy of the Chinese Revolution* (second revised edition) New York 1968, p.160
33 Lu Da-xiu, Interview, 24 August 1958. Quoted in Perry, E. op. cit. p.152
34 Chesnaux, J. op. cit. p. 359
35 Isaacs, H. R. *The Tragedy of the Chinese Revolution,* Stanford 1938; Brandt, C. *Stalin's Failure in China,* New York 1958
36 Isaacs, H. R. op. cit. p.160
37 Isaacs op. cit. p.177
38 Mann, T. op. cit. p.15
39 Valtin, J. op. cit. p.139
40 Wang Cheng op. cit. p.95
41 Tsai Shu-fan op. cit. p.87

8. Heaven and earth will hear us

1 Blanket-Sulkowicz, A. 'Destruction of Brzezin' p.140, *Brzeziny memorial book* ed. Alperin, A. and Summer, N. New York: Brzeziner Book Committee, 1961. Excerpts used with kind permission of the YIVO Institute, New York.
2 Ibid.
3 Fogel, A. 'Past Generations', ibid.
4 Lencicki, D. 'Brzeziner Tailors', ibid. pp.40–3
5 Fogel, A. 'Past Generations', ibid. pp.21–30
6 Frank, M. 'A Bundle of Memories', ibid. pp.69–71
7 Ibid.
8 Ibid.
9 Shaibowicz, J. 'Brzeziny in History', ibid. pp.3–20
10 Ibid.
11 Quoted in Tobias, H.J. *The Jewish Bund in Russia: From its origins to 1905,* Stanford 1972, p.9
12 Patai, J. *Complete Diaries of Theodor Herzl,* vol. III, p.729
13 An-sky, S. 'Di Shvue', 1902. Translation courtesy Taube Center for Jewish Studies, Stanford University
14 Fogel, A. op. cit.

15 Litvak, A. *Geklibene shriften*, New York 1945, p.180. Quoted in Tobias, H.J. *The Jewish Bund in Russia from its Origins to 1905*, Stanford 1972, p.309 (Khaim Helfand)
16 Fogel, A. op. cit.
17 Ibid.
18 Ibid.
19 Abramowicz, A. 'The Workers' Movement in Brzezin', ibid. pp.104–7
20 Frank, M. op. cit.
21 Fogel, A. op. cit.
22 Abramowicz, A. op. cit. pp.104–7
23 Ibid.
24 Ibid.
25 Wisse, R.R. (ed.) *The I.L. Peretz Reader*, Yale 2002
26 Kreingold, P. 'I.L. Peretz, Father of the Yiddish Renaissance', *Fidelio* summer 2003, Vol. XII No. 2 p.35
27 Fiszel Maliniak in Alperin et al., op. cit.
28 Sh. Tshernetski 'Unsere sportier marshirn faroys' *Yngt-veker* 10, 15 May 1929, p.4 quoted in Jacobs, J. ed. *Jewish Politics in Eastern Europe: the Bund at 100*, New York, 2001 p.61
29 Rosenberg, A. 'Jewish sports in Brzezin' in Alperin, A. and Summer, N. op. cit. pp.118–21
30 Ibid.
31 Pat, J. 'About Sefer Brzezin and the Destroyed Town of Brzeziny' in Alperin, A. and Summer, N. op.cit. pp. xvii–xx
32 Hertz, S. 'Aynike Shtrikhn Vegn de Idisher Arbeiter Bavegung', *Socialistisze Bleter* I June 1931 pp. 41–3. Quoted in Johnpoll, B. op. cit. p.179
33 Abramowicz. A, op. cit.
34 Maliniak F., Brzezin Between Two World Wars, in Alperin, A. and Summer, N. op. cit. p.87–9
35 Colonel Jan Kowalewski, *Gazeta Polska* 22 April 1937. Quoted in Johnpoll, B. op. cit. p.208
36 Erlich, H. 'Naye Folkstsaytung', 31 July 1938. Quoted in Polonsky, A. 'The New Jewish Politics and its Discontents' in Gitelman, Z. (ed.) *The New Emergence of Modern Jewish Politics*, Pittsburgh 2003, p.37
37 Janasowicz, I. 'My Gate to the Great World' in Alperin, A. and Summer, N. op. cit.
38 Goldstein, B. *Five Years in the Warsaw Ghetto*, London 2005
39 Ibid. p. 95
40 *Oyf der Vakh*, 20 September 1942. Quoted in Blatman, D. *For Our Freedom and Yours: The Jewish Labour Bund in Poland 1939–1949*, London 2003, p.103
41 Edelman, M. *The Ghetto Fights*, London 1990
42 Ibid.
43 Goldstein, B. op. cit. p. 130
44 'Second Report from the Jewish Workers' Underground Movement 15 November 1943' in Edelman, M. op. cit. p. 97
45 Mawult, J. in Grynberg, M. (ed.) *Words to Outlive Us: Eyewitness Accounts from the Warsaw Ghetto*, London 2004, p.253
46 Goldstein, B. op. cit. p.156
47 Ibid. p.152
48 Kann, M. *Na oczach swiata*, Warsaw 1943, p.33
49 ZOB 23 April 1943, in Goldstein, B. op. cit. p.168

50 Goldstein, B. op. cit. p.171
51 Zygelboym, A. 11 May 1943, Yad Vashem Archives, O-55
52 Goldstein, B. op. cit. p.169.
53 *The Stroop Report*, Jewish Virtual Library
(http://www.jewishvirtuallibrary.org/jsource/Holocaust/nowarsaw.html)
54 Deutscher, I. Preface to Mendel, H. *Memoirs of a Jewish Revolutionary*, London 1989
55 Rose, J. 'Interview with Marek Edelman at his home in the Polish city of Lodz',
21 March 1989 in Edelman, M. op. cit. p.116

9. Joy brought on by hope

1 *Il Domani*, 11 September 1920. Quoted in Bell, D.H. *Sesto San Giovanni: Workers, Culture and Politics in an Italian Town*, 1880–1922, New Brunswick 1986, p.122
2 'Intervista a Maurizio Garino' FIOM, Turin
(http://www.pmt.cgil.it/Fiomtorino/Scuolo-moderna.htm)
3 Garino, M. op. cit.
4 Gramsci, A. *L'Ordine Nuovo*, 13 September 1920. Quoted in Williams, G.A. *Proletarian Order: Antonio Gramsci, Factory Councils and the Origins of Communism in Italy 1911–1921*, p.115
5 Programme of the Workshop Councils. Quoted in Williams, G.A. op. cit., p.130
6 Garino, M. 'Consigli di fabbrica e di azienda. Relazione presentata al Congresso dell'Unione Anarchica Italiana' (Bologna 1–4 luglio 1920) in *Umanità Nova*, 1 July 1920. Quoted in *Class War, Reaction & the Italian Anarchists*, FCdAI, n.d, p.26
7 Buozzi, B. 'L'occupazione delle fabbriche', *Almanaco Socialista Italiana,* Paris 1936, p.79
8 Buozzi, B. Quoted in memorial speech, 'Bruno Buozzi, il Riformista' Cordova, F. (http://www.fondazionebrunobuozzi.org/documenti.htm)
9 Summary by the prefect of Turin. Quoted in Spriano, P. *The Occupation of the Factories: Italy 1920*, London 1974, p.143
10 Ibid.
11 *Il Corriere della Serra*, 31 August 1920. Quoted in Spriano, P. op. cit.
12 Massoul, H. 'La lecon de Mussolini' *Mercure de Paris*, 1934. Quoted in Spriano, P. op. cit.
13 Parodi, G. 'La Fiat Centro in mano agli operai' in *Lo Stato Operaio*, iv 1930 number 10, Bureau d'Editions. Paris, p.638
14 Colombino, E. article in *Avanti*, 2 September 1920
15 Telephone conversation transcript in Spriano, P. op. cit. p.190
16 *Il Domani*, 25 September 1920. Quoted in Bell, D. H. op. cit. p.128
17 Buozzi, B. 'L'occupazione delle fabbriche'. Quoted in Spriano, P. op. cit. p.135
18 Ford, H. *My Life and Work*, New York 1922, p.147
19 CGT pamphlet, 1913. Reproduced in *Histoire Economique et sociale de la France*, vol. IV p.528, Paris, PUF 1976–80; cited in Beaud, M. *A History of Capitalism 1500–1980*, London 1981
20 Buozzi, B. 'La razionalizzazione' *La Libertà*, Paris, 16 December 1928. Quoted in Buozzi, B. *Le condizone della classe lavoratrice in Italia 1922–1943*, Milan 1973, p.10
21 Guigui, A. and Ganivet, P. 'Le contrôle ouvriere' in *L'Homme Réel*, June 1934. Quoted in Dolleans, E. *Histoire du Mouvement Ouvrier: De 1921 à nos jours*, Paris 1953, p.102

22 http://www.historicalvoices.org

23 Weil, S. *La Condition Ouvrière,* Paris 1951, p.95

24 Ibid. p. 144

25 Danos, J. and Gibelin, M. *June '36: Class Struggle and the Popular Front in France,* London, 1986, p.249

26 Weil, S. op. cit. p.148

27 'Leon Blum devant la Cour de Riom'. Quoted in Danos, J. and Gibelin, M. op. cit.

28 Cited in Danos, J. and Gibelin, M. ibid.

29 Graham, H. and Preston, P. *The Popular Front in Europe,* London 1987, p.67

30 Danos, J. and Giblein, M. op. cit. p.132

31 Weil, S. op. cit.

32 PSA Peugeot-Citroen, 2004 Corporate History (http://www.psa-peugeot-citroen.com/en/psa_group/history_b4.php)

33 Wharton, A. Directive to IAM chairmen, 30 April 1937. Quoted in Matles, J. and Higgins, J. *Them and Us: Struggles of a Rank and File Union,* New Jersey 1974

34 http://www.historicalvoices.org. The University of Michigan oral history archive of the Flint dispute is an invaluable online resource.

35 Ibid.

36 Ibid.

37 Ibid.

38 http://lib.umflint.edu/archives/knotts.html

39 Linder, W. *The Great Sit Down Strike Against GM,* New York 1965

40 http://www.marxists.org/history/etol/newspape/amersocialist/bullsrun.htm

41 Linder, W. op. cit.

42 Skunda, J. (in http://lib.umflint.edu/archives/JSkunda.html)

43 Quoted in Linder, W. op. cit.

44 Ibid.

45 Michigan State University, U-M Flint Labor History Project, interview transcript

46 http://lib.umflint.edu/archives/Markanovich.html

47 Weil, S. op. cit.

Louise Michel with fairy wings

1 Freeman, R. 'Doubling the Global Workforce', 8 November 2004, Centre for Economic Performance, London School of Economics paper (http://www.petersoninstitute.org/publications/papers/freeman1104.pdf)

2 Bluestone, I. 'Walter Reuther', *Time,* 7 December 1998

Acknowledgements

Authors: though much of this book is based on primary sources, language was a barrier in two chapters: on Shanghai and on the Bund. In Chapter 9, the account of the Warsaw Ghetto Uprising follows that in Marek Edelman's *The Ghetto Fights*, with boundless respect to its author. Chapter 7 quotes heavily from secondary sources, and I very gratefully acknowledge the work of the historians from whose translations I have drawn, in particular Steve Smith, Professor of History at the University of Essex; Gail Hershatter, Professor of History, UC Santa Cruz; Emily Honig, Professor of Women's Studies at UC Santa Cruz; and Elizabeth Perry, Professor of Government, Harvard University. The 'typical German worker' depicted in Chapter 6 was drawn in part from research by Professor Vernon Lidtke of Johns Hopkins University, whose work I gratefully acknowledge.

Institutions: thanks to the staff of the British Library for their dedicated service to this marvellous institution. I am grateful to the YIVO Institute, New York, for permission to quote from their online archive of Yizkor Books, and to the Jewish Bund, New York, for providing valuable out-of-print material. Also to the historicalvoices.org archive hosted by Michigan State University, whose online archive of the Flint strike formed the core material for that section of Chapter 9. Massive new insight into the lives of the Lyon silk workers was provided by the online publication of their newspaper and other documents by the Bibliothèque Municipale de Lyon. The International Institute for Social History in Amsterdam was invaluable for chasing down details in numerous chapters. The Labadie Collection at the University of Michigan's superb photographic collection assisted the writing of Chapter 5. Porcupine Bookcellar, a dingy basement at Houseman's Bookshop in north London, was an invaluable source of out-of-print material; thanks to its proprietors Andrew Burgin and Barry Buitekant.

Jane Bell's Druidstone Hotel provided the calm that helped me draft large parts of the book.

People: thanks first to my agent, Peter Tallack, for helping me discover the book I really wanted to write, and to Stuart Williams at Harvill Secker for believing it could work. Thanks also to BBC *Newsnight* editor Peter Barron and BBC News editor Helen Boaden for permission to write it. Thanks to Christina Purcell, who helped me research and translate various French language sources, especially in Chapters 2, 3 and 5; and to Alejandra Crosta who helped with Argentine sources and translated the interview with Raul Godoy. Thanks to Ewa Jasciewicz for facilitating my contacts with the Southern Oil Workers Union of Iraq. Alina Teran was my interpreter on the trip to Bolivia and accompanied me, above and beyond the call of duty, a mile and a half into the Dolores mine in Huanuni; Luis Gomez of NarcoNews facilitated crucial meetings in El Alto. The redoubtable Edera Liang fixed and translated on both my trips to China, and inspired me with her ability to overcome all bureaucratic obstacles calmly. Thanks to Sam Goddard of ActionAid UK, who invited me on her field trip to Varanasi, and to Dr Lenin Raghuvanshi, who acted as interpreter with the silk weavers there. In Nigeria I was privileged to work with Sam Olukoye, a renowned freelance journalist in Lagos, who arranged my trip into Amukoko and organised interviews with workers in the city. Catherine Howarth, Neil Jameson and Matthew Bolton of London Citizens facilitated meetings with migrant cleaners in London for me. In Delhi, Pallavi Mansingh at the Centre for Education and Communication alerted me to the case of the Honda strikers. Thanks are also due to the following *Newsnight* producers and cameracrew who worked with me during the trips I have described here: Joe Mather (Bolivia); Sara Afshar, Julie Ritson, Ruth Parkinson and Ian Pritchard (China); Ian O'Reilly (Nigeria). Gratitude also to Kevin Curran, International Union of Food Workers, and to Ben Hurley formerly of the TUC press office, for various contacts and introductions. I consulted numerous issues of *Revolutionary History* and greatly missed being able to consult its late editor, Al Richardson. Thanks to Matthew Cobb and Keith Hassell and Dave Stocking for helpful comments. Thanks to my mother and my sister for their tireless support. Finally to Jane Bruton, my wife and comrade, limitless love and gratitude.

Index

Index

and Holocaust 214–15, 232–41
Kapp Putsch (1920) 174–5
March Madness (1921) 175–6
naval mutiny (1918) 165–7
Nazi Party rise 176, 179–81
Spartacus Rising (1919) 173
Weimar Republic 173–9
workers' attitude to First World War 160–5
workers' life before First World War 152–9
workers' life after First World War 173–6
Gibelin, M. 263
Gilimón, Eduardo 109, 127, 129
Giolitti, Giovanni 250, 253, 254
Giovannitti (IWW organiser) 144, 145
globalisation
19th century 110
anti-globalisation movement 281–2, 283
link to labour movements 280
modern 278, 280–3
GLU see General Labour Union
Godoy, Raul 242–3, 244–5
Goldstein, Bernard 233–4, 235, 236–7, 238, 240
Gompers, Samuel 141, 256
Goncalves, Benedita 107, 108
Gould, Jay 85, 89–90, 92, 95
Gramsci, Antonio 246, 247, 254
Grangers 84
Great Southwest Strike (1886) 92–6, 102
Great Unrest 139–46
Griffuelhes, Victor
background 109, 117, 118
and CGT 119–20, 124, 125
First World War evacuation 162
stands down from CGT 139
Guigui, Albert 257
Guild of Women 42

Haase, Hugo 161
Hamburg 152–7, 176–7
uprising (1923) 178–9
Hardie, James Keir 278–9
Harvard University 144
hat makers 127
Haviland, Charles 122
Haviland, Theodore 121, 122, 123
Le Havre 259
Haymarket Massacre (1886) 102–3
Haywood, Bill 109, 131–5, 140, 144, 283
Hechalutz youth movement 234, 235
Henry, Alice 141
Herzl, Theodore 219
Hill, Joe 106
Hind Mazdoor Sabha (HMS; India) 185–6
Hippe, Oskar
background 159
demonstrates against First World War 161, 163–4
as First World War conscript 165, 167
last days 180–1
postwar KPD activism 170, 171, 172–3, 174, 175–6
Hitler, Adolf 176, 180
HMS see Hind Mazdoor Sabha
Holland, Ray 267
Holocaust 214–15, 232–41
Honda 182–3
hospital cleaners 108
Hotchkiss 260

housing
Buenos Aires 129–30
London's East End 112
Lyon 31–2
Manchester 15–16
Nigeria 47–9
Paris 59–60
slumdweller statistics 49
Hoyker, Baruch 216, 220, 221, 222
HSBC 106
Huanuni 147–52
Huaylla, Marisol 147–8
Hunt, Henry 8–9, 11, 22
Huxley, Aldous 188

Ikeja 49–51
Independent Social Democratic Party of Germany
(USPD)
and 1918–19 Revolution 167–8, 170, 171, 172–3
formation 165
and German naval mutiny (1918) 166
split and demise 174
India 25–9, 182–7
industrial accidents 1–3, 15
The Industrial Syndicalist (newspaper) 139
Industrial Workers of the World (IWW; 'Wobblies')
133–6, 144–5
International (Workingmen's International
Association)
bannings 59, 64
foundation 56
and Franco-Prussian War (1870–71) 65
and the Paris Commune 69, 70, 71
and public meeting movement 61, 62
and Varlin 66
on women 57, 61
Iquipaza, Eliodoro 211
Iraq 79–81
Ireland and Irish 125–6, 141
Irons, Martin
background 83–5
and Knights of Labor 89–90, 92, 95–6
last days 103, 104–5
political beliefs 86, 97
Italian Socialist Party 248–9, 252–3
Italy 245–55
IWW see Industrial Workers of the World

Jacquard, Joseph 26, 30
Janasowicz, Icchok 232
Japan: and China 192, 197–8
Jaurès, Jean 161
Jewish Fighting Organisation (ZOB) 237–40
Jews 214–41
Joffe, Adolf 200
Jouhaux, Leon 139, 261–2
Juma, Hassan 79–81
Jünger, Ernst 173–4

Kapp Putsch (1920) 174–5
Karski, Jan 236
Knights of Labor (USA) 82–5, 86–96, 98–100,
102
Knotts, Roy 267
KPD see Communist Party: Germany
Kraus, Henry 272
Kuomintang 195, 196, 199, 200–9

301

Index